LIVING LANGUAGE®

COMPLETE JAPANESE

THE BASICS

REVISED & UPDATED

COMPLETE JAPANESE

THE BASICS

REVISED & UPDATED

REVISED BY HIROKO STORM, PH.D.

University of Arizona

Assistant Professor of Japanese
Lafayette College

◆

Based on the original by Ichiro Shirato

LIVING LANGUAGE®

Published in the United States by Living Language, A Random House Company

www.livinglanguage.com

Editor: Suzanne J. Podhurst
Production Editor: David Downing
Production Managers: Helen Kilcullen and Heather Lanigan

ISBN 1-4000-2145-6

Library of Congress Cataloging-in-Publication Data available upon request.

This book is available for special discounts for bulk purchases for sales promotions or premiums. Special editions, including personalized covers, excerpts of existing books, and corporate imprints, can be created in large quantities for special needs. For more information, write to Special Markets/Premium Sales, 1745 Broadway, MD 6-2, New York, New York 10019 or e-mail specialmarkets@randomhouse.com.

PRINTED IN THE UNITED STATES OF AMERICA

10 9 8 7 6 5 4 3

CONTENTS

Introduction	xvii
Course Material	xix
Instructions	xxi

LESSON 1   1
A. A Preliminary Note   1
B. The Alphabet: The Letters   2
C. Accent   3
D. The Alphabet: The Sounds   4
E. Loan Words: English Words
Used in Japanese   4

LESSON 2   6
A. Vowels   6
B. Vowel Clusters   7
C. Devoiced Vowels   8

LESSON 3   9
A. Consonants I   9

LESSON 4   12
A. Consonants II   12
B. Semi-Vowels   16

LESSON 5   17
  A. The Japanese Syllabary   17
  B. General Sound Equivalents   18
  C. More Loan Words   20

LESSON 6   23
  A. Days and Months   23
  B. Numbers 1–10   24
  C. Colors   24
  D. North, South, East, West   24
    QUIZ 1   24
  E. Word Study   25

Supplemental Vocabulary List 1: At School   26

LESSON 7   27
  A. Greetings   27
  B. How's the Weather?   29
    QUIZ 2   30

Supplemental Vocabulary List 2: The Weather   30

LESSON 8   31
  A. Do You Have?   31
  B. In a Restaurant   32
    QUIZ 3   34
  C. Word Study   34

Supplemental Vocabulary List 3: Food   35

LESSON 9   36
  A. Pronouns   36
  B. To Be or Not to Be   37
  C. *Desu*   40
    QUIZ 4   43
    REVIEW QUIZ 1   44

Supplemental Vocabulary List 4: Family and
  Relationships   47

LESSON 10   48
  A. Common Verb Forms   48
  B. Asking a Question I   51
  C. Where Is It?   52
  D. Here and There   53
  E. Near and Far   54
    QUIZ 5   55

Supplemental Vocabulary List 5: Around Town   56

LESSON 11   58
  A. Nouns and Noun Particles   58
  B. Common Adjective Forms   65
    QUIZ 6   71

LESSON 12   72
  A. Plain or Polite   72
  B. To Construct the Polite Form of a Verb   74
  C. The -te and -ta Forms   76
  D. Various Usages of the -te Form   80
    QUIZ 7   82

LESSON 13   82
  A. My, Your, His, Her, etc.   82
  B. Some Comparisons   84
  C. Asking a Question II   85
    QUIZ 8   87
  D. Word Study   88

Supplemental Vocabulary List 6:
  The Human Body   89

LESSON 14   90
  A. To Have and Have Not   90
  B. Also   93

QUIZ 9   94
   C. Word Study   94

LESSON 15   95
   A. I Have Been to . . .   95
   B. Sometimes I Go . . .   96
   C. I Can, I Am Able to . . .   96
   D. I've Decided to . . .   96
      QUIZ 10   97

Supplemental Vocabulary List 7:
   Travel and Tourism   98

LESSON 16   99
   A. Do You Speak Japanese?   99
   B. Please Speak a Little Slower   100
   C. Thanks!   101
      QUIZ 11   102
   D. Word Study   102

LESSON 17   103
   A. This and That   103
      QUIZ 12   105
   B. Not   105
   C. Isn't It? Aren't You? etc.   106
      QUIZ 13   107
   D. Word Study   107

LESSON 18   108
   A. It's Me (I), etc.   108
   B. It's Mine, etc.   108
   C. About Me, etc.   109
   D. To Me, etc.   109
   E. The Modifiers   109
   F. The Noun-Maker *No*   111
      QUIZ 14   111

LESSON 19   112
  A. Hello, How Are You?   112
  B. I'd Like You to Meet . . .   113
  C. What's New?   113
  D. See You Soon!   114
    QUIZ 15   114

Supplemental Vocabulary List 8: People   115

LESSON 20   116
  A. Have You Two Met?   116
  B. Glad to Have Met You   117
    QUIZ 16   119
  C. Word Study   119
    REVIEW QUIZ 2   120

Supplemental Vocabulary List 9: Sports and
Recreation   123

LESSON 21   124
  A. Numbers   124
  B. More Numbers   126
  C. Pronunciation of Numbers
    Before Certain Counters   127
  D. First, Second, Third   128
    QUIZ 17   130
  E. Two and Two   130

Supplemental Vocabulary List 10: In the Office   131

LESSON 22   132
  A. It Costs . . .   132
  B. The Telephone Number Is . . .   132
  C. My Address Is . . .   133
  D. Some Dates   134
    QUIZ 18   134

LESSON 23   135
    A. What Time Is It?   135
    B. The Time Is Now . . .   136
    C. When Will You Come?   137
    D. It's Time   138
      QUIZ 19   139
    E. Word Study   140

LESSON 24   140
    A. Ago   140
    B. Morning, Noon, and Night   141
    C. This Week, Next Month, etc.   142
    D. Expressions of Past, Present, and Future   143

LESSON 25   144
    A. Days of the Week   144
    B. Days of the Month   144
    C. What's the Date Today?   146
      QUIZ 20   147
    D. Months of the Year   148
    E. The Seasons   149
      QUIZ 21   150

Supplemental Vocabulary List 11: Nature   151

LESSON 26   152
    A. *Iku:* To Go   152
    B. A Few Action Phrases   155
    C. Word Study   156
    D. *Shinbun Uriba De*   156

LESSON 27   157
    A. They Say That . . .   157
    B. I Have to, I Must . . .   158
    C. Something to Drink   159
      QUIZ 22   161
    D. Word Study   162

Supplemental Vocabulary List 12:
   In the Kitchen   162

LESSON 28   163
   A. A Little and a Lot   163
   B. Too Much/Not Too Much   164
   C. More or Less   165
   D. Enough and Some More   165
      QUIZ 23   166

LESSON 29   167
   A. I Want to . . .   167
   B. I Intend to . . .   168
   C. It Is Supposed to . . .   169
   D. Something, Everything, Nothing   170
      QUIZ 24   172
   E. Word Study   173

LESSON 30   174
   A. Of Course! It's a Pity!
      It Doesn't Matter!   174
      QUIZ 25   175
   B. The Same   176
   C. Already   176
   D. Word Study   176

LESSON 31   177
   A. I Like It, It's Good   177
   B. I Don't Like It, It's Bad   178
      QUIZ 26   179
      REVIEW QUIZ 3   179
   C. Word Study   182
   D. *Waraibanashi*   183

Supplemental Vocabulary List 13:
   Entertainment   184

LESSON 32   186
  A. Who? What? When? etc.   186
    QUIZ 27   190
  B. Word Study   191
  C. How Much?   192
  D. How Many?   192
    QUIZ 28   192

LESSON 33   193
  A. Some, Someone, Something   193
  B. Once, Twice   195
  C. Up to   196
  D. I Need It, It's Necessary   196
  E. I Feel Like   197
  F. At the Home of   197
    QUIZ 29   198
    REVIEW QUIZ 4   198

Supplemental Vocabulary List 14: At Home   201

LESSON 34   203
  A. On the Road   203
  B. Bus, Train, Subway, Taxi   204
  C. Writing and Mailing Letters, E-mails, and
    Faxes   205
  D. Telephoning   207
  E. Word Study   208

Supplemental Vocabulary List 15: Computers
and the Internet   208

LESSON 35   210
  A. What's Your Name?   210
  B. Where Are You From?
    How Old Are You?   211
  C. Professions   213
  D. Family Matters   213
    REVIEW QUIZ 5   214

Supplemental Vocabulary List 16: Jobs   218

LESSON 36	219
A. *Kaimono:* Shopping	219
QUIZ 30	223
B. Word Study	225
Supplemental Vocabulary List 17: Clothing	225
LESSON 37	227
A. *Asagohan:* Breakfast	227
B. A Sample Menu	231
REVIEW QUIZ 6	232
LESSON 38	234
A. In, On, Under	234
B. If, When	236
C. Without	238
QUIZ 31	239
REVIEW QUIZ 7	240
D. *Shakuya Sagashi:* House Hunting	243
QUIZ 32	249
Supplemental Vocabulary List 18:	
In the Bathroom	250
LESSON 39	251
A. *Kuru:* To Come	251
B. *Iu (yuu):* To Say	253
QUIZ 33	254
C. *Suru:* To Do	255
QUIZ 34	256
REVIEW QUIZ 8	257
D. I'm a Stranger Here	260
QUIZ 35	265
LESSON 40	267
A. The Most Common Verb Forms	267
B. *Kyuuyuu to No Saikai:* Meeting an Old Friend	277
QUIZ 36	281

C. The Most Common Verbs
and Verb Phrases 282
QUIZ 37 298
D. Public Notices and Signs 299
FINAL REVIEW QUIZ 305

SUMMARY OF JAPANESE GRAMMAR 309
1. The Alphabet and Romanization 309
2. Simple Vowels 313
3. Vowel Clusters 314
4. Consonants and Semi-Vowels 315
5. Double Consonants 316
6. The Syllabic *N* 317
7. Contractions 318
8. Accent 319
9. Intonation 320
10. Nouns 320
11. Counters 328
12. Pronouns 332
13. Demonstratives 336
14. *Ko-So-A-Do* Words 336
15. Adjectives 337
16. Comparisons 339
17. The Classes and Forms of Verbs 343
18. Particles Used with Verbs 353
19. Negatives 360
20. Word Order 363
21. Questions 364
22. Question Words 365
23. Something, Everything,
Nothing, Anything 367
24. Even If, Even Though 370
25. Hearsay 371
26. Seeming 372
27. Imminence 374
28. Obligation and Prohibition 374
29. Permission 377
30. Alternatives 377

31. Passive, Potential, and Respect 378
32. Causative 379
33. Desideratives 380
34. To Do (Something) for . . . 382
35. May, Perhaps, Probably 383
36. If and When 383
37. Whether . . . or . . . , If . . . or . . . 387
38. Indefinite Pronouns 388
39. In Order to 389
40. Requests, Commands 390
41. Adverbial Expressions 392
42. The Writing System 395

LETTER WRITING 410
1. Formal Letters 410
2. Business Letters 413
3. Informal Letters 416
4. Electronic Mail 420
5. Addressing an Envelope 422
6. Internet Resources 423

INTRODUCTION

Living Language® Complete Japanese: The Basics
makes it easy to learn how to speak, read, and write
Japanese. This course is a thoroughly revised and
updated version of *Living Japanese: The Complete
Living Language® Course*. The same highly effective
method of language instruction is still used, but the
content has been updated to reflect modern usage, and
the format has been clarified. In this course, the basic
elements of the language have been carefully selected
and condensed into forty short lessons. If you can
study about thirty minutes a day, you can master this
course and learn to speak Japanese in a few weeks.

You'll learn Japanese the way you learned English,
starting with simple words and progressing to more
complex phrases. Just listen and repeat after the native
instructors on the recordings. To help you immerse
yourself in the language, you'll hear only Japanese
spoken. Hear it, say it, absorb it through use and repetition.

This *Living Language® Complete Japanese: The
Basics* coursebook provides English translations and
brief explanations for each lesson. The first five
lessons cover pronunciation, laying the foundation for

learning the vocabulary, phrases, and grammar components that are explained in the later chapters. If you already know a little Japanese, you can use the book as a phrase book and reference. In addition to the forty lessons, there is a summary of Japanese grammar, plus verb conjugations and a section on writing letters.

Also included in the course package is the *Living Language® Japanese Dictionary*. It contains more than 15,000 entries, with many of the definitions illustrated by phrases and idiomatic expressions. More than 1,000 of the most essential words are capitalized to make them easy to find. You can increase your vocabulary and range of expression just by browsing through the dictionary.

Practice your Japanese as much as possible. Even if you can't manage a trip abroad, watching Japanese movies, reading Japanese magazines, eating at Japanese restaurants, and talking with Japanese-speaking friends are enjoyable ways to help you reinforce what you have learned with *Living Language® Complete Japanese: The Basics*. Now, let's begin. The following instructions will tell you what to do.

COURSE MATERIAL

1. Three 60-minute compact discs.

2. *Living Language® Complete Japanese: The Basics* coursebook. This book is designed for use with the recorded lessons, but it may also be used alone as a reference. It contains the following sections: basic Japanese in forty lessons, a summary of Japanese grammar, verb conjugations, and a section on letter writing.

3. *Living Language® Japanese Dictionary.* The Japanese/English–English/Japanese dictionary contains more than 15,000 entries. Phrases and idiomatic expressions illustrate many of the definitions. More than 1,000 of the most essential words are capitalized.

INSTRUCTIONS

1. Look at page 4. The words in **boldface** type are the ones you will hear on the recording.

2. Now read Lesson 1 all the way through. Note the points to listen for when you play the recording. The first word you will hear is **Akira.**

3. Start the recording, listen carefully, and say the words aloud in the pauses provided. Go through the lesson once and don't worry if you can't pronounce everything correctly the first time around. Try it again and keep repeating the lesson until you are comfortable with it. The more often you listen and repeat, the longer you will remember the material.

4. Now go on to the next lesson. If you take a break between lessons, it's always good to review the previous lesson before starting a new one.

5. In the manual, there are two kinds of quizzes. With matching quizzes, you must select the English translation of the Japanese sentence. The other type requires you to fill in the blanks with the correct Japanese word chosen from the three given directly below the sentence. If you make any mistakes, reread the section.

6. There are 18 supplemental vocabulary sections in the course. Each one focuses on a useful theme that is related to the content of the surrounding lessons. Practice the lists through repetition, self-quizzes, or with flash cards to build a solid foundation in Japanese vocabulary.

7. Even after you have finished the forty lessons and scored 100 percent on the final quiz, keep practicing your Japanese by listening to the recordings and speaking with Japanese-speaking friends.

For further study, we recommend *Ultimate Japanese Beginner-Intermediate* and *Ultimate Japanese Advanced*, both from the experts at Living Language. Or, go to our website at www.livinglanguage.com for more information on the available Japanese courses and reference materials.

LIVING LANGUAGE®

COMPLETE JAPANESE

THE BASICS

REVISED & UPDATED

LESSON 1

DAI IKKA

A. A Preliminary Note

Japanese, as spoken by the majority of Japan's 127 million people, is the language you will be learning in this course. Japanese is peculiarly original among the world's languages. Despite the fact that more than half the words in Japanese were borrowed from Chinese, the linguistic structure of Japanese is quite different from that of Chinese. Although Japanese grammar is amazingly similar to Korean, and both languages share some vocabulary adopted from Chinese, the two differ in virtually all other respects.

There are several things you should know and remember to make your understanding of Japanese easier:

1. Japanese syllables can be classified into five kinds:

   a. a vowel by itself
   b. a consonant by itself
   c. a consonant + a vowel
   d. a semi-vowel + a vowel
   e. a consonant + *y* + a vowel

2. In Japanese, verbs, adjectives, copulas (linking words), and certain endings are inflected in a number of categories.

3. Japanese has many so-called "particles." They are used very frequently to show the grammatical relationship within a sentence of one word to

another. Mastering these particles is key to rapidly learning Japanese.

4. Punctuation is used in Japanese as it is in English. The use of punctuation marks in the Japanese writing system is relatively new, and rules governing punctuation usage have not yet been firmly established.

5. The word order of Japanese sentences differs from the word order of English sentences. In Japanese, verbs come at the end of a sentence, rather than following the subject and preceding the object, as they do in English.

6. Japanese has a complex system of "honorifics," words that reflect the relationship between the speakers and whom they are speaking about. Different words and word forms are used to indicate the degrees of politeness. The degree of politeness is typically expressed by verb forms in Japanese. There are also more than a dozen ways to say "you" (similar to the French differentiation between "vous" and "tu"); however, speakers often avoid using "you" in conversation, instead preferring to address the hearer by name or by position/title. This book uses the most standard forms of the language, so that, unless otherwise indicated, each phrase can be said by both men and women in most situations without sounding too casual or too formal.

B. THE ALPHABET: THE LETTERS

All Japanese words and sentences in this course have been transcribed into Roman letters, and all the letters of

the English alphabet (except for "l,"[1] "q," and "x")
appear in the transcription. Note, however, that the letter
"c" appears only in combination with "h" and that these
two letters together (ch) are *always treated as one letter*.

A comprehensive list of signs and instructions in
Japanese characters (including their English mean-
ings) appears in Lesson 40. An explanation of the tra-
ditional Japanese writing system and a description of
Japanese characters appear in the section called "The
Writing System." For a discussion of the Japanese
Syllabary, see Lesson 5.

C. ACCENT

Regardless of their length, Japanese words may or
may not be accented. When a word is accented, there
is a drop in the pitch of the voice in the syllable that
directly follows the accented syllable. If a word is
unaccented, the pitch is always slightly lower on the
first syllable, and thereafter the pitch is held at an even
level. In accented words, the pitch drops directly after
the accented syllable and then is held at an even level
throughout the rest of the word. If a one-syllable word
is accented, the drop in pitch occurs after that word.

Note that accents may be dropped in certain cases,
depending on the placement of a word in a sentence and
on the dialect of the speaker. The best way for a student
to grasp the complex rules governing accentuation in
Japanese is to listen closely to the recordings that ac-
company this course or to native speakers of Japanese.

---

[1] The sound of *l* is sometimes heard in the pronunciation of
Japanese by Japanese nationals. But this sound is always interchangeable with the Japanese variety of *r*. For the sake of simplic-
ity, all sounds that might sometimes be pronounced *l* are written
throughout this course as *r*.

D. THE ALPHABET: THE SOUNDS

Many Japanese sounds are like sounds in English. Listen and repeat the following Japanese first names, and notice which sounds are similar and which are different:

Akira	Haruo	Noboru
Aiko	Hideko	Nobuko
Atsuko	Isoo	Osamu
Chieko	Itoko	Rentaroo
Emiko	Jiroo	Ryuuichi
Eijiroo	Jun	Shinzoo
Fusao	Kiyoshi	Susumu
Fusako	Kuniko	Takashi
Gantaroo	Makoto	Teruko
Giichi	Mariko	Umeko

NOTE

1. Each sound is pronounced clearly and crisply; sounds are not slurred over as they often are in English.

2. Each syllable is spoken evenly for almost an equal length of time.

3. Some names or words have an accented syllable and some don't.

E. LOAN WORDS: ENGLISH WORDS USED IN JAPANESE

Now listen to and repeat the following words. These are some of the thousands of English "loan words" used in Japan. While the meanings of these loan words are the same as those of their English counterparts, notice how the Japanese spelling and pronunciation differ from the English:

akusento	accent
amachua	amateur
Amerika	America
baree	ballet
basu	bus
bataa	butter
beru	bell
booto	rowboat
chokoreeto	chocolate
daiyamondo	diamond
dansu	dance
dezaato	dessert
dezain	design
enameru	enamel
erebeetaa	elevator
esukareetaa	escalator
furanneru	flannel
gaido	guide (for travelers)
gasorin	gasoline
gareeji	garage
gorufu	golf
haihiiru	high heel
handobaggu	handbag
herikoputaa	helicopter
hisuterii	hysteria, hysterics
hoosu	water hose
hoomushikku	homesick
hoteru	hotel
infure	inflation
inku	ink
interi	intelligentsia
jaanarisuto	journalist

jamu	jam, jelly
jazu	jazz
kappu	cup (trophy, measuring)
koppu	drinking glass
karee raisu	curried rice
karendaa	calendar
maagarin	margarine
maaketto	market
maaku	mark
modan	modern
nairon	nylon

LESSON 2

DAI NIKA

A. VOWELS

The following groups of words will give you some additional practice in spelling and pronunciation. Listen to the vowel sounds in each word.

1. The sound *a* is pronounced as in the English word "ah" or "father," but short and crisp:

hanasu	tell	**kata**	shoulder
akai	red	*wakai*	young

2. The sound *i* is pronounced like the "e" in the English word "keep," but short and crisp:

i	stomach	**ni**	two
ki	tree	*hi*	fire

3. The sound *u* is pronounced as in the English word "put," but spoken without rounding the lips:

ushi	cow, bull	**kutsu**	shoes
kushi	comb	*tsukue*	desk

4. The sound *e* is pronounced like the "a" in the English word "may," but without the final "y":

e	picture	**te**	hand
ke	hair	*me*	eye

5. The sound *o* is pronounced as in the English word "go," but sharply cut off:

o	tail	**otoko**	male
oto	sound	*soto*	outside

B. VOWEL CLUSTERS

1. When two identical vowels such as *aa, ii, uu, ee,* or *oo* appear together, they form a sound twice as long as that of a single vowel. Compare the following pairs:

kado	corner	**kaado**	card
chizu	map	**chiizu**	cheese
su	nest	**suu**	number (*particle*)
deta	came out	**deeta**	data
to	door	**too**	ten

Sometimes a pair of identical vowels is called a "long vowel" or a "double vowel," and it can be written as a single letter with a macron over it, e.g., *ā*, *ū*, *ē*, and *ō*. However, "long" or "double" *i* is usually written *ii*:

koohii,	coffee	**kuuki,**	air
kōhii		*kūki*	
kaaten,	curtain	*keeki,*	cake
kāten		*kēki*	

2. In a succession of two or more different vowels, each vowel is pronounced clearly and distinctly, and each is articulated for the same length of time:

ue	top	**akai**	red
tsukue	desk	**aoi**	blue
chiisai	small	*aoi umi*	blue ocean
chiisai ie	small house	*aoi kao*	pale face

The combination *ei* forms an exception to this rule, for in everyday speech *ei* is often pronounced like *ee:*

keiko	practice	**Beikoku**	The United
(said		(said	States of
keeko)		*Beekoku*)	America
seito	pupil,	*seinen*	youth
(said	student	(said	
seeto)		*seenen*)	

C. DEVOICED VOWELS

The vowels *i* and *u* are "weak" or "devoiced" vowels. Unless they are accented, they sometimes disappear altogether or are whispered in rapid conversation.

Devoicing usually occurs when these vowels are surrounded by such voiceless consonants as *ch, f, h, k, p, s, sh, t,* and *ts;* or in a word immediately following one of the voiceless consonants. In the following examples, the vowel with a circle underneath is a devoiced vowel:

ki̥tte	postage stamp	**zehi̥**	by all means
ku̥tsushi̥ta	socks	**su̥kkari**	entirely

However, the devoicing of vowels is not crucial. Unlike the case of single vowel vs. double vowel shown in B-1, voicing vs. devoicing does not change the meaning.

LESSON 3

DAI SANKA

A. CONSONANTS I

1. *B* is generally pronounced like the English "b," but less explosively:

bentoo	box lunch	*binsen*	writing pad
kaban	bag	*obon*	tray

2. *Ch* is pronounced like the English "ch" in "cheese":

ocha	tea	*uchi*	house
chotto	a little bit	*chuui*	caution

3. *D* is pronounced with the tip of the tongue touching the back of the upper teeth and is less explosive than the English "d":

dare	who	*densha*	train
doko	where	*kado*	corner

4. *F* is usually pronounced by forcing the air out between the lips as though blowing out a candle. Note that this consonant resembles the English "wh":

fune	ship	*furo*	bath
fukai	deep	*futatsu*	two

5. The Japanese *g* has two sounds:

   a. At the beginning of a word, it is pronounced like the English "g" in "go":

gaikoku	foreign country	*genryoo*	raw material
gin	silver	*go*	five

   b. In the middle of a word, it usually has some nasal quality and sounds something like the "ng" of the English word "singer":

hagaki	postcard	*kagi*	key
kage	shadow	*kagu*	household furniture

6. The Japanese *h* has two sounds:

   a. Before *a, e,* and *o,* it is pronounced like the English "h" in "high":

hai	yes	**hon**	book
hei	fence	*hoo*	cheek

  b. Before *i* or *y*, it is pronounced like the English "h" in "hue":

higashi	east	**hyaku**	one hundred
hiru	noon	*hyooshi*	rhythm

7. *J* is pronounced like the English "j" in "jeep":

jagaimo	potato	**shookaijoo**	letter of introduction
jibiki	dictionary	*juku*	cram school

8. *K* is pronounced like the English "k" in "kite":

kasa	umbrella	**koya**	hut
kesa	this morning	*kutsu*	shoes

9. *M* is pronounced like an English "m," but without tightening the lips as much:

maiasa	every morning	**mikan**	tangerine
me	eye	*mushi*	bug

10. *N* has two sounds in Japanese:

  a. Before *a, e, o,* and *u*, it is pronounced with the tip of the tongue touching the back of the upper teeth:

nashi	pear	**nodo**	throat
neko	cat	*numa*	marsh

b. Before *i* or *y*, it is pronounced like the "n" in the English word "news" (with the tip of the tongue touching the back of the lower teeth and the middle part of the tongue touching the roof of the mouth):

niku	meat	**gyuunyuu**	cow's milk
nishi	west	*nyuuin*	hospitalization

11. *P* is pronounced like the English "p," but less explosively:

pan	bread	**pin**	pin
pen	pen	*sanpun*	three minutes

12. *R* is pronounced by first placing the tip of the tongue at the back of the upper teeth and then flapping it.[1]

raigetsu	next month	**riku**	land
renga	brick	*roku*	six

LESSON 4

DAI YONKA

A. CONSONANTS II

1. *S* is pronounced like the English "s" in "song," but with less hiss:

---

[1] For more on the sound of *r*, refer to the footnote on page 3.

saka   slope   **sora**   sky
sekai   world   *su*   vinegar

2. *Sh* resembles the English "sh" in "she":

shashin   photograph   **shooko**   proof
shichi   seven   *shuto*   capital city

3. *T* is pronounced with the tip of the tongue touching the back of the upper teeth and is less explosive than the English "t":

tamago   egg   **te**   hand
takusan   a lot   *to*   door

4. *Ts* is pronounced like the English "ts" in "cats":

natsu   summer   *atsui*   hot
tsunami   tidal wave   *tsutsuji*   azalea

5. *V* is pronounced like the English "v" in "vain." This sound appears only in words borrowed from Occidental languages. Note that most Japanese do not use this sound at all but replace it with a *b*, as follows:

vaiorin   violin   **baiorin**   violin
veeru   veil   **beeru**   veil
viniiru   vinyl   *biniiru*   vinyl
revyuu   revue   *rebyuu*   revue

6. *Z* usually has two sounds in Japanese:

a. At the beginning of a word it has a sound similar to the English "ds" in "beds":

zaisei	finance	**zoo**	elephant
zeitaku	luxury	*zutto*	by far

b. In the middle of a word it is pronounced like the English "z" in "zero":

kaze	wind	*mizu*	water
suzume	sparrow	*kazoku*	family

Note that some Japanese mix the *dz* and *z* sounds described above without regard to the position of the letter in the word.

7. *P, t, k,* or *s* can be a syllable by itself.[1] To pronounce such a syllabic consonant, hold the tongue position abruptly for one beat before the next syllable is pronounced.

a. When a syllabic consonant (*p, t, k,* or *s*) is followed by the same consonant, they are called "double consonants" and the sound is doubled in length. Note the differences in pronunciation between the following pairs of words. The first word in each pair contains a single consonant and the second contains double consonants:

haka	tomb	**hakka**	peppermint
kasai	fire damage	**kassai**	applause
moto	formerly	*motto*	more

b. Syllabic *t* can be followed by *ch* or *ts*, and *s* can be followed by *sh:*

---

[1] In words borrowed from Western languages (loan words), *d* or *g* can also be a syllable by itself.

| **itchi** | agreement | **irasshai** | welcome |
| *ittsuu* | one letter | *kesshin* | determination |

8. The syllabic *n* represents another group of sounds that is independent of the *n* described above in Item 10. In this manual, the syllabic *n* is written like the ordinary *n*. Remember, however, that it differs in pronunciation from the ordinary *n* as follows:

   a. It is always held as long as one full syllable.
   b. Its own sound value changes, depending on what follows.

    (1) Before *n, t,* and *d,* it is pronounced like the English "n" in "pen":

| **anna** | that sort of | **santoo** | third class |
| *onna* | female | *kondo* | this time |

    (2) Before *m, p,* or *b,* it is pronounced like the English "m":

SPELLED	PRONOUNCED	
sanmai	**sammai**	three sheets
shinpai	*shimpai*	worry
kanban	*kamban*	signboard

    (3) Before a vowel or a semi-vowel (*y* or *w*), it is pronounced somewhat like the English *ng* in "singer," but without finishing the *g* sound; the preceding vowel is often nasalized:

gen'an[1]   original plan

---

[1] Notice that an apostrophe is placed after a syllabic *n* when it precedes a vowel or *y*.

tan'i	unit
hon'ya	bookstore
minwa	folklore

Note that in the following pairs of words, the first has an ordinary *n* and the second has a syllabic *n:*

tani	valley	**tan'i**	unit
zenin	approval	*zen'in*	all members

(4) Before *k, g,* and *s,* or when it is the final letter in a word, the syllabic *n* sounds somewhat like the English "ng" in "singer" described in (3) above:

kankei	relationship	*sensei*	teacher
ningen	human beings	*san*	three
sen	one thousand	*kin*	gold

B. Semi-Vowels

1. *W* is pronounced somewhat like the English "w" in "want," but without rounding or protruding the lips:

watakushi[1]	I (formal)	**kawa**	river
watashi	(informal)	*uwagi*	jacket

2. *Y* occurs in two kinds of environments:

a. It occurs before a vowel (e.g., *ya, yu, yo*) and is pronounced like the English "y" in "yellow":

[1] The use of formal and informal forms is very complicated. It depends on the speaker and the particular situation. Women are more likely than men to use the formal form of the word.

yama	mountain	**hayai**	fast
yoru	night	*fuyu*	winter

  b. It occurs between a consonant and a vowel.
     Then the consonant is palatalized (said with
     the tongue touching the palate):

kyaku	guest	**ryoodo**	territory
happyoo	announcement	*kyuu*	nine

LESSON 5

DAI GOKA

A. THE JAPANESE SYLLABARY

The traditional writing system used in Japan is based
on two different types of symbols: phonetic and ideographic. (See "The Writing System" for a detailed
explanation.) The phonetic symbols are the Japanese
equivalents of our alphabet and are called *kana*. Each
kana symbol stands for a syllable.

  These are the basic syllables represented in *kana*:[1]

a	ka	sa	ta	na	ha	ma	ya	ra	wa	n (syllabic)
i	ki	shi	chi	ni	hi	mi		ri		
u	ku	su	tsu	nu	fu	mu	yu	ru		
e	ke	se	te	ne	he	me		re		
o	ko	so	to	no	ho	mo	yo	ro	o[2]	

[1] For non-basic syllables, see "The Writing System," pages 397- 403.
[2] These two *o* sounds are pronounced the same but their uses differ.
For details, see "The Writing System," page 397.

B. GENERAL SOUND EQUIVALENTS

1. Japanese *aa* = English "ar," "er," "ir," "or":

apaato	apartment	*saakasu*	circus
pitchaa	pitcher (baseball)	*mootaa*	motor

2. Japanese *ee* = English "a":

geemu	game	*teeburu*	table
keeki	cake	*keeburu*	cable (car)

3. Japanese *oo* = English "o," "oa":

boonasu	bonus	*hoomuran*	home run
booto	boat	*koochi*	coach (athletic)

4. Japanese *ui* = English "ui," "wi":

kuizu	quiz (radio, TV program)	*uitto*	wit

5. Japanese *b* = English "v":

terebi	television	*shaberu*	shovel

6. Japanese *chi* = English "ti":

chippu	tip	*chiimu*	team

7. Japanese *ji* = English "di":

rajio   radio   *jirenma*   dilemma
sutajio   studio
          (art, broadcasting, movie)

8. Japanese *k* = English "c":

kakuteru   cocktail   *kamera*   camera
Amerika   America   *konsarutanto*   consultant

9. Japanese *kku* = English "ack," "ock":

barakku   barrack
dokku   dock

10. Japanese *kki* = English "eck," "ick":

dekki   deck
sutekki   stick (walking)

11. Japanese *ru* = English "l," "rl":

hoteru   hotel   *kaaru*   curl
booru   ball

12. Japanese *suto* = English "st":

sutoraiki,   strike   *jaanarisuto*   journalist
  or **suto**   (labor)   *pianisuto*   pianist

13. Japanese *tto* = English "t":

maaketto   market   *soketto*   socket
pan-   pamphlet   *yotto*   yacht
  furetto

14. Japanese *tsu* = English "t":

shatsu   shirt
omuretsu   omelet

15. Japanese *s* = English "th":

suriru   thrill   *oosoritii*   authority

C. MORE LOAN WORDS

As you have already observed, a great number of English words have been adopted by the Japanese and are in everyday use. The following is a list of some more loan words.

apaato	apartment house	*geemu*	game
		gorira	gorilla
aribai	alibi	*guruupu*	group
arufabetto	alphabet	*haamonika*	harmonica
arukooru	alcohol	*hoomuran*	home run
asupirin	aspirin	*infuruenza*	influenza
batto	bat (baseball)	*iyahoon*	earphone
		jiguzagu	zigzag
booi sukauto	boy scout	*jirenma*	dilemma
boonasu	bonus	*karorii*	calorie
booru	ball	*keeki*	cake (Occidental)
burashi	brush		
daasu	dozen	*konkuriito*	concrete
dainamaito	dynamite	*kooto*	coat
damu	dam	*koruku*	cork
dorama	drama	*kurabu*	club

doru	dollar	*kureyon*	crayon
emerarudo	emerald	*kuriimu*	cream
episoodo	episode	*kuriiningu*	cleaning
feruto	felt	*kuupon*	coupon
gaaru sukauto	girl scout	*makaroni*	macaroni
		massaaji	massage
masukotto	mascot	*ribon*	ribbon
medaru	medal	*roketto*	rocket
megahon	megaphone	*romansu*	romance
memo	memo	*saakasu*	circus
menyuu	menu	*sairen*	siren
mootaa	motor	*sakkarin*	saccharine
motto	motto	*sandoitchi*	sandwich
neonsain	neon sign	*sararii*	salary
onsu	ounce	*shaberu*	shovel
oosoritii	authority	*shoouindoo*	show window
ootobai	motorcycle (auto-bicycle)	*soketto*	socket
		sooseeji	sausage
ootomiiru	oatmeal	*supai*	spy
Orinpikku	Olympic Games	*supiido*	speed
		surippa	slipper
paasento	percent	*sutereo*	stereo
pai	pie	*suutsu*	suitcase
painappuru	pineapple	*keesu*	
panfuretto	pamphlet	*taipuraitaa*	typewriter
panku	flat tire (puncture)	*tairu*	tile
		takushii	taxi
panorama	panorama	*tanku*	tank
parupu	pulp	*taoru*	towel
pasupooto	passport	*teeburu*	table
pianisuto	pianist	*tonneru*	tunnel
poketto	pocket	*torakku*	truck
raion	lion	*ueetoresu*	waitress
rajuumu	radium	*uranyuumu*	uranium

reinkooto	raincoat	*yotto*	yacht
resutoran	restaurant (Occidental)	*yuumoa*	humor

Note that when a word from English is used in Japanese, not only is the *sound* of the word changed to harmonize with the Japanese sound system, but the *length* of the word may be cut, as in the following examples:

infure	inflation
panku	puncture (flat tire)
pasokon	personal computer
terebi	television

Notice that some words are used in a more restricted sense in Japanese than in English. Here are some more words borrowed from English that are used in a restricted or altered sense in Japanese:

JAPANESE FORM	WORD OF ORIGIN	BUT MEANS IN JAPANESE
barakku	barrack	shack; shabby-looking, flimsy wooden house
biru *birudingu*	building	Occidental-style concrete office building
bisuketto	biscuits	tea biscuits and cookies
doa	door	Occidental-style door
doramu	drum	drum (musical only; refers mainly to types used in jazz)
jamu	jam	jam and jelly
kappu	cup	trophy, measuring cup
konpasu	compass	compass (instrument for drawing circles)

manshon	mansion	condominium (or high-class apartment)
mishin	machine	sewing machine
nooto	note	notebook
paipu	pipe	pipe
raitaa	lighter	cigarette lighter
sutoroo	straw	drinking straw

LESSON 6

DAI ROKKA

A. DAYS AND MONTHS

Getsuyoobi	Monday
Kayoobi	Tuesday
Suiyoobi	Wednesday
Mokuyoobi	Thursday
Kin'yoobi	Friday
Doyoobi	Saturday
Nichiyoobi	Sunday
Ichigatsu	January
Nigatsu	February
Sangatsu	March
Shigatsu	April
Gogatsu	May
Rokugatsu	June
Shichigatsu	July
Hachigatsu	August
Kugatsu	September
Juugatsu	October

Juuichigatsu   November
Juunigatsu   December

B. NUMBERS 1–10

ichi	one
ni	two
san	three
shi, yon	four
go	five
roku	six
shichi, nana	seven
hachi	eight
kyuu, ku	nine
juu	ten

C. COLORS

ao	blue
aka	red
kiiro	yellow
midori	green
shiro	white
kuro	black
chairo	brown
nezumiiro, haiiro	gray

D. NORTH, SOUTH, EAST, WEST

kita	north	**higashi**	east
minami	south	**nishi**	west

QUIZ 1

Match the Japanese and English words in these two columns:

1. *Nichiyoobi*	a. Thursday
2. *Hachigatsu*	b. brown
3. *Suiyoobi*	c. ten
4. *nezumiiro*	d. Sunday
5. *Mokuyoobi*	e. red
6. *ku*	f. August
7. *chairo*	g. Monday
8. *hachi*	h. July
9. *Shichigatsu*	i. five
10. *kiiro*	j. white
11. *aka*	k. gray
12. *Getsuyoobi*	l. nine
13. *go*	m. Wednesday
14. *shiro*	n. yellow
15. *juu*	o. eight

ANSWERS

1—d; 2—f; 3—m; 4—k; 5—a; 6—l; 7—b; 8—o;
9—h; 10—n; 11—e; 12—g; 13—i; 14—j; 15—c.

E. WORD STUDY

fiito	feet
garon	gallon
guramu	gram
inchi	inch
kiromeetoru	kilometer
mairu	mile
meetoru	meter
pondo	pound
rittoru	liter
yaado	yard

Supplemental Vocabulary List 1: At School

at school	*gakkoo ni, gakkoo de*
school	*gakkoo*
university	*daigaku*
classroom	*kyooshitsu*
course	*katei, kamoku, kooza*
teacher	*sensei, kyooshi*
professor	*kyooju*
student	*gakusei, seito*
subject	*kamoku, gakka*
notebook	*nooto*
textbook	*kyookasho*
math	*suugaku*
history	*rekishi*
chemistry	*kagaku*
biology	*seibutsugaku*
literature	*bungaku*
language	*gogaku, gengo*
art	*geijutsu, bijutsu*
music	*ongaku*
gym	*taisoo, taiiku, jimu*
recess	*kyuukei, yasumi, kyuuka*
test	*tesuto, shiken*
grade	*seiseki*
report card	*tsuuchihyoo*
diploma	*sotsugyooshoosho, gakuimenjoo*
degree	*gakui, shoogoo*
difficult / easy	*muzukashii / yasashii*
to study	*benkyoosuru*
to learn	*narau*
to pass	*ukaru, gookakusuru*
to fail	*ochiru, rakudaisuru*

LESSON 7

DAI NANAKA

A. GREETINGS

Now let's study some of the greetings you'll use right from the start. The words in brackets are literal translations.

Ohayoo gozaimasu.	Good morning.
Yamada-san[1]	Mr. Yamada
Yamada-san, ohayoo gozaimasu.	Good morning, Mr. Yamada.
Konnichi wa.	Good afternoon. [Good day.]
Konban wa.	Good evening.
Oyasumi nasai.	Good night (*said just before going to bed*).
Ogenki desu ka?	How are you? [Are you in good spirits?]
genki	well [good spirits]
Genki desu.	I am very well.
Arigatoo gozaimasu.	Thank you.
Okagesama de.	Thank you. [Due to your kind thought, am well.]
Onamae wa nan to osshaimasu ka?	What is your name?
Onamae wa?	What is your name?

watashi wa Erin desu.

[1] The suffix *-san* is used in Japanese as a term of respect meaning "Mr.," "Mrs.," "Miss," "Sir," or "Madam."

Yamada Masao to mooshimasu.[1]	My name is Yamada Masao.[1]
Yamada desu.	I am Yamada.
Watakushi no namae wa Yamada desu.	My name is Yamada.
Gomen nasai.	Excuse me. I'm sorry.
Ii desu.	That's all right.
yukkuri	slowly
Yukkuri hanashite kudasai.	Please speak slowly.
doozo	please
Doozo yukkuri hanashite kudasai.	Please speak slowly.
moo ichido	once more
Itte kudasai.	Please say [it].
Moo ichido itte kudasai.	Please repeat that. [Say it once more, please.]
Doozo moo ichido itte kudasai.	Please repeat that. [Please say it once more.]
doomo	very much [indeed!]
Doomo arigatoo gozaimasu.	Thank you very much.
Doo itashimashite.	Not at all.
Arigatoo gozaimashita.	Thank you (*for what you have done*).
Kochira koso.	It was a pleasure. [It was my side (that should have thanked).]

[1] Japanese people use their last names before their first names; therefore, Yamada is the last name of the person speaking. When giving their names in English, however, Japanese people usually adopt the Western order. For a Western name, even while speaking Japanese, the Western order is also usually used.

Dewa ashita.	Till tomorrow. See you tomorrow. [Well, then, tomorrow.]
Dewa Doyoobi ni.	Till Saturday. See you Saturday. [Well, then, on Saturday.]
Dewa Getsuyoobi ni.	Till Monday. See you Monday.
Dewa Mokuyoobi ni.	Till Thursday. See you Thursday.
Dewa konban.	Till this evening. See you this evening.
Dewa ashita no ban.	Till tomorrow evening. See you tomorrow evening.
Dewa raishuu.	Till next week. See you next week.
Dewa mata.	See you later. [Well, then, again.]
Dewa sono uchi ni.	See you sometime.
Sayoonara.	Good-bye.

B. How's the Weather?

Kyoo no tenki wa doo desu ka?	How's the weather today? What's the weather like today?
Ii tenki desu.	It's nice weather.
Kyoo wa tenki ga warui desu.	The weather is bad today.
Ame ga futte imasu.	It's raining.
Yuki ga futte imasu.	It's snowing.
Atsui desu.	It's hot.
Samui desu.	It's cold.
Suzushii desu.	It's cool.

QUIZ 2

1. *Genki desu.*	a. Please speak.
2. *Konban wa.*	b. once more
3. *Hanashite kudasai.*	c. It's hot.
4. *Arigatoo gozaimasu.*	d. See you tomorrow.
5. *moo ichido*	e. How are you?
6. *Doozo.*	f. I am very well.
7. *Atsui desu.*	g. slowly
8. *Dewa ashita.*	h. Thank you.
9. *Ogenki desu ka?*	i. Please.
10. *yukkuri*	j. Good evening.

ANSWERS

1—f; 2—j; 3—a; 4—h; 5—b; 6—i; 7—c; 8—d; 9—e; 10—g.

SUPPLEMENTAL VOCABULARY LIST 2: THE WEATHER

weather	*tenki*
It's raining.	*Ame ga futteiru.*
It's snowing.	*Yuki ga futteiru.*
It's hailing.	*Arare ga futteiru.*
It's windy.	*Kaze ga tsuyoi.*
It's hot.	*Atsui.*
It's cold.	*Samui.*
It's sunny.	*Hareteiru.*
It's cloudy.	*Kumotteiru.*
It's beautiful.	*Subarashii.*
storm	*arashi*
wind	*kaze*
sun	*taiyoo, nikkoo*
thunder	*arashi*
lightening	*kaminari*

hurricane	*boofuu, harikeen*
temperature	*ondo*
degree	*do*
rain	*ame*
snow	*yuki*
cloud	*kumo*
fog	*kiri*
smog	*sumoggu*
umbrella	*kasa*

LESSON 8

DAI HACHIKA

A. DO YOU HAVE?

In the phrases below, you will see the particles *ka* and *ga*. Particles are an important part of basic grammar and will be studied in Lesson 11. For now, understand that particles indicate the relationship between the words or parts of a phrase. For example, the particle *ka* is used at the end of an interrogative sentence and shows that what precedes it is a question. The particle *ga* is used to show that what precedes it is the grammatical subject, or in some cases object, of a verb. Also, note that there is usually no translation in Japanese for "some" or "any."

Arimasu ka?   Do you have . . . ? [Is
                         there . . . ?]

   mizu ga   some water (*as the
                         subject of the verb*)

tabako ga	some (any) cigarettes
hi ga	a light
matchi ga	some matches
sekken ga	some soap
kami ga	some paper
Mizu ga¹ arimasu ka?	Do you have some water?
Tabako ga arimasu ka?	Do you have any cigarettes?

B. IN A RESTAURANT

asagohan	breakfast
hirugohan	lunch
bangohan	supper
Irasshaimase.	Welcome.
Nani o meshiagari-masu ka?	What would you like to eat?
Misete kudasai.	Show me . . . , please.
Menyuu o misete kudasai.	Show me a menu, please.
. . . kudasai.	I'd like [Please give me . . .]
Pan o kudasai.	I'd like some bread, please.
pan o	some bread
bataa o	some butter
suupu o	some soup
niku o	some meat
gyuuniku o	some beef
tamago o	some eggs
yasai o	some vegetables
jagaimo o	some potatoes
sarada o	some salad
miruku o	some milk

¹ Note that in the English equivalent, "water" is the object of "have," but *mizu* (water) is followed by the particle *ga* (the subject marker; see above). This also holds true for the rest of the sentences in the section.

wain o	some wine
satoo o	some sugar
shio o	some salt
koshoo o	some pepper
yakizakana o	some broiled fish
miso shiru o	some miso soup (made with bean paste)
sashimi o	some sashimi (raw fish)
tenpura o	some tempura (fritter; deep-fried food)
Motte kite kudasai . . .	Please bring me . . .
Suupu o motte kite kudasai.	Please bring me some soup.
tiisupuun o	a teaspoon
fooku o	a fork
naifu o	a knife
napukin o	a napkin
sara o	a plate
koppu o	a glass
. . . ippai kudasai.	I'd like [Please give me] a glass of . . .
. . . hitobin kudasai.	I'd like [Please give me] a bottle of . . .
Mizu o ippai kudasai.	Please give me a glass of water.
ocha o ippai	a cup of tea
koohii o ippai	a cup of coffee
wain o ippon	a bottle of wine
biiru o ippon	a bottle of beer
tamago o moo hitotsu	another egg
sore o sukoshi	a little of that
sore o moo sukoshi	a little more of that
pan o moo sukoshi	some more bread, a little more bread

niku o motto	some more meat
niku o moo sukoshi	a little more meat
Chekku o motte kite kudasai.	The check, please.

QUIZ 3

1.	*niku o*	a.	please bring me
2.	*biiru o*	b.	matches
3.	*arimasu ka?*	c.	please give me
4.	*miruku o*	d.	meat
5.	*bataa o*	e.	some water
6.	*kudasai*	f.	a light
7.	*matchi o*	g.	milk
8.	*niku o moo sukoshi*	h.	eggs
9.	*motte kite kudasai*	i.	beer
10.	*mizu o*	j.	the check
11.	*hi o*	k.	Do you have . . .
12.	*shio o*	l.	butter
13.	*tamago o*	m.	a cup of coffee
14.	*koohii o ippai*	n.	some more meat
15.	*chekku o*	o.	salt

ANSWERS
1—d; 2—i; 3—k; 4—g; 5—l; 6—c; 7—b; 8—n; 9—a; 10—e; 11—f; 12—o; 13—h; 14—m; 15—j.

C. WORD STUDY

burausu	blouse
hankachi	handkerchief
nekutai	necktie
oobaakooto	overcoat
seetaa	sweater
shatsu	shirt
sukaafu	scarf

sukaato	skirt
surippu	slip

SUPPLEMENTAL VOCABULARY LIST 3: FOOD

food	*tabemono*
dinner	*yuushoku, bangohan*
lunch	*chuushoku, hirugohan*
breakfast	*chooshoku, asagohan*
meat	*niku*
chicken	*toriniku, chikin*
beef	*gyuuniku, biifu*
pork	*butaniku, pooku*
fish	*sakana*
shrimp	*ebi*
lobster	*robusutaa*
bread	*pan*
egg	*tamago*
cheese	*chiizu*
rice	*(o)kome, gohan (cooked rice)*
vegetable	*yasai*
lettuce	*retasu*
tomato	*tomato*
carrot	*ninjin*
cucumber	*kyuuri*
pepper	*koshoo*
fruit	*kudamono, furuutsu*
apple	*ringo*
orange	*orenji*
banana	*banana*
pear	*nashi*
grapes	*budoo*
drink	*nomimono*
water	*mizu*
milk	*gyuunyuu, miruku*

juice	*juusu*
coffee	*koohii*
tea	*koocha, ocha*
wine	*wain*
beer	*biiru*
soft drink / soda	*seiryooinryoo,*
	sofutodorinku / sooda
salt	*shio*
pepper	*koshoo*
sugar	*satoo*
honey	*hachimitsu*
hot / cold	*atsui / tsumetai*
sweet / sour	*amai / suppai*

LESSON 9

DAI KYUUKA

This lesson and several of the following lessons are longer than the others. They contain the grammatical information you need to know from the start. Don't try to memorize anything; just read each section until you understand every point. Then, as you continue with the course, try to observe examples of the points mentioned. Refer back to these sections and to the Summary of Japanese Grammar at the back of the book as necessary. In this way, you will eventually find that you have a good grasp of the basic features of Japanese grammar without any deliberate memorization of rules.

A. PRONOUNS

Personal pronouns are used much less frequently in Japanese than in English. The context clarifies what or who is being referred to or addressed. In addition, in Japanese there are more varieties of words that correspond to English pronouns. The list below will help you follow the sections to come, but be sure to study Section 12 of the Summary of Japanese Grammar for more information.

I	**watashi,** watakushi[1]
you	**anata**[2]
he/she	**ano hito**
he	**kare**
she	**kanojo**
we	**watashitachi,** watakushitachi
you (*pl.*)[3]	**anatagata**[4]
they	**ano hitotachi,** karera

B. TO BE OR NOT TO BE

1. There is more than one way to say "is" in Japanese. A different word is used for this English verb in each of the following sentences:

Enpitsu desu.	It is a pencil.
Enpitsu ga arimasu.[5]	There is a pencil.
Nyuu Yooku ni imasu.	He is in New York.

[1] The form *watakushi*, while official, is less conversational than *watashi*.

[2] *Anata* and *anatagata* are usually to be avoided. It is more polite to use the person's name.

[3] Throughout this book *pl.* stands for "plural" and *sg.* stands for "singular."

[4] *Anata* and *anatagata* are usually to be avoided. It is more polite to use the person's name.

[5] This sentence is ambiguous; it can also mean "(I) have a pencil." See Lessons 8 and 14 for phrases with "have."

    a. When you say that one thing is equal to another, you use *desu*. Its meaning roughly corresponds to "am, is, are."

    b. When you are talking about something being located or situated in a place, use *arimasu* if the thing referred to is inanimate.

    c. Use *imasu* if the thing referred to is animate.

Note that *desu* is called the *copula*. *Arimasu* and *imasu* are ordinary verbs and are inflected like other verbs, which you will begin to study in Lesson 10. Also, the negative of *desu* has its own particular forms; see below.

  2. Study these examples with *desu*, *arimasu*, and *imasu*:

a. *Sore wa enpitsu desu.* — That is a pencil. (A equals B.)

b. *Soko ni enpitsu ga arimasu.* — There is a pencil there. (A—inanimate—is located at B.)

c. *Soko ni kodomo ga imasu.* — There is a child there. (A—animate—is located at B.)

a. *Sore wa tabako desu ka?* — Is that a cigarette?

b. *Tabako ga arimasu ka?* — Is a cigarette there?

c. *Yamada-san wa soko ni imasu ka?* — Is Mr. Yamada there?

a. *Shikago wa ookii machi desu.* — Chicago is a big city.

b. *Shikago wa Irinoishuu ni arimasu.* — Chicago is in the state of Illinois.

c. *Yamada-san wa Shikago ni imasu.* — Mr. Yamada is in Chicago.

3. Listen for examples of these forms in the phrases that follow. Notice that the word or phrase that equals the element "A" (as used in the phrases above) is marked with the particle *wa* or *ga*. *Wa* is used when the emphasis in the sentence is not on "A." *Ga* is used to emphasize "A." The word or phrase equaling the element "B" always comes immediately before *desu*. (If no specific noun is used for "B," use *soo* in its place, as *desu* can never be used alone.)

Anata wa Amerikajin desu ka?	Are you an American?
Hai, soo desu.	Yes, I am. [Yes, am so.]
tatemono	building
taishikan	embassy
Dono tatemono ga Amerika Taishikan desu ka?	Which building is the American Embassy?
Ano tatemono wa Amerika Taishikan desu.	That building is the American Embassy.
Ano tatemono ga soo desu.	That building is. [That building is so.]
Ano tatemono ga Amerika Taishikan desu ka?	Is that building the American Embassy?
Hai, soo desu.	Yes, it is. [Yes, is so.]
Sumisu-san wa Amerika Taishikan ni imasu.	Mr. Smith is in the American Embassy.

Tanaka-san wa Too-kyoo ni imasu.	Ms. Tanaka is in Tokyo.
Okinawa wa doko ni arimasu ka?	Where is Okinawa?
Nippon to Taiwan no aida ni arimasu.	It is between Japan and Taiwan.
Dono kata ga Tanaka-san desu ka?	Which person is Ms. Tanaka?
Watashi ga Tanaka desu.	I am. [Am Tanaka.]
Watashi ga soo desu.	I am [so].
Sore wa tabako desu.	That is a cigarette.
Enpitsu ga arimasu ka?	Do you have a pencil? Is there a pencil?
Kodomo wa Tookyoo ni imasu.	The child is in Tokyo.
Tabako ga arimasu.	I have a cigarette. There is a cigarette.

C. *DESU*

1. Compare the following different forms of *desu* in the affirmative:

present or future	*A wa B desu.*	A is B.
past	*A wa B deshita.*	A was B.
tentative	*A wa B deshoo.*	A is probably B.
tentative past	*A wa B datta deshoo.*	A was probably B.

2. The negative forms of the above are:

present or future	*A wa B*	{ *ja* / *dewa* }	*arimasen.* A is not B.
	A wa B	{ *ja* / *dewa* }	*nai desu.*

past	A wa B	{ja / dewa}	arimasen deshita.[1]	A was not B.
	A wa B	{ja / dewa}	nakatta desu.	
tentative	A wa B	{ja / dewa}	nai de-shoo.	A is prob-ably not B.
tentative past	A wa B	{ja / dewa}	nakatta deshoo.	A was probably not B.

Ja is a contraction of *dewa* that you will hear in conversation, while you are more likely to see *dewa* in written material. Their meaning is the same. Most of the examples in this book will use *ja*, since our focus is on conversational Japanese.

3. Study these examples with *desu* and its forms:

gakusei	student
Watashi wa gakusei desu.	I'm a student.
kaishain[2]	businessperson
Watashi wa kaishain desu.	I'm a businessperson.
Watakushi wa Amerika-jin desu.	I'm American.

---

[1] This form of the negative is not heard in colloquial conversation as often as the second (tentative) form. However, it is included here for reference, since some forms of adjectives follow this pattern, as you will see in Lesson 11.

[2] *Kaishain* actually means "employee of a business firm." You will often hear *bijinesuman* for "businessman" or *sarariiman* for "person earning a salary."

Kono tatemono wa Igirisu Taishikan desu ka?	Is that building the British Embassy?
Igirisu Taishikan ja arimasen.	It is not the British Embassy.
Watashi wa gakusei ja arimasen.	I'm not a student.
Ano hito wa kaishain ja arimasen.	He [that person] is not a businessperson.
Ano hito wa Nihonjin ja arimasen.	She [that person] is not Japanese.
Watashi wa gakusei deshita.	I was a student.
sensei	teacher
Tanaka-san wa sensei deshita.	Ms. Tanaka was a teacher.
hoteru	hotel
Ano tatemono wa hoteru deshita.	That building was a hotel.
Kare wa gakusei ja arimasen deshita.	He was not a student.
Yamada-san wa kaishain ja arimasen deshita.	Ms. Yamada was not a businessperson.
Amerika Taishikan ja arimasen deshita.	That was not the American Embassy.
Kore wa hoteru deshoo.	This is probably a hotel.
Kanojo wa Amerikajin deshoo.	She's probably American.
Ano hito wa sensei ja nai deshoo.	He is probably not a teacher.
kuruma	car
Kuruma wa Nihonsei ja nai deshoo.	The car is probably not Japanese.

Igirusu Taishikan ja nai deshoo.

That is probably not the British Embassy.

Ano hito wa sensei ja nakatta deshoo.

He was probably not a teacher.

Kuruma wa Nihonsei ja nakatta deshoo.

The car was probably not Japanese.

QUIZ 4

1. *Tabako ga arimasu ka?*
2. *Watashi wa gakusei ja arimasen.*
3. *Sore wa enpitsu desu.*
4. *Kono tatemono wa Igirisu Taishikan desu ka?*
5. *Tanaka-san wa sensei ja arimasen deshita.*
6. *Nyuu Yooku ni imasu.*
7. *Kuruma desu.*
8. *Kore wa hoteru deshoo.*
9. *Kodomo wa Tookyoo ni imasu.*
10. *Yamada-san wa kaishain desu.*

a. Is this building the British Embassy?
b. Mr. Yamada is a businessperson.
c. Ms. Tanaka was not a teacher.
d. It's a car.
e. The child is in Tokyo.
f. This is probably a hotel.
g. Do you have a cigarette?
h. I'm not a student.
i. That is a pencil.
j. I'm in New York.

ANSWERS
1—g; 2—h; 3—i; 4—a; 5—c; 6—j; 7—d; 8—f; 9—e; 10—b.

REVIEW QUIZ 1

Choose the correct Japanese equivalent for the English word or phrase:

1. five =
    a. *roku*
    b. *shichi*
    c. *go*

2. eight =
    a. *hachi*
    b. *ku*
    c. *shi*

3. Tuesday =
    a. *Suiyoobi*
    b. *Kayoobi*
    c. *Kin'yoobi*

4. Sunday =
    a. *Nichiyoobi*
    b. *Doyoobi*
    c. *Getsuyoobi*

5. March =
    a. *Sangatsu*
    b. *Kugatsu*
    c. *Shigatsu*

6. June =
    a. *Shichigatsu*
    b. *Rokugatsu*
    c. *Gogatsu*

7. red =
   a. *ao*
   b. *kiiro*
   c. *aka*

8. green =
   a. *kiiro*
   b. *midori*
   c. *haiiro*

9. black =
   a. *kuro*
   b. *chairo*
   c. *shiro*

10. brown =
   a. *kuro*
   b. *aka*
   c. *chairo*

11. Good morning =
   a. *Ohayoo gozaimasu.*
   b. *Konban wa.*
   c. *Genki desu.*

12. I'm not a student =
   a. *Kare wa Kaishain desu.*
   b. *Watashi wa gakusei ja arimasen.*
   c. *Igirisu Taishikan ja arimasen.*

13. Thank you =
   a. *Itte kudasai.*
   b. *Arigatoo gozaimasu.*
   c. *Doo itashimashite.*

14. Please =
    a. *Hanashite kudasai.*
    b. *Arigatoo gozaimasu.*
    c. *Doozo.*

15. Good-bye =
    a. *Dewa ashita.*
    b. *Sayonara.*
    c. *Konnichi wa.*

16. car =
    a. *kuruma*
    b. *kaishain*
    c. *kodomo*

17. She's probably American =
    a. *Kanojo wa Amerikajin ja arimasen.*
    b. *Kanojo wa Amerikajin deshita.*
    c. *Kanojo wa Amerikajin deshoo.*

18. businessperson =
    a. *kaishain*
    b. *hoteru*
    c. *kodomo*

19. There's a cigarette =
    a. *Tabako ga arimasu.*
    b. *Tabako desu.*
    c. *Tabako ga imasu.*

20. He is in New York =
    a. *Nyuu Yooku ga arimasu.*
    b. *Nyuu Yooku ni imasu.*
    c. *Nyuu Yooku desu.*

ANSWERS

1—c; 2—a; 3—b; 4—a; 5—a; 6—b; 7—c; 8—b;
9—a; 10—c; 11—a; 12—b; 13—b; 14—c; 15—b;
16—a; 17—c; 18—a; 19—a; 20—b.

SUPPLEMENTAL VOCABULARY LIST 4: FAMILY AND RELATIONSHIPS

family and relationships	*kazoku to shinrui kankei*
mother	*okaasan, okaasama* (respect), *haha* (one's own)
father	*otoosan, otoosama* (respect), *chichi* (one's own)
son	*musuko, musukosan* (polite)
daughter	*musume, musumesan* (polite), *ojoosan* (polite)
older sister	*oneesan, ane* (one's own)
younger sister	*imooto, imootosan* (polite)
baby	*akanboo, akachan*
older brother	*oniisan, ani* (one's own)
younger brother	*otooto, otootosan* (polite)
husband	*dannasama* (someone else's), *goshujin* (someone else's), *otto* (one's own), *shujin* (one's own)
wife	*okusan* (someone else's), *tsuma* (one's own), *kanai* (one's own)
aunt	*obasan, oba* (one's own)
uncle	*ojisan, oji* (one's own)
grandmother	*obaasan, sobo* (one's own)
grandfather	*ojiisan, sofu* (one's own)
cousin	*itoko*
mother-in-law	*giri no okaasan, giri no haha* (one's own)

father-in-law	*giri no otoosan, giri no chichi* (one's own)
stepmother	*keebo, mamahaha*
stepfather	*keefu, mamachichi*
stepson	*keeshi, mamako*
stepdaughter	*keeshi, mamako*
boyfriend	*kare, kareshi, booifurendo*
girlfriend	*kanozyo, gaarufurendo*
fiancé(e)	*konyakusha*
friend	*tomodachi, yuuzin*
relative	*shinrui, shinseki*
to love	*aisuru*
to know (a person)	(X *o*) *shitteiru*
to meet (a person)	(X *ni*) *au*
to marry (someone)	(X *to*) *kekkonsuru*
to divorce (someone)	(X *to*) *rikonsuru*
to get a divorce	*rikonsuru*
to inherit	*soozokusuru*

LESSON 10

DAI JIKKA

A. COMMON VERB FORMS

In Japanese, main verbs come at the ends of sentences (similarly to *desu*). You will also see that Japanese verbs make no distinction of person or number; the same forms are used for first, second, and third persons in both the singular and plural. And, as you have probably noticed, in Japanese it is the verb endings that determine tenses.[1]

---

[1] You will learn more about verb forms in Lesson 12.

1. I speak/talk, I spoke/talked, I'm speaking/talking, etc.

Hanashimasu.	I speak/talk. I will speak/talk.
Hanashimashita.	I spoke/talked. I have spoken/talked.
Hanashimashoo.	Let's talk/speak. I think I'll talk/speak.
Hanashite imasu.	I am talking/speaking.
Hanashite imashita.	I was talking/speaking.
Hanashite kudasai.	Please talk/speak.

NOTE

a. The endings denoting tense are:

present or future	*(hanashi)masu*
past	*(hanashi)mashita*
tentative	*(hanashi)mashoo*
present progressive	*(hanashi)te imasu*
past progressive	*(hanashi)te imashita*
polite request	*(hanashi)te kudasai*

b. The same forms are used for singular and plural and for the first, second, and third persons. The subject of a sentence does not have to be mentioned when the context clarifies who is speaking or what is being spoken about.

Hanashimasu.	I speak/talk.
Hanashimasu.	You (*sg.*) speak/talk.
Hanashimasu.	He/she speaks/talks.

Hanashimasu.	We speak/talk.
Hanashimasu.	You (*pl.*) speak/talk.
Hanashimasu.	They speak/talk.

2. I don't speak, I didn't speak, I wasn't speaking, etc.

Hanashimasen.	I don't speak. I will not speak.
Hanashimasen deshita.	I didn't speak.
Hanashite imasen.	I am not speaking.
Hanashite imasen deshita.	I wasn't speaking.
Hanasanaide kudasai.	Please don't speak.

NOTE

a. The negative is formed as follows:

negative present or future	*(hanashi)masen*
negative past	*(hanashi)masen deshita*
negative present progressive	*(hanashi)te imasen*
negative past progressive	*(hanashi)te imasen deshita*
negative polite request	*(hanasa)naide kudasai*

b. Note, again, that the subject of each of these sentences could be "I," "you," "he/she," "we," or "they." "I" is arbitrarily used as the subject in the English translations.

3. Study these examples:

Tabemasu.	I eat. I will eat.
Tabete imasu.	I am eating.
Tabemashita.	I ate.
Tabete imashita.	I was eating.
Tabete kudasai.	Please eat.
Tabemashoo.	Let's eat.
Tabemasen.	I do not eat. I will not eat.
Tabete imasen.	I am not eating.
Tabemasen deshita.	I did not eat.
Tabete imasen deshita.	I was not eating.
Tabenaide kudasai.	Please don't eat.
Donna mono o tabemashita ka?	What kinds of things did you eat?
Sukiyaki ya tenpura o tabemashita.	We ate sukiyaki, tempura, and things like that.
koohii	coffee
Koohii o nomimasu.	I drink coffee.
ocha	tea
Ocha o nomimashoo.	Let's drink (Japanese) tea.
Ocha o nomimashita.	They drank (Japanese) tea.

As the lessons proceed, you'll see more verbs in these forms, and after a while, you'll become more familiar with them. Be sure to refer to Lesson 40 for even more instruction on verbs.

B. ASKING A QUESTION I

1. As we have seen, one way to ask a question is to add the particle *ka* to the end of the sentence and use either a rising or falling intonation:

Naraimasu.	You learn.
Naraimasu ka?	Do you learn?
Naraimashita.	You learned. You have learned.
Naraimashita ka?	Did you learn? Have you learned?
Naratte imasu.	You are learning.
Naratte imasu ka?	Are you learning?
Naratte imashita.	You were learning.
Naratte imashita ka?	Were you learning?

2. To ask a question with a negative, use the particle *ka* in the same way:

Naraimasen ka?	Don't you learn?
Naraimasen deshita ka?	Didn't you learn?
Naratte imasen ka?	Aren't you learning?
Naratte imasen deshita ka?	Weren't you learning?

C. WHERE IS IT?

Chotto sumimasen.	Excuse me for a moment. [I am asking a question, but . . .]
doko	where
arimasu	there is
Doko ni arimasu ka?	Where is it?
Hoteru wa doko ni arimasu ka?	Where is a hotel?
resutoran	restaurant
Resutoran wa doko ni arimasu ka?	Where is a restaurant?
denwa	telephone
Denwa wa doko ni arimasu ka?	Where is a telephone?
uketsuke	reception desk

Uketsuke wa doko ni arimasu ka?	Where is the reception desk?
eki	station
Eki wa doko ni arimasu ka?	Where is the station?
yuubinkyoku	post office
Yuubinkyoku wa doko ni arimasu ka?	Where is the post office?

D. HERE AND THERE

koko	here, this place
soko	there, that place (near to person addressed by speaker)
asoko	there, that place over there (far from both speaker and person addressed)
doko	where, which place
Doko desu ka?	Where is it? Which place is it?
kochira	this way
sochira	that way
achira	that way over there
dochira	which way
Dochira desu ka?	Which way is it?
Achira desu	It is over that way.
Kochira desu.	It's this way.
migi no hoo ni	to the right [in the direction of the right]
hidari no hoo ni	to the left [in the direction of the left]
Migi no hoo ni arimasu.	It's to the right. [It is in the direction . . .]

Hidari no hoo ni arimasu.	It's to the left.
Migi e magarimasu.	You turn right.
Hidari e magarimasu.	You turn left.
Massugu ikimasu.	You go straight ahead.
Massugu saki desu.	It's straight ahead.
Choodo hantaigawa desu.	It's directly opposite.
Kado ni arimasu.	It's on the corner.
Koko ni wa arimasen.	It's not here.
Soko ni wa arimasen.	It's not there.
Asoko ni arimasu.	It's over there.
Koko ni imasu.	He is here.
Koko ni kite kudasai.	Come here, please.
Koko ni ite kudasai.	Stay here, please.
Soko de matte ite kudasai.	Wait there, please.
Kochira e itte kudasai.	Go this way, please.
Achira e itte kudasai.	Go that way, please.
Soko ni dare ga imasu ka?	Who's there?
Koko ni oite kudasai.	Put it here, please.
Soko ni oite kudasai.	Put it there, please.

E. NEAR AND FAR

Chikai desu.	It's near.
Koko kara chikai desu.	It's near here. [Near from here.]
Totemo chikai desu.	It's very near. It's quite close.
Mura no chikaku[1] desu.	It's near the village.
Michi no chikaku desu.	It's near the road.

[1] *chikaku:* nearby place (*a noun*).

Kare no uchi no chikaku desu.	It's near his house.
Koko kara totemo chikai desu.	It's very near here.
tooi	far
Tooi desu ka?	Is it far?
Tooi desu.	It's far.
Tooku arimasen.	It's not far.
Koko kara tooi desu.	It's far from here.

QUIZ 5

1. *Denwa wa doko ni arimasu ka?*
2. *Hanashimasu.*
3. *Kochira desu.*
4. *Massugu saki desu.*
5. *Migi no hoo ni arimasu.*
6. *Mura no chikaku desu.*
7. *Soko de matte ite kudasai.*
8. *Kochira e itte kudasai.*
9. *Hidari e magarimasu.*
10. *Choodo hantaigawa desu.*
11. *Tooku arimasen.*
12. *Soko ni oite kudasai.*
13. *Koko ni arimasen.*
14. *Koko ni ite kudasai.*
15. *Soko ni dare ga imasu ka?*

a. It's this way.
b. It's to the right.
c. He's/I'm turning left.
d. It's directly opposite.
e. It's straight ahead.
f. Where is a telephone?
g. He speaks.
h. It's near the village.
i. It's not here.
j. Stay here, please.
k. Wait there, please.
l. Go this way, please.
m. Who's there?
n. Put it there, please.
o. I'm eating.

16. *Hoteru wa doko ni*   p. Let's eat.
    arimasu ka?
17. *Naraimashita ka?*   q. I drink coffee.
18. *Tabete imasu.*   r. Where is a hotel?
19. *Tabemashoo.*   s. It's not far.
20. *Koohii o nomimasu.*   t. Did you learn?

ANSWERS
1—f; 2—g; 3—a; 4—e; 5—b; 6—h; 7—k; 8—l;
9—c; 10—d; 11—s; 12—n; 13—i; 14—j; 15—m;
16—r; 17—t; 18—o; 19—p; 20—q.

SUPPLEMENTAL VOCABULARY LIST 5: AROUND TOWN

around town	*machi no shuuhen*
town	*machi*
city	*toshi, shi*
village	*mura*
car	*kuruma, jidoosha*
bus	*basu*
train	*densha*
taxi	*takushii*
subway / metro	*chikatetsu*
traffic	*kootsuu*
building	*tatemono, biru* (highrise)
apartment building	*apaato*
library	*toshokan*
restaurant	*resutoran*
store	*mise*
street	*michi, toori*
park	*kooen*
train station	*eki*
airport	*kuukoo*

airplane	*hikooki*
intersection	*koosaten*
lamp post	*gaitoobashira*
street light	*gaitoo*
bank	*ginkoo*
church	*kyookai*
temple	*(o)tera*
mosque	*mosuku*
sidewalk	*hodoo*
bakery	*panya, beekarii*
butcher shop	*nikuya*
café / coffee shop	*kissaten*
drugstore	*yakkyoku, kusuriya*
supermarket	*suupaa*
market	*ichiba, maaketto*
shoe store	*kutsuya*
clothing store	*yoohinten, iryoohinten*
electronics store	*denkiya*
bookstore	*honya, shoten*
department store	*depaato*
mayor	*shichoo, choochoo*
city hall / municipal building	*shiyakusho*
to buy	*kau*
to go shopping	*kaimono ni iku*
near / far	*chikai / tooi*
urban	*tokai no*
suburban	*koogai no*
rural	*inaka no, den' en no, nooson no*

LESSON 11

DAI JUUIKKA

A. NOUNS AND NOUN PARTICLES

In Japanese, the form of a noun remains the same no matter where it appears in a sentence. Normally, every noun is followed by at least one particle when it is used in a sentence.[1] A particle, which is often not translatable, is the "tag" or "signpost" that tells what relation the word it accompanies has to another word or part of a sentence. For instance, one particle may show that the noun it follows is the *subject* of the sentence; another may show that the noun it follows is the *object* of the sentence; and still another may show that the noun it follows is the *modifier of another noun*. Remember, however, that *all* particles must follow the words with which they are used.

Following is a list of important noun particles with a brief description of how they are used:[2]

1. *Wa* shows that the noun it follows is the topic of the sentence. Here the word "topic" is deliberately employed as a contrast to the word "subject," which we often use in grammar. A topic in Japanese—that is, a word or group of words that is followed by the particle *wa*—serves as advance notice of what the speaker will talk about. This practice of isolating a topic and setting it off with the particle *wa* is frequently used to start a sentence in Japanese, and can be compared to the occasional practice in English of beginning a sen-

---

[1] There are some exceptions to this rule, but only a few.
[2] See the Summary of Japanese Grammar for a more complete list of particles and their uses.

tence with "As for . . ." or "Speaking of. . . ." For instance, in Japanese you would say:

As for Mr. Yoshida, (he) came to this country again this year.
Speaking of this morning's *New York Times,* have (you) read (it)?

Notice how a topic is first singled out and then followed by a simplified statement. Note also that a topic can be either an *implied subject* or an *implied object* of the verb, and that it may even specify a *time* or *place.*

Additional examples with *wa:*

Kabukiza wa Tookyoo ni arimasu.	(The) Kabuki Theatre is in Tokyo. [As for the Kabuki Theatre, (it) is in Tokyo.]
Bunraku wa mimasen deshita.	I didn't see (the) Bunraku (Puppet Play). [As for Bunraku, I didn't see (it).]
Boardman-san wa Amerika e kaerimashita.	Speaking of Mr. Boardman, he returned to America.
Kinoo wa Tanaka-san no uchi e ikimashita.	Speaking of yesterday, I went to Tanaka's house.

2. *Ga* shows that the noun it follows is both the grammatical subject of a verb and also an "emphatic" subject. In English, you place emphasis on a subject by raising your voice. In Japanese you can create the same emphasis, usually without raising your voice, by using the particle *ga.*

If you do *not* want to emphasize the subject, you can either introduce the subject with the topic particle *wa* or avoid mentioning it altogether. In English you always mention the subject, except when using the imperative. In Japanese you may omit specifically naming the subject when you feel that the person to whom you are speaking already knows what the subject is.

Watashi ga ikimashita.	I (not he) *(spoken with emphasis)* went. [(It) was I who went.]
Tanaka-san ga kimashita.	*Ms. Tanaka (spoken with emphasis) came.*
Jikan ga arimasen.	There isn't *time*.

3. *O* shows that the noun it follows is *the thing acted upon* by the verb. It roughly corresponds to the direct object of a transitive verb. Yet, *O* also implies the notion of a place in which movements (transitions) such as going, coming, passing, walking, running, swimming, flying, and departing take place.

Kippu o kaimashita.	I bought some tickets.
Tegami o dashimashita.	I sent a letter.
Ginza Doori o arukimashita.	We walked on Ginza Street.
Saka o hashirimashita.	We ran on the slope.

4. *No* shows that the noun it follows modifies (i.e., explains or characterizes) another noun that comes after it. It is most frequently used for the possessive ("of"):

Tookyoo no machi desu.	It is the city of Tokyo.
Yamada-san no uchi desu.	It is Mr. Yamada's house. [(It) is the house of Mr. Yamada.]
Tanaka-san no kodomo desu.	He is Ms. Tanaka's child. [He is the child of Ms. Tanaka.]

5. *Ni* is used in the following ways:

    a. The noun with *ni* may tell *where* a thing or person is (in the sense of being "in" or "at" a place):

Tanaka-san wa Tookyoo ni imasu.	Ms. Tanaka is in Tokyo.
Ginza wa Chuuoo-ku ni arimasu.	Ginza is in the Chuo ward (of Tokyo).

    b. The noun with *ni* may tell the *purpose* for which the action is performed (in the sense of "for" or "in order to"):

Nihon e benkyoo ni kimashita.	I came to Japan to study.

    c. The noun with *ni* may tell the *person* or *thing* to which the action of the verb is directed (in the sense of "to," "from," or "of"):

Yamada-san ni agemashita.	I gave it to Mr. Yamada.

    d. The noun with *ni* may tell the *thing into*

which something changes (there is usually no translation for this usage):

Tookyoo Daigaku no gakusei ni narimashita.	I became a student at [of] Tokyo University.

   e. The noun with *ni* is the direction toward which a motion takes place ("to," "toward"):

Nara ni ikimashita.	I went to Nara.
Amerika ni okurimashita.	I sent it to America.

  6. *De* signifies that the noun preceding it is:

   a. The *place* of action ("at," "in"):

Kyooto de kaimashita.	I bought it in Kyoto.

   b. The *means* of action ("by," "through"):

Hikooki de ikimashita.	I went by [means of a] plane.

   c. The *limit* to which the predicate is restricted ("in," "within"):

Nihon de ichiban takai yama desu.	It is the highest mountain in Japan. [Restricting ourselves to Japan, (it) is the highest mountain.]

  7. *Kara* shows that the noun it follows is the *beginning point* in space or time of an action or state ("from," "since"):

Amerika kara kimashita.	I came from America.
Nigatsu kara koko ni sunde imasu.	I have been living here since February.

8. *Made* shows that the noun it follows is the *ending point* of an action or event ("up to," "by," "until"):

Hiroshima made ikimashita.	I went as far as Hiroshima.
Juugatsu made Kyooto ni imasu.	I'll be in Kyoto until October.

Kara and *made* are often used together:

Tookyoo kara Oosaka made ikimashita.	I went from Tokyo to Osaka.

9. *E* shows that the noun it follows is the *direction toward which* a motion takes place ("to," "toward"). *E* and *ni* (in 5.e. above) are usually interchangeable:

Nara e ikimashita.	I went to Nara.
Amerika e okurimashita.	I sent it to America.

10. *To* shows that the preceding noun is one of the following:

a. A part of a complete list ("and"):

Tookyoo to Kyooto to Oosaka e ikimashita.	I went to Tokyo, Kyoto, and Osaka. (These are the places I went to.)
Yamada-san to Tanaka-	Mr. Yamada, Ms.

*san to Takeda-san
ga kimashita.*

Tanaka, and Ms.
Takeda came. (These
are the people who
came.)

b. The one with whom the action of the verb is
performed ("with"):

Kanai to ikimashita. I went with my wife.
*Tanaka-san to hanashi-
mashita.*
I spoke with Mr.
Tanaka.

c. The thing into which something or somebody
changes:

**Ano tatemono wa
Tanaka-san no
mono to narima-
shita.**
That building became
Ms. Tanaka's (prop-
erty).

*Nihon no daihyoo to
narimashita.*
She became the repre-
sentative of Japan.

Daigishi to narimashita. He became a member
of Parliament.

Note that in this usage *to* is often interchangeable
with *ni* (shown above).

11. *Ya* shows, as *to* sometimes does, that the noun it
follows is part of a list; however, the fact that *ya*
is used implies that the list is not a complete one:

*Niku ya pan ya sarada
o tabemashita.*
I ate meat, bread, and
salad (and some
other things).

B. COMMON ADJECTIVE FORMS

There are two types of adjectives in Japanese: *i*-adjectives and *na*-adjectives.

1. *I*-adjectives
   I-adjectives all end in *-i*. They are used very much like verbs. They have their own forms for present, past, etc., and they have "plain" and "polite" forms, as do verbs (see Lesson 12).

   a. Below are some commonly used conjugations of the *i*-adjective *takai* (expensive):

Takai desu.	It is expensive. It will be expensive.
Takakatta desu.	It was expensive.
Takai deshoo.	It is probably expensive.
Takakatta deshoo.	It was probably expensive.
Takaku arimasen.⎤ *Takaku nai desu.*⎦	It is not expensive.
Takaku arimasen deshita.⎫ *Takaku nakatta desu.*⎭	It was not expensive.
Takaku nai deshoo.	It is probably not expensive.
Takaku nakatta deshoo.	It was probably not expensive.

   (1) Notice how the endings differ for affirmative and negative forms (parentheses set off the adjectival root "expensive" from the ending):

AFFIRMATIVE

present	*(taka)i desu*
past	*(taka)katta desu*
tentative	*(taka)i deshoo*
tentative past	*(taka)katta deshoo*

NEGATIVE

present	*(taka)ku arimasen*
	(taka)ku nai desu
past	*(taka)ku arimasen deshita*
	(taka)ku nakatta desu
tentative	*(taka)ku nai deshoo*
tentative past	*(taka)ku nakatta deshoo*

(2) Notice how the same forms are used for both singular and plural in all persons (I, you, he, she, it, we, you, they):

Takai desu.	It is expensive.
Takai desu.	They are expensive.
Takakatta desu.	It was expensive.
Takakatta desu.	They were expensive.
Kashikoi desu.	You are wise.
Kashikoi desu.	She is wise.

(3) Notice that the present negative and the past negative of *i*-adjectives have two forms. The *-ku nai* (present) and *-ku nakatta* (past) forms are used more often in colloquial conversation:

Takaku nai desu.	It is not expensive.
Hoteru wa takaku na- *katta desu.*	The hotel was not expensive.

See parts d and f in what follows, as well.

b. *I*-adjectives modifying a noun:

takai kuruma	expensive car
Takai kuruma desu.	It is an expensive car.
Takai kuruma ja nai desu.	It is not an expensive car.
ookii	big
ookii hoteru	big hotel
Ookii hoteru deshita.	It was a big hotel.

c. Sentences with present, affirmative *i*-adjectives:

Yasui desu.	It's inexpensive/cheap.
Oishii desu.	It's delicious/tasty.
Ookii desu.	It's big.
Chiisai desu.	It's small.
Ii desu. Yoi desu.[1]	It's good/nice.
Warui desu.	It's bad.
Warui tenki desu.	It's bad weather.
Tenki wa warui desu.	The weather is bad.
Chiisai hon desu.	It's a small book.
Ookii kuruma desu.	It's a big car.
Oishii koohii desu.	It's delicious coffee.
Yasui hon desu.	It's an inexpensive book.

d. Sentences with present, negative *i*-adjectives:

---

[1] Both *ii* and *yoi* mean "good," but *ii* is more colloquial and more commonly used. However, conjugations (such as the negative or past forms), are based on *yoi* and not *ii*.

Takaku nai desu. **Takaku arimasen.**	It is not expensive.
Yoku nai desu. **Yoku arimasen.**	It is not good.
omoshiroi	interesting
Omoshiroku nai desu. **Omoshiroku arimasen.**	It is not interesting.
atarashii	new
Atarashiku nai desu. *Atarashiku arimasen.*	It is not new.
furui[1]	old
Furuku nai desu. *Furuku arimasen.*	It is not old.
tooi	far
Tooku nai desu. *Tooku arimasen.*	It is not far.
atsui	hot
Atsuku nai desu. *Atsuku arimasen.*	It is not hot.
Tenki wa waruku nai desu.	The weather is not bad.
Kuruma wa yoku nai desu.	The car is not good.
Furui kuruma wa takaku arimasen.	The old cars are not expensive.

    e. Sentences with past, affirmative *i*-adjectives:

Ookikatta desu.	It was big.
Atsukatta desu.	It was hot.
Atarashikatta desu.	It was new.

---

[1] *Furui*, "old," is used to describe inanimate things and not animate beings.

Yokatta desu.	It was good.
Kuruma wa takakatta desu.	The car was expensive.
Heya wa chiisakatta desu.	The room was small.
Tenki wa warukatta desu ka.	Was the weather bad?

f. Sentences with past, negative *i*-adjectives:

Takaku nakatta desu. / **Takaku arimasen deshita.**	It was not expensive.
Omoshiroku nakatta desu. / *Omoshiroku arimasen deshita.*	It was not interesting.
Ooikiku nakatta desu.	It was not big.
Kuruma wa ookiku nakatta desu.	The car was not big.
Koohii wa oishiku nakatta desu.	The coffee was not tasty.
Hoteru wa yoku nakatta desu.	The hotel was not good.
Resutoran wa atarashiku nakatta desu.	The restaurant was not new.

2. *Na*-adjectives

   Na-adjectives are used very much like nouns. Unlike *i*-adjectives, they do not conjugate—that is, change their forms according to tense, etc. Instead, the copula *desu* that follows *na*-adjectives conjugates.

a. Below are some sentences with *na*-adjectives. Notice that the sentence patterns are just like those with nouns (see Lesson 9):

shizuka	quiet
Shizuka desu.	It is quiet.
Shizuka deshita.	It was quiet.
Shizuka deshoo.	It is probably quiet.
Shizuka datta deshoo.	It was probably quiet.
Shizuka {ja / dewa} arimasen.	It is not quiet.
Shizuka {ja / dewa} nai desu.	
Shizuka {ja / dewa} arimasen deshita.	It was not quiet.
Shizuka {ja / dewa} nakatta desu.	
Shizuka {ja / dewa} nai deshoo.	It is probably not quiet.
Shizuka {ja / dewa} nakatta deshoo.	It was probably not quiet
kirei	pretty/clean
Kirei ja arimasen.	It is not pretty/clean.
fukuzatsu	complicated
Fukuzatsu ja arimasen.	It is not complicated.
Fukuzatsu dewa nakatta desu.	It was not complicated.
Kono mondai wa fukuzatsu desu.	This problem is complicated.
Shigoto wa fukuzatsu ja nai desu.	The job is not complicated.
shinsetsu	kind

Yamada-san wa shinsetsu desu.	Mr. Yamada is kind.
Tanaka-san wa shinsetsu deshita.	Ms. Tanaka was kind.
kantan	simple/brief
Kantan deshita.	It was simple/brief.
Shigoto wa kantan deshita.	The job was simple.

b. *Na*-adjectives modifying a noun

Na-adjectives are used with *na* before a noun:

shizuka na apaato	quiet apartment
kirei na shashin	pretty photograph
fukuzatsu na mondai	complicated problem
shinsetsu na sensei	kind teacher
taisetsu	important
taisetsu na mono	important thing
genki	healthy
genki na kodomo	healthy child
rippa	magnificent
rippa na tatemono	magnificent building
raku	easy/comfortable
raku na shigoto	easy task
Kantan na setsumei deshita.	It was a brief explanation.
Taisetsu na mono ja nai desu.	It is not an important thing.

QUIZ 6

1. Takai desu.
2. *Omoshiroku nai desu.*
3. *Yoi hoteru desu.*

a. It's not a good car.
b. It's delicious.
c. It was good.

4. *Ii kuruma ja nai desu.*	d. It is probably expensive.
5. *Yokatta desu.*	e. It was probably expensive.
6. *Ii eiga deshita.*	f. It's a good hotel.
7. *Takai deshoo.*	g. It is pretty.
8. *Takakatta deshoo.*	h. It is expensive.
9. *Oishii desu.*	i. It's not interesting.
10. *Kirei desu.*	j. It was a good movie.

ANSWERS
1—h; 2—i; 3—f; 4—a; 5—c; 6—j; 7—d; 8—e; 9—b; 10—g.

LESSON 12

DAI JUUNIKA

A. PLAIN OR POLITE

For each of the forms of *i*-adjectives, verbs, and copulas used at the end of sentences, there is an additional form called a "plain form." The forms we have seen at the end of a sentence are called "polite forms." The polite forms are derived from plain forms and are characterized by ending with -*desu* or -*masu* or a form derived from one of these. The plain form is usually used in the *middle* of a sentence, while the polite form is usually at the *end* of a sentence. However, the plain form can also be used at the end of a sentence, but only when the speaker is very familiar and has a casual relationship with the person to whom he/she is speaking. A husband, for example, may use this form with his wife, or a high-school boy with his classmates. But for anyone learning Japanese as a foreign language, it is best to use the polite form at the end of a sentence.

Dictionaries and glossaries usually list the plain present affirmative form of *i*-adjectives, verbs, and the copula. Here is a table showing the plain and polite present affirmative forms of some words that you have already seen:

PLAIN PRESENT AFFIRMATIVE	POLITE PRESENT AFFIRMATIVE	MEANING
	I-ADJECTIVES	
takai	*takai desu*	it is expensive
tooi	*tooi desu*	it is far
	VERBS	
hanasu	*hanashimasu*	I speak
kau	*kaimasu*	I buy
aru	*arimasu*	there is
taberu	*tabemasu*	I eat
kuru	*kimasu*	I come
	COPULA	
da[1]	*desu*	A is B

To construct the polite present affirmative form of an *i*-adjective, add *desu* to the plain present affirmative.

Construct the polite present affirmative of a verb according to the rules presented in the next section.

The polite present affirmative of the copula *da* is *desu*. Rarely, *de arimasu* can also be used, but this form is considered very formal.

---

[1] *Na* or *no* is used in place of *da* in certain contexts.

B. To Construct the Polite Form of a Verb

In order to construct the polite form of a verb from its plain present form, you must learn to identify the class or conjugation to which that verb belongs. To do so, you need to know the following basic facts:

1. The plain present affirmative form of all verbs ends in -*u*.

2. All verbs belong to one of three classes: *consonant, vowel,* or *irregular.* Consonant verbs make up the largest group and irregular verbs the smallest.

3. There are only two verbs that are entirely irregular, and they are the most common: *suru* [do] and *kuru* [come]. Although there are a few other verbs that are somewhat irregular, even those are basically consonant verbs. Two such examples are *iku* [go] and *kudasaru* [give].

4. The vast majority of verbs that end in -*eru* or -*iru* are vowel verbs—for example, *taberu* [eat] and *miru* [see]—so called because the base[1] (which remains unchanged most of the time) ends in a vowel. However, there are a few verbs that end in -*eru* or -*iru* that are not vowel verbs, such as *keru* [kick], *kaeru* [return], and *hairu* [enter]. Since the bases of these verbs end in -*r* (*ker-, kaer-,* and *hair-,* respectively), they are classified as consonant verbs.

---

[1] The base of a vowel verb is that part remaining after the final -*ru* is dropped; i.e., *tabe(ru), mi(ru).*

5. All other verbs are consonant verbs—so called because the base ends in a consonant.[1] Verbs that end in two vowels, such as *kau* [buy], or *iu*, which is *yuu* [say], are also included in this class because they add -*w* at the end of the base when appending an ending that begins with -*a*, e.g., -*anai* [not], -*areru* (*passive*), or -*aseru* (*causative*).

Once you can identify the class to which a given verb belongs, you can form the polite, present affirmative forms as follows:

I. Consonant verbs

Add -*imasu* to the base, which remains the same except for two special circumstances:

a. When the base ends in *s*, the letter is changed to *sh* before adding -*imasu*. For example: *hanasu* becomes *hanashimasu*.

b. When the base ends in *ts*, the latter is changed to *ch* before adding -*imasu*. For example: *tatsu* becomes *tachimasu*.

II. Vowel verbs

Add -*masu* to the base.

III. Irregular verbs

Learn the polite form of each individually.

---

[1] The base of a consonant verb is that part remaining after the final *u* has been dropped. For example: *das(u)* [put out, send out], *ar(u)* [there is], *ka(w)(u)* [buy], *kak(u)* [write].

Note: In the following examples, the end of the base has been marked with a hyphen.

PLAIN PRESENT AFFIRMATIVE	POLITE PRESENT AFFIRMATIVE	MEANING
	CONSONANT VERBS	
kak-u	*kakimasu*	write(s)
kas-u	*kashimasu*	lend(s)
mats-u	*machimasu*	wait(s)
mots-u	*mochimasu*	hold(s)
hair-u	*hairimasu*	enter(s)
ka(w)-u	*kaimasu*	buy(s)
	VOWEL VERBS	
tabe-ru	*tabemasu*	eat(s)
tome-ru	*tomemasu*	stop(s)
mi-ru	*mimasu*	see(s)
oki-ru	*okimasu*	get(s) up
	IRREGULAR VERBS	
suru	*shimasu*	do(es)
kuru	*kimasu*	come(s)

C. THE -*TE* AND -*TA* FORMS

When the -*te* form of a verb appears in a sentence, it signifies that one or more additional verbs will also appear in that sentence.

The -*te* form of a verb is used in such expressions as *hanashite kudasai* [please speak] and *hanashite imasu* [I'm speaking]. Although the verb in such a construction most often ends in -*te,* it can also end in -*tte* or in -*de.* The way the -*te* form ends or the way it is formed from the plain, present, affirmative (which is the dictionary form) depends on (a) the *class of verb* to which it belongs, and (b) if it is a consonant verb, the *pronunciation of the last syllable* of the plain present.

The *-te* form is sometimes called a gerund; but unlike a proper gerund, it is never used as a noun. (See page 80 for uses of the *-te* form.)

The *-ta* form is another way to distinguish the plain past affirmative from the polite past affirmative. In dependent clauses, the *-ta* form is usually used in place of the polite form.

Remember that the polite past affirmative always ends in *-mashita*, whereas the *-ta* form can end not only in *-ta* but also in *-tta* or *-da*. The *-ta* form is derived from the plain present affirmative in exactly the same way as the *-te* form.

When using either of these forms, be careful not to interchange the final *-e* and *-a*. Follow these instructions:

1. For consonant verbs:

   a. When the last syllable of the plain present is *-u*, *-tsu*, or *-ru*, drop that syllable and add *-tte* or *-tta*:

PLAIN PRESENT AFFIRMATIVE	*-TE* FORM	*-TA* FORM	MEANING OF PLAIN PRESENT AFFIRMATIVE
kau	**katte**	**katta**	buy
omou	*omotte*	*omotta*	think
matsu	**matte**	**matta**	wait
motsu	*motte*	*motta*	hold
okuru	**okutte**	**okutta**	send
toru	*totte*	*totta*	take

Note: To learn this rule it might be helpful to memorize the following fictitious word, which is made up by stringing together the three final syllables involved and the *-tta*.

Mnemonic device: *u-tsu-ru-tta (utsurutta)*

b. When the last syllable of the plain present affirmative is *-mu, -nu,* or *-bu,* drop that and replace it with *-nde* or *-nda:*

PLAIN PRESENT AFFIRMATIVE	*-TE* FORM	*-TA* FORM	MEANING OF PLAIN PRESENT AFFIRMATIVE
yomu	**yonde**	**yonda**	read
nomu	*nonde*	*nonda*	drink
shinu	**shinde**	**shinda**	die
yobu	**yonde**	**yonda**	call
tobu	*tonde*	*tonda*	fly

Mnemonic device: *mu-nu-bu-nda (munubunda).*

c. When the last syllable of the plain present affirmative is *-ku,* drop that and replace it with *-ite* or *-ita.* If the last syllable is *-gu,* drop that and replace it with *-ide* and *-ida:*

PLAIN PRESENT AFFIRMATIVE	*-TE* FORM	*-TA* FORM	MEANING OF PLAIN PRESENT AFFIRMATIVE
kaku	**kaite**	**kaita**	write
saku	*saite*	*saita*	bloom
oyogu	**oyoide**	**oyoida**	swim
kagu	*kaide*	*kaida*	smell

Mnemonic device: *ku-gu-ita-ida (kuguitaida).*

Note: *iku* [go] is one exception. Its *-te* and *-ta* forms are *itte* and *itta,* respectively.

   d. When the last syllable of the plain present is
      -su, drop that and add -shite or -shita:

PLAIN PRESENT AFFIRMATIVE	-TE FORM	-TA FORM	MEANING OF PLAIN PRESENT AFFIRMATIVE
hanasu	**hanashite**	**hanashita**	speak
kasu	**kashite**	**kashita**	lend
hosu	*hoshite*	*hoshita*	dry
moyasu	*moyashite*	*moyashita*	burn

   Mnemonic device: *su-shita (sushita)*.

  2. For vowel verbs:

    Simply drop the final syllable -*ru* and add -*te* or
    -*ta*.

PLAIN PRESENT AFFIRMATIVE	-TE FORM	-TA FORM	MEANING OF PLAIN PRESENT AFFIRMATIVE
taberu	**tabete**	**tabeta**	eat
akeru	**akete**	**aketa**	open
miru	*mite*	*mita*	see
kiru	*kite*	*kita*	wear

  3. For irregular verbs:

PLAIN PRESENT AFFIRMATIVE	-TE FORM	-TA FORM	MEANING OF PLAIN PRESENT AFFIRMATIVE
suru	**shite**	**shita**	do
kuru	**kite**	**kita**	come

D. Various Usages of the *-te* Form

The basic function of a *-te* form can be to name an action or condition. It serves to show that the sentence is not complete. That is why, as a rule, it does not appear at the end of a sentence.

The *-te* form verb can be used in many ways. Some of the more important follow:

1. When a sentence contains several different verbs, the *-te* form is usually used for all but the last:

Nippon e itte kaimashita.	I bought it in Japan. [(I) went to Japan and bought it (there).]
Eiga o mite Ginza de gohan o tabete uchi e kaerimashita.	I saw a movie, ate [my meal] in Ginza, and returned home.

Notice that the tense is expressed in *the terminal verb only* and not in the *-te* form verbs. In translation, however, the tense is expressed for the *-te* form verbs, as well.

2. Sometimes the function of a *-te* form verb is merely to explain *how* the action of the following verb is performed:

Hashitte[1] ikimashita.	He went running.
Isoide[2] kimashita.	He came hurriedly.

---

[1] *hashiru* = run.
[2] *isogu* = hurry.

3. The phrase *-te imasu* is used to express an action taking place or a state or condition resulting from an action that occurred in the past:

Ame ga futte imasu.	It is raining. [The rain is falling.]
Ima gohan o tabete imasu.	We are eating [the meal] now.
Okyaku sama ga kite imasu.	We have a visitor. [(A) visitor came and is with us.]

4. The phrase *-te arimasu* is used to express a state or condition that is the result of the past action of a transitive verb. In English, it is often translated using the passive voice.

Sore wa haratte arimasu.	That has been paid for. That is paid. [That is in the state of my having paid for it.]
Sono tegami wa moo kaite arimasu.	That letter (of which you are speaking) is already written. [The letter is already in the state of my having written it.]

5. The phrase *-te kudasai* is used to express a request and corresponds most closely to the imperative in English:

Kippu o katte kudasai.	Please buy a ticket.
Doyoobi ni kite kudasai.	Come on Saturday, please.

QUIZ 7

1. *Nippon e itte kaimashita.*	a. He came hurriedly.
2. *Isoide kimashita.*	b. I went to Japan and bought it there.
3. *Ame ga futte imasu.*	c. That letter is already written.
4. *Doyoobi ni kite kudasai.*	d. Come on Saturday, please.
5. *Hashitte ikimashita.*	e. We have a visitor.
6. *Sono tegami wa moo kaite arimasu.*	f. He went running.
7. *Okyaku sama ga kite imasu.*	g. It is raining.
8. *Sore wa haratte arimasu.*	h. That has been paid for.
9. *Ima gohan o tabete imasu.*	i. We are eating the meal now.
10. *Eiga o mite Ginza de gohan o tabete uchi e kaerimashita.*	j. I saw a movie, ate in Ginza, and returned home.

ANSWERS
1—b; 2—a; 3—g; 4—d; 5—f; 6—c; 7—e; 8—h;
9—i; 10—j.

LESSON 13

DAI JUUSANKA

A. MY, YOUR, HIS, HER, ETC.

There are no separate words for "my," "your," "his,"
"her," etc. To express the idea of these words, add the
particle *no* to the words for "I," "you," "he," "she."

Watashi no hon wa doko ni arimasu ka?	Where is my book?
Anata no hon wa doko ni arimasu ka?	Where is your book?
Sono hito no hon wa doko ni arimasu ka?	Where is his/her [that person's] book?
Sono hitotachi no hon wa doko ni arimasu ka?	Where are their [those people's] books?
Anata no tegami wa doko ni arimasu ka?	Where is your letter?
Sono hito no tegami wa doko ni arimasu ka?	Where is his/her [that person's] letter?
Sono hitotachi no tegami wa doko ni arimasu ka?	Where are their [those people's] letters?

Sometimes the idea of "your" may be suggested by prefixing the noun referred to with *o-* or *go-*. In such cases, *anata no* [your] is usually not used. Notice that the nouns to which *o-* or *go-* can be added are limited in number.

Gokazoku[1] *wa?*	How about your family?
Okuni[2] *wa dochira desu ka?*	Where are you from?
Onamae[3] *wa nan desu ka?*	What is your name?

[1] *kazoku* = family.
[2] *kuni* = country, hometown.
[3] *namae* = name.

B. SOME COMPARISONS

Here are a few forms of comparisons. Refer to Section 16 in the Summary of Japanese Grammar for more information.

1. More . . . than:

Sono densha wa hayai desu.	That train is fast.
Sono densha wa basu yori hayai desu.	That train is faster than the bus.
Sono kuruma wa atarashii desu.	That car is new.
Sono kuruma wa watashi no kuruma yori atarashii desu.	That car is newer than my car.
Tanaka-san no heya wa shizuka desu.	Ms. Tanaka's room is quiet.
Tanaka-san no heya wa kono heya yori shizuka desu.	Ms. Tanaka's room is more quiet than this room.

2. The most . . .

Kono kuruma ga ichiban atarashii desu.	This car is the newest.
Watashi no shigoto ga ichiban raku desu.	My job is the easiest.
Kono resutoran ga ichiban kirei desu.	This restaurant is the cleanest.
Kono mondai ga ichiban fukuzatsu desu.	This problem is the most complicated.

3. Not as . . . as . . .

Tanaka-san wa Harada-san hodo[1] sei ga takaku arimasen.	Ms. Tanaka is not as tall as Ms. Harada.
Nara wa Kyooto hodo ookiku arimasen.	Nara is not as big as Kyoto.
Watashi no heya wa Tanaka-san no heya hodo kirei ja arimasen.	My room is not as clean as Ms. Tanaka's room.
Kyoo no shiken wa mae no shiken hodo kantan dewa nakatta desu.	Today's test was not as simple as the previous test.

4. As . . . as possible:

Dekiru dake kuwashiku kaite kudasai.	Please write it as detailed (with as much detail) as possible.
Dekiru dake kitsuku shimete kudasai.	Please tie it as tightly as possible.
Dekiru dake hayaku shite kudasai.	Do it as soon as possible.

C. Asking a Question II

There are several ways to ask a question:

1. Add the particle *ka* at the end of a declarative sentence, and either raise the pitch of your voice at the end (i.e., use the "question intonation"), or not, as you like.

[1] *hodo* = not as . . . as

2. Phrase the sentence like a declarative statement and use the question-intonation but do not use the particle *ka* at the end. This is a very informal usage.

3. When you ask a question that demands an answer, and the answer can be one of several alternatives, add *ka* to each of the alternatives you offer.

Kore desu ka?	Is it this?
Kore desu.	It's this.
Sore desu ka?	Is it that?
Kore desu ka? Sore desu ka?	Is it this, or is it that?
Koko ni imasu ka?	Is he here?
Asoko ni imasu ka?	Is he over there?
Koko ni imasu ka? Asoko ni imasu ka?	Is he here, or is he over there?
Doko ni imasu ka?	Where is he?
Doko desu ka?	Where is it? [Which place is (it)?]
Dare desu ka?	Who is it?
Donata[1] desu ka?	Who is it *(respect)?*
Nan desu ka?	What is it?
Itsu desu ka?	When is it?
Ikura desu ka?	How much is it?
Ikutsu desu ka?	How many? How old is he?
Naze desu ka?	Why is it?
Dooshite[2] desu ka?	Why is it?

---

[1] *Donata* is more polite than *dare*. *Donata* is referred to as the respect form of *dare*. The respect form of words is used only when someone is talking about someone else in a more polite way. The humble form, in contrast, is used to demote someone's status.

[2] *Dooshite* is less formal than *naze*.

Doo desu ka?	How is it?
Dochira desu ka?	Which of the two is it? Which way is it?
Dore desu ka?	Which is it *(used for more than two)?*
Dono tatemono desu ka?	Which building is it?
Dono hito desu ka?	Which person is it?
Ikimashita ka?	Did you go?
Dare ga ikimashita ka?	Who went?
Naze ikimashita ka?	Why did you go?
Itsu ikimashita ka?	When did you go?
Nan de ikimashita ka?	How did you go? [By what means (of transportation) did (you) go?]
Dare to ikimashita ka?	With whom did you go?
Itsu dare to ikimashita ka?	When and with whom did you go?
Dooshite Tanaka-san to ikimashita ka?	Why did you go with Ms. Tanaka?
Kabuki wa doo deshita ka?	How was the Kabuki play?
Bunraku wa dooshite mimasen deshita ka?	Why didn't you see the Bunraku (puppet play)?
Kabuki e dare to ikimashita ka?	With whom did you go to the Kabuki?

QUIZ 8

1. *Watakushi no hon wa doko ni arimasu ka?*

   a. Where is your book?

2. *Anata no hon wa doko ni arimasu ka?*

   b. What is your name?

3. *Sono hitotachi no tegami wa doko ni arimasu ka?*

c. That train is not as fast as this train.

4. *Onamae wa nan desu ka?*

d. Which building is it?

5. *Sono densha wa kono densha hodo hayaku arimasen.*

e. Where are their [those people's] letters?

6. *Kono kuruma no hoo ga ano ji-doosha yori atarashii desu.*

f. Where is my book?

7. *Dono tatemono desu ka?*

g. When is it?

8. *Dekiru dake haya-ku shite kudasai.*

h. This car is newer than that one.

9. *Kore desu ka?*

i. Do it as soon as possible, please.

10. *Itsu desu ka?*

j. Is it this?

ANSWERS

1—f; 2—a; 3—e; 4—b; 5—c; 6—h; 7—d; 8—i; 9—j; 10—g.

D. WORD STUDY

aisukuriimu	ice cream
bifuteki	beefsteak
chiizu	cheese
kechappu	ketchup
mayoneezu	mayonnaise
omuretsu	omelet
sarada	salad
soosu	sauce
suupu	soup
toosuto	toast

SUPPLEMENTAL VOCABULARY LIST 6: THE HUMAN BODY

the human body	*ningen no karada*
head	*atama*
face	*kao*
forehead	*hitai, odeko*
eye	*me*
eyebrow	*mayuge*
eyelashes	*matsuge*
ear	*mimi*
nose	*hana*
mouth	*kuchi*
tooth	*ha*
tongue	*shita, bero*
cheek	*hoo, hoho, hoppeta*
chin	*ago*
hair (on head)	*kami no ke*
hair (on body)	*ke*
neck	*kubi*
chest	*mune*
breast	*nyuuboo, mune*
shoulders	*kata*
arm	*ude*
elbow	*hiji*
wrist	*tekubi*
hand	*te*
stomach / abdomen	*hara / onaka*
penis	*penisu*
vagina	*chitsu*
leg	*ashi*
knee	*hiza*
ankle	*kakato*
foot	*ashi*
finger	*yubi*
toe	*ashi no yubi*

skin	*hifu, hada*
blood	*chi, ketsueki*
brain	*noo*
heart	*shinzoo*
lungs	*hai*
bone	*hone*
muscle	*kinniku*
tendon	*ken*

LESSON 14

DAI JUUYONKA

A. TO HAVE AND HAVE NOT

1. I have (you have, he/she has . . .)

Motte imasu.[1]

    I have. [Am holding.]
    You have. [Are holding.]
    He has. [Is holding.]
    They have. [Are holding.]

2. I don't have (you don't have, he/she doesn't have . . .)

Motte imasen.	I don't have. (You don't have, etc.)[2]
Nani mo motte imasen.	I have nothing. I don't have anything.
Okane o motte imasu.	I have money.

---

[1] Another expression for "have" was introduced in Lesson 8.
[2] "I" is arbitrarily used as the subject in these English translations.

Okane o juubun motte imasu.	I have enough money.
Okane o sukoshi mo motte imasen.	I don't have any money. [I don't have even a little bit of money.]

3. Do I (you . . .) have?

Motte imasu ka?	Do I have (it)?

4. Don't I (you . . .) have?

Motte imasen ka?	Don't you have (it)?
Okane o motte imasu ka?	Does he have (any) money?
Okane o juubun motte imasu ka?	Does he have enough money?
Enpitsu o motte imasu ka?	Do you have a pencil?
Pen o motte imasu ka?	Do you have a pen?
Okane o juubun motte imasen ka?	Don't you have enough money?
Enpitsu o motte imasen ka?	Don't you have a pencil?
Pen o motte imasen ka?	Don't you have a pen?

5. I (you . . .) have to have:

Motte inakereba narimasen.	I have to have (it). [If (I) don't have (it), it won't do.]

6. Do I (you . . .) have to have?

Motte inakereba narimasen ka?	Do I have to have (it)?

7. I (you . . .) don't have to have:

Motte inakute mo ii desu.	I don't have to have (it). [Even if (I) don't have (it), I will be all right.]

8. Don't I (you . . .) have to have?

Motte inakute mo ii desu ka?	Don't I have to have it?
Pasupooto o motte inakereba narimasen.	You have to have a passport.
Kippu o motte inakereba narimasen.	You have to have a ticket.
Shookaijoo o motte inakereba narimasen.	You have to have a letter of introduction.
Pasupooto o motte inakereba narimasen ka?	Do you have to have a passport?
Kippu o motte inakereba narimasen ka?	Do you have to have a ticket?
Shookaijoo o motte inakereba narimasen ka?	Do you have to have a letter of introduction?
Pasupooto o motte inakute mo ii desu.	You don't have to have a passport.
Kippu o motte inakute mo ii desu.	You don't have to have a ticket.
Shookaijoo o motte inakute mo ii desu.	You don't have to have a letter of introduction.

Pasupooto o motte inakute mo ii desu ka? — Don't I have to have a passport? [Is it all right (to go) even if I don't have a passport?]

9. I (you . . .) may have it:

Motte iru ka mo shiremasen. — I may have (it). [I cannot tell if I have (it).]

10. I (you . . .) may not have it:

Motte inai kamoshiremasen. — I may not have (it).
Okane o motte iru kamoshiremasen. — He may have (some) money.
Kippu o motte iru kamoshiremasen. — He may have the ticket.
Okane o motte inai kamoshiremasen. — He may not have any money.
Kippu o motte inai kamoshiremasen. — He may not have the ticket.

B. ALSO

mo	also, too
watashi mo	I also, I too
anata mo	you also
ano hito mo	he/she also
watashitachi mo	we also
anatatachi mo	you (pl.) also
ano hitotachi mo	they also
Ano hitotachi mo kimasu.	They are coming too.
Watashi mo kimasu.	I'm coming too.

QUIZ 9

1. *Oishii desu.*	a. He may have a ticket.
2. *Atarashii desu.*	b. I don't have any money.
3. *Nan desu ka?*	c. You don't have to have a ticket.
4. *Dono tatemono desu ka?*	d. You have to have a passport.
5. *Okane o juubun motte imasu.*	e. I have enough money.
6. *Enpitsu o motte imasu ka?*	f. It's delicious.
7. *Pasupooto o motte inakereba narimasen.*	g. Which building is it?
8. *Okane o sukoshi mo motte imasen.*	h. It's new.
9. *Kippu o motte inakute mo ii desu.*	i. Do you have a pencil?
10. *Kippu o motte iru kamoshiremasen.*	j. What is it?

ANSWERS
1—f; 2—h; 3—j; 4—g; 5—e; 6—i; 7—d; 8—b; 9—c; 10—a.

C. WORD STUDY

burausu	blouse
mafuraa	muffler (heavy scarf)
nekutai	necktie

oobaakooto	overcoat
seetaa	sweater
shatsu	shirt
sukaafu	scarf
sukaato	skirt
surippu	slip

LESSON 15

DAI JUUGOKA

A. I HAVE BEEN TO . . .

Hakone e itta koto[1] ga arimasu.	I have been to Hakone. [(I) have the experience of having gone to Hakone.]
Taiwan e itta koto ga arimasu.	I have been to Taiwan.
Nihon ryoori o tabeta koto ga arimasu.	I have eaten Japanese cooking. [(I) have had the experience of eating Japanese cooking.]
Kabuki o mita koto ga arimasu.	I have seen (the) Kabuki.

[1] *koto* = act, event, experience.

B. SOMETIMES I GO . . .

Hakone e iku koto ga arimasu.	Sometimes I go to Hakone. [The act of my going to Hakone exists.]
Taiwan e iku koto ga arimasu.	Sometimes I go to Taiwan.
Nihon ryoori o taberu koto ga arimasu.	Sometimes I eat Japanese cooking.
Kabuki o miru koto ga arimasu.	Sometimes I see Kabuki plays.

C. I CAN, I AM ABLE TO . . .

Ashita wa Hakone e iku koto ga dekimasu.	Tomorrow I can go to Hakone. [The act of my going to Hakone tomorrow is possible.]
Rainen wa Taiwan e iku koto ga dekimasu.	Next year I can go to Taiwan.
Nihon ryoori o taberu koto ga dekimasu.	I can eat Japanese cooking.
Nyuu Yooku de Kabuki o miru koto ga dekimashita.	I was able to see the Kabuki in New York.

D. I'VE DECIDED TO . . .

Ashita wa Hakone e iku koto ni shimashita.	I've decided to go to Hakone tomorrow.

*Rainen wa Taiwan e
    iku koto ni shima-
    shita.*
**Nihon ryoori o taberu
    koto ni shimashita.**
**Kabuki o miru koto
    ni shimashita.**

I've decided to go to
    Taiwan next year.
I've decided to have
    [eat] Japanese cooking.
We've decided to see
    the Kabuki plays.

QUIZ 10

1. *Sore desu ka?*

2. *Doko ni imasu ka?*

3. *Ookii deshoo.*

4. *Itsu desu ka?*

5. *Dare to ikimashita
    ka?*
6. *Ookiku arimasen
    deshita.*
7. *Kabuki wa doo
    deshita ka?*
8. *Itsu ikimashita ka?*
9. *Dare ga ikimashita ka?*
10. *Sore wa kore hodo
    ookiku arimasen.*
11. *Kabuki o mita koto
    ga arimasu.*
12. *Nihon ryoori o
    taberu koto ga de-
    kimashita.*
13. *Dekiru dake ha-
    yaku shite kudasai.*

a. We've decided to
    see the Kabuki plays.
b. Please do it as soon
    as possible.
c. I have seen (the)
    Kabuki.
d. Why didn't you see
    the Bunraku?
e. That one isn't as big
    as this one.
f. I was able to eat
    Japanese cooking.
g. When is it?

h. It is probably big.
i. Where is he?
j. Is it that?

k. It wasn't big.

l. When did you go?

m. Who went?

14. *Bunraku wa doo*　　n. With whom did
　　shite mimasen　　　　you go?
　　deshita ka?
15. *Kabuki o miru koto*　o. How was the Ka-
　　ni shimashita.　　　　buki play?

ANSWERS
1—j; 2—i; 3—h; 4—g; 5—n; 6—k; 7—o; 8—l;
9—m; 10—e; 11—c; 12—f; 13—b; 14—d; 15—a.

SUPPLEMENTAL VOCABULARY LIST 7:
TRAVEL AND TOURISM

travel and tourism	*ryokoo to kankoojigyoo*
tourist	*ryokoosha*
hotel	*hoteru*
youth hostel	*yuusuhosuteru*
reception desk	*furonto desuku*
to check in	*chekkuinsuru*
to check out	*chekkuautosuru*
reservation	*yoyaku*
passport	*pasupooto*
tour bus	*kankoobasu*
guided tour	*gaidotsuki no tsuaa*
camera	*kamera*
information center	*annaijo, infomeeshonsentaa*
map	*chizu*
brochure	*panfuretto*
monument	*kinenhi*
to go sightseeing	*kankoo ni iku, kenbutsu ni iku*
to take a picture	*shashin o toru*
Can you take our picture?	*Watashitachi no shashin o totte kudasai masu ka?*

LESSON 16

DAI JUUROKKA

A. DO YOU SPEAK JAPANESE?

Nihongo ga dekimasu ka?	Do you speak Japanese? [Is Japanese possible?]
Iie, dekimasen.	No, I don't speak Japanese.
heta desu.	speak poorly [be poor (in skill)]
taihen heta desu	speak very poorly [be very poor]
Taihen heta desu.	I (speak) very poorly.
sukoshi	a little
Hai, sukoshi dekimasu.	Yes, I speak a little.
honno sukoshi	just a little
Honno sukoshi dekimasu.	I speak just a little.
amari . . . dekimasen	not much *(used with a negative verb)*
wazuka dake	just a little
Wakarimasu ka?	Do you understand (it)?
Iie, wakarimasen.	No, I don't understand (it).
Amari yoku wakarimasen.	I don't understand (it) very well.
Nihongo wa amari yoku wakarimasen.	I don't understand Japanese very well.
Hai, wakarimasu.	Yes, I understand.
Hai, sukoshi wakarimasu.	Yes, I understand a little.

Yomemasu[1] ga,[2] hanasemasen.	I can read, but I can't speak.
Wakarimasu ka?	Do you understand?
Sukoshi mo wakarimasen.	Not at all.
Yoku wakarimasen.	I don't understand very well.
Kaite kudasai.	Write it, please.
Doo kakimasu ka?	How do you write it?
Sono kotoba wa shirimasen.	I don't know that word.
Sore wa Nihongo de doo iimasu ka?	How do you say that in Japanese?
"Thank you" wa Nihongo de doo iimasu ka?	How do you say "Thank you" in Japanese?

B. PLEASE SPEAK A LITTLE SLOWER

Yukkuri hanashite kudasareba . . .	If you speak slowly (for me) . . .
Yukkuri hanashite kudasareba wakarimasu.	If you speak slowly, I'll be able to understand you.
Yukkuri hanashite kudasai.	Please speak slowly.
Nan to osshaimashita ka?	What did you say?

---

[1] *Yomemasu* = can read; *hanasemasu* = can speak. These examples present a way of saying "can . . ." different from the one introduced in Section C of Lesson 15. See also Section C (p. 285) of Lesson 40 and Section 31 of the Summary of Japanese Grammar.
[2] *ga* = but.

Doo yuu imi desu ka?	What do you mean?
. . . *kudasaimasen ka?*	Wouldn't you . . . ?
hanasu	speak
motto yukkuri	slower
Motto yukkuri hanashite kudasaimasen ka?	Would you please speak slower? [Wouldn't you speak . . .]
doozo	please
Doozo motto yukkuri hanashite kudasaimasen ka?	Would you mind speaking a little slower, please?
Moo ichido itte kudasaimasen ka?	Would you please say (that) again?

C. THANKS!

Arigatoo.	Thanks.
Doomo arigatoo gozaimasu.	Thank you very much.
Doo itashimashite.	Don't mention it.
Arigatoo gozaimasu.	Thanks. [(I) thank (you).]
Doo itashimashite.	You're welcome.
Gomennasai.	Excuse me.
Doozo.	Certainly. [Please (go ahead).]
Doozo osaki ni.	Go ahead!
Sumimasen. Nan to osshaimashita ka?	Pardon? What did you say?
Dewa mata.	See you soon.
Dewa nochihodo.	See you later.
Dewa konban.	See you this evening.

QUIZ 11

1. *Kaite kudasai.*	a. I don't speak Japanese.
2. *Nihongo wa deki-masen.*	b. Just a little.
3. *Nihongo wa yoku wakarimasen.*	c. Do you understand?
4. *Wakarimasu ka?*	d. I don't understand Japanese very well.
5. *Honno sukoshi.*	e. Write it down, please.
6. *Moo ichido itte kudasaimasen ka?*	f. How do you write it?
7. *"Thank you" wa Nihongo de doo iimasu ka?*	g. I don't know that word.
8. *Doo yuu imi desu ka?*	h. How do you say "Thank you" in Japanese?
9. *Doo kakimasu ka?*	i. What do you mean?
10. *Sono kotoba wa shirimasen.*	j. Would you please say that again?

ANSWERS
1—e; 2—a; 3—d; 4—c; 5—b; 6—j; 7—h; 8—i; 9—f; 10—g.

D. WORD STUDY

banana	banana
karifurawaa	cauliflower
kyabetsu	cabbage
meron	melon
orenji	orange
paseri	parsley
remon	lemon

retasu	lettuce
serori	celery
tomato	tomato

LESSON 17

DAI JUUNANAKA

A. THIS AND THAT

1. *Kono:* This

kono hon	this book
kono hito	this person
kono hoteru	this hotel
kono tegami	this letter
kono hanashi	this story

2. *Sono:* That

Sono refers to a thing or place that is nearby.

sono hon	that book
sono hi	that day
sono kotoba	that word
sono hito	that person
sono hoteru	that hotel
sono tegami	that letter

3. *Ano:* That

Ano refers to something outside of immediate reach.

ano uchi	that house (over there)
ano ki	that tree (over there)
ano neko	that cat (over there)

The distinction among *kono, sono,* and *ano* is similar to that among *kore, sore,* and *are,* respectively. The difference between the *kono-sono-ano* series and the *kore-sore-are* series below is that a member of the former series must be followed by a noun (e.g., *kono hon* [this book]); whereas a member of the latter series cannot be followed by a noun.

4. *Kore:* This

Kore wa doo yuu imi desu ka?	What does this mean?
Kore wa watakushi no desu.	This is mine.

5. *Sore:* That

Sore desu.	That's it. It's that.
Sore o totte kudasai.	Please pick that one.
Sore wa ii kangae desu ne.	That is a good idea.
Kore mo sore mo dame desu.	Both this one and that one are no good.

6. *Are:* That

Are desu.	It's that (over there).
Are ja arimasen.	It isn't that. That's not it.
Are o kudasai.	Give me that (over there), please.
Kore wa watakushi no desu; are wa anata no desu.	This one is mine; that one (over there) is yours.

QUIZ 12

1. *Are wa anata no desu ka?*	a. What does this mean?
2. *Kore wa doo yuu imi desu ka?*	b. It isn't that.
3. *Are o kudasai.*	c. That is mine.
4. *Ano hon o kudasai.*	d. This one is mine; that one is yours.
5. *Sore desu.*	e. This is mine.
6. *Kore wa watakushi no desu.*	f. Give me that, please.
7. *Are desu.*	g. It's that.
8. *Sore wa watakushi no desu.*	h. Please give me that book (over there).
9. *Kore wa watakushi no desu; are wa anata no desu.*	i. It's that.
10. *Are ja arimasen.*	j. Is that yours?

ANSWERS
1—j; 2—a; 3—f; 4—h; 5—g; 6—e; 7—i; 8—c; 9—d; 10—b.

B. NOT

Yoku arimasen.	It's not good.
Waruku arimasen.	It's not bad.
Sore ja arimasen.	It's not that.
Koko ni arimasen.	It's not here.
Amari takusan dewa naku.	Not too much.
Amari hayaku naku.	Not too fast.
Mada desu.	Not yet. [It's yet (to come).]
Sukoshi mo . . . masen.	Not at all *(with a negative predicate).*

Sukoshi mo jikan ga arimasen.	I don't have any time.
Doo suru ka shirimasen.	I don't know how to do it.
Itsu ka shirimasen.	I don't know when.
Doko ka shirimasen.	I don't know where.
Nani mo shirimasen.	I don't know anything.
Nani mo iimasen deshita.	He didn't say anything.
Nani mo arimasen.	Nothing. [There is nothing.]
Nani mo motte imasen.	I don't have anything.
Kesshite.	Never *(with a negative predicate)*.
Kesshite kimasen.	She never comes.
Dare ga kimashita ka?	Who came?
Dare mo kimasen deshita.	Nobody came.
Dare mo miemasen.	I don't see anyone. [No one is in sight.]
Moo soko e ikimasen.	I don't go there anymore.
Moo kimasen.	She doesn't come anymore.
Hyakuen shika arimasen.	I have only a hundred yen. [(I) don't have but a hundred yen.]
Ichijikan shika arimasen.	You have only one hour.

C. ISN'T IT? AREN'T YOU? ETC.

Hontoo desu ne?	It's true, isn't it?
Kimasu ne?	You are coming, aren't you?
Juubun motte imasu ne?	You have enough of it, don't you?

Sukoshi mo motte   You don't have any of
  imasen ne?   it, do you?
Sensei desu ne?   You're a teacher,
       aren't you?

QUIZ 13

1. *Sore ja arimasen.*
2. *Itsu ka shirimasen.*

3. *Sukoshi mo jikan
   ga arimasen.*
4. *Nani mo arimasen.*

5. *Kimasu ne?*

6. *Ichijikan shika
   arimasen.*
7. *Dare mo miemasen.*
8. *Hyakuen shika
   arimasen.*
9. *Sukoshi mo motte
   imasen ne?*
10. *Nani mo iimasen
    deshita.*

a. I don't see anyone.
b. I have only a hun-
   dred yen.
c. You have only one
   hour.
d. You are coming,
   aren't you?
e. You don't have any
   of it, do you?
f. It's not that.

g. I don't have any time.
h. I don't know when.

i. He didn't say any-
   thing.
j. There's nothing.

ANSWERS
1—f; 2—h; 3—g; 4—j; 5—d; 6—c; 7—a; 8—b;
9—e; 10—i.

D. WORD STUDY

baree booru   volleyball
basuketto booru   basketball
bokushingu   boxing
gorufu   golf

haikingu	hiking
pinpon	Ping-Pong (table tennis)
resuringu	wrestling
sukeeto	skating
sukii	ski, skiing
tenisu	tennis

LESSON 18

DAI JUUHACHIKA

A. IT'S ME (I), ETC.

Watashi desu.	It's me (I).
Anata desu.	It's you.
Kare desu.	It's him (he).
Kanojo desu.	It's her (she).
Watashitachi desu.	It's us (we).

B. IT'S MINE, ETC.

Notice that when a noun appears together with *no,* but the combination is not followed by another noun, it often means, literally, "a thing pertaining to (that noun)." For example:

watakushi no	a thing pertaining to me; my thing; mine
Watashi no desu.	It's mine.
Anata[1] no desu.	It's yours.

---

[1] It is more polite to use the person's name rather than the personal pronoun "you" *(anata, anatagata).* If you want to say "it's yours" and you are speaking to Mr. Yamada, you would say *Yamada-san no desu.*

Kare (kanojo) no desu.	It's his (hers).
Watashitachi no desu.	It's ours.
Anatagata no desu.	It's yours *(pl.)*.
Karera no desu.	It's theirs.

C. ABOUT ME, ETC.

Anata no koto o hanashite iru no desu.[1]	I'm talking about you. [(I'm) talking of things pertaining to you.]
Watashi no koto o hanashite iru no desu ne?	You are talking about me, aren't you? [. . . that's what it is, isn't it?]

D. TO ME, ETC.

Watashi ni kudasai.	Give it to me, please.
Watashitachi ni kudasai.	Give it to us, please.
Watashi ni kudasaimashita.	She gave it to me.
Watashitachi ni kudasaimashita.	She gave it to us.

E. THE MODIFIERS

In Japanese, a modifier *always* precedes the word that it modifies, whether the modifier is a single word, a phrase, or a clause. An adjective that modifies a noun

---

[1] Notice that when the sequence *no desu* (or *n desu*) immediately follows a predicate, it means, "That's what it is," or "It's a fact that," and the predicate itself is usually in the plain form.

is always placed before the noun, and an adverb that
modifies a verb is always placed before the verb. Even
a long clause, which in English would follow the
noun, precedes it in Japanese. In fact, the very act of
placing a clause before a noun makes it a modifier of
that noun.

Here are some examples:

ie	a house
akai	it is red *(plain)*
akai ie	a red house
yane	a roof
Yane ga akai.	The roof is red.
yane ga akai ie⎫ **yane no akai ie**⎭	the house whose roof is red [the-roof-is-red house]
Yane no akai ie ni sunde imasu.	He lives in a house with a red roof.
hito	a person
sunde imasu	he lives [is residing]
sunde iru	he lives *(plain)*
sunde iru hito	the person who lives (there)
sono ie ni sunde iru hito	the person who lives in that house
yane no akai ie ni sunde iru hito	the person who lives in the house with a red roof
Ano yane no akai ie ni sunde iru hito ga kyonen Amerika kara kita hito desu.	The person who lives in that house with a red roof is the person who came from America last year.

F. THE NOUN-MAKER *NO*

In addition to the particle *no* that follows a noun and links it to another noun, there is a "noun-maker" *no* which appears only *after* a clause. (As you have already seen, a clause *can* consist of a single adjective or a verb or a series of words ending in an adjective or verb.) This *no* makes a noun out of the clause and is usually translated "one who," "one which," "the act of doing," "the time when," or "the place where."

Akai no o kudasai.	Please give me one that is red. Please give me a red one.
Akaku nai no o kuda-sai.	Give me one that is not red, please.
Yane ga akai no ga watashi no ie desu.	The one (house) with a red roof is my house. [The-roof-is-red one (house) is my house.]
Tabemashita.	I ate.
Tabeta.	I ate *(plain)*.
sakana	fish
Tabeta no wa sakana deshita.	The food [thing] that I ate was fish.
Sakana o tabeta.	I ate fish *(plain)*.
Sakana o tabeta no wa kinoo deshita.	It was yesterday that I ate fish. [The day that (I) ate fish was yesterday.]

QUIZ 14

1. *Watashi no desu.*   a. It was yesterday that I ate fish.

2. *Tabeta no wa sa-   b. Give me one that
   kana deshita.*   is not red, please.

3. *Anata no koto o   c. Give it to us, please.
   hanashite iru no
   desu.*

4. *Anatagata no desu.*   d. Give me one that
                             is red, please.

5. *Watashitachi ni   e. He lives in a house
   kudasai.*   with a red roof.

6. *Watashi ni kuda-   f. It's yours.
   saimashita.*

7. *Yane no akai ie ni   g. He gave it to me.
   sunde imasu.*

8. *Akaku nai no o   h. The food that I ate
   kudasai.*   was fish.

9. *Akai no o kudasai.*   i. It's mine.

10. *Sakana o tabeta no   j. I'm talking about
    wa kinoo deshita.*   you.

ANSWERS
1—i; 2—h; 3—j; 4—f; 5—c; 6—g; 7—e; 8—b;
9—d; 10—a.

LESSON 19

DAI JUUKYUUKA

A. HELLO, HOW ARE YOU?

Konnichi wa.   Hello. Good afternoon.
Ohayoo gozaimasu.   Good morning.
Ogenki desu ka?   How are you?
Okagesama de genki   Very well, thanks.
  desu.   [Thanks to your
                             thinking of me . . .]

Betsu ni kawari arimasen.	So-so. [No special change.]
Anata wa?	And how are you? [And you?]
Doo ni ka yatte orimasu.	Not bad.
Okagesama de doo ni ka yatte orimasu.	Not bad, thanks.

B. I'd Like You to Meet . . .

Sakata-san o goshookai itashimasu.	Allow me to present Ms. Sakata. [May (I) introduce Ms. Sakata?]
Hajimemashite.	How do you do?
Sakata desu. Doozo yoroshiku.	I am Sakata. Glad to meet you.
Doozo yoroshiku.	Glad to meet you.

C. What's New?

Konnichi wa.	Hello.
Ogenki desu ka?	How are you?
Okage sama de.	Fine, thanks.
Kawatta koto wa arimasen ka?	What's new?
Betsu ni arimasen.	Nothing much. [There isn't anything especially.]
Nisannichi shitara denwa o kakete kudasai.	Call me one of these days, please.
Wasurenaide kudasai.	Please don't forget.

Kashikomarimashita.	I'll certainly do so.
Daijoobu desu ne?	Are you sure it's OK? You're sure it's OK?
Daijoobu desu.	Sure!

D. SEE YOU SOON!

Dewa mata.	See you soon. [Well, then, again.]
Getsuyoobi ni ome ni kakarimasu.	See you on Monday.
Isshuukan shitara ome ni kakarimasu.	I'll see you in a week.
Nishuukan shitara ome ni kakarimasu.	I'll see you in two weeks.
Kin'yoobi no yoru ome ni kakarimasu.	I'll see you Friday night.
Kono Mokuyoobi ni ome ni kakarimasu.	I'll see you this coming Thursday.
Kono Mokuyoobi no ban hachiji ni ome ni kakarimasu.	I'll see you this coming Thursday at eight o'clock in the evening. [This coming Thursday evening at eight o'clock (I'll) see you.]
Kon'ya ome ni kakarimasu.	I'll see you tonight.

QUIZ 15

1. *Ogenki desu ka?*   a. So-so.
2. *Ashita ome ni*   b. Very well, thanks.
   kakarimasu.
3. *Doozo yoroshiku.*   c. Not too bad.

4. *Kawatta koto wa arimasen ka?*
   d. How are you?

5. *Mokuyoobi ni ome ni kakarimasu.*
   e. I'll see you tomorrow.

6. *Okagesama de.*
   f. I'm happy to know you.

7. *Betsu ni arimasen.*
   g. What's new?

8. *Konnichi wa.*
   h. I'll see you on Thursday.

9. *Doo ni ka yatte orimasu.*
   i. Good afternoon. Hello.

10. *Betsu ni kawari arimasen.*
   j. Nothing much.

11. *Isshuukan shitara ome ni kakarimasu.*
   k. Allow me . . . (I would like to introduce . . .)

12. *Nisannichi shitara denwa o kakete kudasai.*
   l. Call me one of these days, please.

13. *Dewa mata.*
   m. See you Monday.

14. *Goshookai itashimasu.*
   n. See you soon.

15. *Getsuyoobi ni ome ni kakarimasu.*
   o. See you in a week.

ANSWERS

1—d; 2—e; 3—f; 4—g; 5—h; 6—b; 7—j; 8—i; 9—c; 10—a; 11—o; 12—l; 13—n; 14—k; 15—m.

SUPPLEMENTAL VOCABULARY LIST 8: PEOPLE

people	*hitotachi, hitobito*
person	*hito*
man	*otoko no hito*

woman	*onna no hito*
adult	*otona, seijin*
child	*kodomo*
boy	*otoko no ko, shoonen*
girl	*onna no ko, shoojo*
teenager	*juudai, tiineijaa*
tall / short	*se (sei) ga takai / se (sei) ga hikui*
old / young	*toshi o totta / wakai*
fat / thin	*futotta / yaseta*
friendly / unfriendly	*shinsetsuna, aiso no ii / fushinsetsuna, aiso no warui*
happy / sad	*ureshii / kanashii*
beautiful / ugly	*kirei, utsukushii / minikui, migurushii*
healthy / sick	*kenkoo na / byooki no*
strong / weak	*tsuyoi / yowai*
famous	*yuumei na*
intelligent	*chiteki na, rikoona*
talented	*sainoo no aru*

LESSON 20

DAI NIJIKKA

A. HAVE YOU TWO MET?

**Kono kata o gozonji
  desu ka?**

Do you know my
  friend [this person]?

**Iie, kyoo hajimete
  ome ni kakarimasu.**

No, I don't think so.
  [Am meeting him for
  the first time today.]

Iie, koremade ome ni kakatta koto wa arimasen.	No, I haven't had the pleasure of meeting [this person] until now.
Mae kara gozonji desu ne?	I believe you already know one another.
Hai, mae kara zonjiagete orimasu.	Yes, we've already met. [Have known him from before.]
Iie, zonjiagete orimasen.	No, I don't believe we've met before. [No, (I) don't know (the gentleman.])]

B. Glad to Have Met You

Hajimemashite.	How do you do?
Ome ni kakarete yokatta desu.	Glad to have met you. [Has been good fortune (for me) to have been able to see you.]
Mata zehi oai shitai to omoimasu.	Hope to see you soon.
Doozo yoroshiku.	Glad to meet you.
Moo ichido sono uchi ni hi o kimete oai shimashoo.	Let's get together again one of these days.
Arigatoo gozaimasu.	Fine. [Thank you.]
Watakushi no juusho to denwa bangoo wa omochi deshoo ka?	Do you have my address and telephone number?
Iie, motte orimasen.	No, I don't.
Itadakemasu ka?	Let me have it. [Can I have it?]

Juusho wa Bunkyoo-ku Oiwake-choo[1] ni-choome[2] juugo banchi desu.	My address is 15 2-choome, Oiwake-choo, Bunkyo-ku.
Denwa bangoo wa san yon hachi san no roku yon roku san ban desu.	My telephone number is 3483-6463.
Jimu︐ o no juusho mo itadakemasu ka?	Could I have your office address, too?
Okaki shimashoo. Ginza yon choome no ni banchi desu.	I'll write it for you. It's 2 Ginza Fourth Street.
Asa wa kuji mae deshitara uchi ni orimasu.	You can get me at home before nine in the morning. [If it is before nine (I'll) be at home.]
Sono ato wa jimusho no hoo ni orimasu.	Otherwise [afterward] at the office.
Aa soo desu ka. Dewa, tashika ni gorenraku shimasu.	Good. I'll be sure to get in touch with you.
Dewa shitsurei shi-masu. Odenwa o omachi shite ori-masu.	Good-bye. [And] (I) will be waiting for your phone call.
Dewa mata.	See you soon.

[1] *Choo* is a word for "street" or "block," and is sometimes added to the name proper, as in *Oiwake-choo*.

[2] *Choome* is a word for "street." *Me* in "*choome*" signifies that the street is an ordinal number (e.g., *Ginza yon choome* = Ginza Fourth Street).

QUIZ 16

1. *Iie, kyoo hajimete ome ni kakarimasu.*

a. Yes, we've already met.

2. *Hai, mae kara zonjiagete orimasu.*

b. No, I haven't had the pleasure of meeting (this person).

3. *Iie, motte orimasen. Itadakemasu ka?*

c. No, not yet. [I am meeting him for the first time today.]

4. *Jimusho no banchi mo itadakemasu ka?*

d. Glad to have met you.

5. *Dewa mata.*

e. I hope to see you soon.

6. *Aa soo desu ka. Dewa tashika ni gorenraku shimasu.*

f. Could I have your office address, too?

7. *Watakushi no juusho to denwa bangoo wa omochi deshoo ka?*

g. No, let me have it.

8. *Iie, ome ni kakatta koto wa arimasen.*

h. Do you have my address and telephone number?

9. *Mata zehi oai shitai to omoimasu.*

i. Good. I will be sure to get in touch with you.

10. *Ome ni kakarete yokatta desu.*

j. See you soon.

ANSWERS

1—c; 2—a; 3—g; 4—f; 5—j; 6—i; 7—h; 8—b; 9—e; 10—d.

C. WORD STUDY

baiorin	violin
furuuto	flute

gitaa	guitar
haapu	harp
kurarinetto	clarinet
mandorin	mandolin
paipu orugan	pipe organ
piano	piano
sakusofon	saxophone
chero	cello

REVIEW QUIZ 2

1. *Doozo moo sukoshi yukkuri* _____ (speak)
   kudasaimasen ka?
   a. *kaite*
   b. *hanashite*
   c. *kakete*

2. *Doozo* _____ (slowly) *hanashite kudasai.*
   a. *hakkiri*
   b. *yoku*
   c. *yukkuri*

3. *Kodomo* _____ (direction-particle) *hon o yarimashita.*
   a. *ga*
   b. *ni*
   c. *no*

4. *Yamada-san ni tegami* _____ (object-particle)
   kakimashita.
   a. *o*
   b. *ga*
   c. *no*

5. *Sonna ni _____* (far) *arimasen.*
    a. *tooku*
    b. *chikaku*
    c. *takaku*

6. *Ano hito _____* (topic-particle) *kodomo ni okane o yarimashita.*
    a. *o*
    b. *wa*
    c. *to*

7. *Watashi wa jimusho ni _____* (am).
    a. *desu*
    b. *imasu*
    c. *arimasu*

8. *_____* (Late) *kimashita.*
    a. *Hayaku*
    b. *Tooku*
    c. *Osoku*

9. *Sono hon wa doko ni _____* (is) *ka?*
    a. *imasu*
    b. *arimasu*
    c. *desu*

10. *Koppu o _____* (bring) *kudasai.*
    a. *katte*
    b. *totte*
    c. *motte kite*

11. *Sore wa _____* (easy) *desu.*
    a. *yasashii*
    b. *muzukashii*
    c. *ookii*

12. *Kodomo no* _____ (room) *desu.*
    a. *mono*
    b. *heya*
    c. *hon*

13. *Okane ga* _____ (there isn't).
    a. *arimasen*
    b. *imasen*
    c. *kimasen*

14. *Tabako o* _____ (have) *imasu ka?*
    a. *mite*
    b. *kaite*
    c. *motte*

15. *Nihongo wa yoku* _____ (don't understand).
    a. *wakarimasen*
    b. *kakemasen*
    c. *shimasen*

16. *Doo mo* _____ (thank) *gozaimasu.*
    a. *osamuu*
    b. *arigatoo*
    c. *otakoo*

17. _____ (Here) *ni imasu ka?*
    a. *Doko*
    b. *Soko*
    c. *Koko*

18. _____ (A little) *wakarimasu.*
    a. *Yoku*
    b. *Takusan*
    c. *Sukoshi*

ANSWERS
1—b; 2—c; 3—b; 4—a; 5—a; 6—b; 7—b; 8—c;
9—b; 10—c; 11—a; 12—b; 13—a; 14—c; 15—a;
16—b; 17—c; 18—c.

SUPPLEMENTAL VOCABULARY LIST 9: SPORTS AND RECREATION

sports and recreation	*supootsu to rikurieeshon*
soccer, football	*sakkaa*
American football	*amerikan futtobooru, amefuto*
basketball	*basukettobooru*
baseball	*yakyuu*
hockey	*hokkee*
tennis	*tenisu*
swimming	*suiei*
judo	*juudoo*
kendo	*kendoo*
sumo	*sumoo*
game	*shiai*
team	*chiimu*
stadium	*kyoogijoo, sutajiamu*
coach	*koochi*
player	*senshu*
champion	*yuushoosha*
ball	*booru, tama*
(to go) hiking	*haikingu (suru / ni iku)*
(to go) camping	*kyanpu (suru / ni iku)*
to play (a sport)	*(undoo o) suru*
to play (a game)	*(shiai o) suru*
to win	*katsu*
to lose	*makeru*
to draw / tie	*hikiwakeru*
cards	*kaado, toranpu*
pool / billiards	*biriyaado*

LESSON 21

DAI NIJUU IKKA

A. Numbers

1. For 1 to 10 only, there are two sets of numbers:

ichi	one
ni	two
san	three
shi, yon	four
go	five
roku	six
shichi, nana	seven
hachi	eight
ku, kyuu	nine
juu	ten

hitotsu	one
futatsu	two
mittsu	three
yottsu	four
itsutsu	five
muttsu	six
nanatsu	seven
yattsu	eight
kokonotsu	nine
too	ten

juuichi	eleven
juuni	twelve
juusan	thirteen
juushi, juuyon	fourteen
juugo	fifteen
juuroku	sixteen

juushichi, juunana	seventeen
juuhachi	eighteen
juuku, juukyuu	nineteen
nijuu	twenty
nijuu ichi	twenty-one
nijuu ni	twenty-two
nijuu san	twenty-three
sanjuu	thirty
sanjuu ichi	thirty-one
sanjuu ni	thirty-two
sanjuu san	thirty-three
yonjuu, shijuu	forty
yonjuu ichi	forty-one
yonjuu ni	forty-two
yonjuu san	forty-three
gojuu	fifty
gojuu ichi	fifty-one
gojuu ni	fifty-two
gojuu san	fifty-three
rokujuu	sixty
rokujuu ichi	sixty-one
rokujuu ni	sixty-two
rokujuu san	sixty-three
nanajuu, shichijuu	seventy
nanajuu ichi	seventy-one
nanajuu ni	seventy-two
nanajuu san	seventy-three
hachijuu	eighty
hachijuu ichi	eighty-one
hachijuu ni	eighty-two
hachijuu san	eighty-three
kyuujuu	ninety
kyuujuu ichi	ninety-one

kyuujuu ni	ninety-two
kyuujuu san	ninety-three

B. MORE NUMBERS

hyaku	one hundred
hyaku ichi	one hundred one
hyaku ni	one hundred two
hyaku san	one hundred three
hyaku nijuu	one hundred twenty
hyaku nijuu ichi	one hundred twenty-one
hyaku sanjuu	one hundred thirty
hyaku yonjuu	one hundred forty
hyaku gojuu	one hundred fifty
hyaku rokujuu	one hundred sixty
hyaku nanajuu	one hundred seventy
hyaku nanajuu ichi	one hundred seventy-one
hyaku hachijuu	one hundred eighty
hyaku kyuujuu	one hundred ninety
hyaku kyuujuu hachi	one hundred ninety-eight
hyaku kyuujuu ku	one hundred ninety-nine
nihyaku	two hundred
sanbyaku[1] nijuu shi	three hundred twenty-four

[1] Notice the *b* in *sanbyaku*, the *p* in *happyaku*, and the *z* in *sanzen*.
See Section 4 of the Summary of Japanese Grammar.

happyaku nanajuu go	eight hundred seventy-five
sen	one thousand
sen ichi	one thousand one
sen ni	one thousand two
sen san	one thousand three
ichi man	ten thousand
juu man	one hundred thousand
hyaku man	one million
sanzen sanbyaku san-juu san	three thousand three hundred thirty-three

C. PRONUNCIATION OF NUMBERS BEFORE CERTAIN COUNTERS

The pronunciation of numbers often differs before "counters" beginning with certain consonants. "Counters" are words like "sheet" in "ten sheets of paper" or "cup" in "ten cups of water." Most things have to be counted with a counter in Japanese.

Before a counter beginning with *h, f, k, s, sh, t, chi,* or *ts,* the pronunciation of the *ichi* [one], *hachi* [eight], and *juu* [ten] usually changes. When a counter begins with *h* or *f,* the *h* or *f* changes to *p.* Before a counter beginning with *h, f,* or *k,* the numbers *roku* [six] and *hyaku* [one hundred] also change form. Following are some examples of these changes:

COUNTER: *-FUN*	MINUTE
ichi, ippun	one, one minute
roku, roppun	six, six minutes

hachi, happun (or) **hachifun**	eight, eight minutes
juu, juppun (or) **jippun**	ten, ten minutes
hyaku, hyappun	one hundred, one hundred minutes

COUNTER: *-KEN*	HOUSE
ichi, ikken	one, one house
roku, rokken	six, six houses
hachi, hakken (or) **hachiken**	eight, eight houses
juu, jukken (or) **jikken**	ten, ten houses
hyaku, hyakken	one hundred, one hundred houses

COUNTER: *-SATSU*	VOLUME
ichi, issatsu	one, one volume
hachi, hassatsu	eight, eight volumes
juu, jussatsu (or) **jissatsu**	ten, ten volumes

COUNTER: *-TEN*	POINT
ichi, itten	one, one point
hachi, hatten	eight, eight points
juu, jutten (or) **jitten**	ten, ten points

D. First, Second, Third

dai ichi[1]	first
dai ni	second

[1] When *dai* precedes a numeral, it shows that the number which follows is an ordinal. Occasionally, an ordinal is used without *dai*.

dai san	third
dai yon	fourth
dai go	fifth
dai roku	sixth
dai nana	seventh
dai hachi	eighth
dai kyuu, dai ku	ninth
dai juu	tenth
Dai Ichiji Taisen	World War I
dai ni maku	the second act
san too	the third class
yon kai	the fourth floor
dai go ka	the fifth lesson
dai rokkai	the sixth time
dai nana shuu	the seventh week
hachikagetsume[1]	the eighth month
dai kyuu nen, dai ku nen	the ninth year
dai juu	the tenth
juuichi ninme no hito	the eleventh person
dai juuni shoo	the twelfth chapter
juusan nichime	the thirteenth day
juuyon seiki	the fourteenth century
juugo kenme no uchi	the fifteenth door, the fifteenth house
juuroku banme no fune	the sixteenth boat
juunana choome	the seventeenth street
dai juuhappan	the eighteenth edition
juukyuu banme no kuruma	the nineteenth car
nijikkenme no ie	the twentieth house

[1] *-me* is another way to indicate an ordinal number.

QUIZ 17

1. *rokkiro*	a. the third class
2. *yon kai*	b. the eighth month
3. *jippun*	c. the ninth year
4. *santoo*	d. six kilometers
5. *juuyon seiki*	e. the fourth floor
6. *juuichi ninme no hito*	f. ten minutes
7. *dai go ka*	g. the eleventh person
8. *hachikagetsume*	h. the thirteenth day
9. *juusan nichime*	i. the fifth lesson
10. *dai kyuunen*	j. the fourteenth century

ANSWERS
1—d; 2—e; 3—f; 4—a; 5—j; 6—g; 7—i; 8—b;
9—h; 10—c.

E. TWO AND TWO

Ichi to ni de san ni narimasu.	Two and one are [become] three.
Ni tasu ichi wa san desu.	Two and [plus] one are three.
Ni to ni wa yon desu.	Two and two are four.
Ni tasu ni wa yon desu.	Two and [plus] two are four.
Yon to san wa shichi desu.	Four and three are seven.
Yon tasu san wa shichi desu.	Four and [plus] three are seven.
Go to ni de shichi ni narimasu.	Five and two are [become] seven.
Go tasu ni wa shichi desu.	Five and [plus] two are seven.

Shichi to ichi de hachi ni narimasu.	Seven and one are [become] eight.
Shichi tasu ichi wa hachi desu.	Seven and [plus] one are eight.

Supplemental Vocabulary List 10: In The Office

in the office	*jimusho ni, jimusho de*
office	*jimusho, ofisu*
desk	*tsukue*
computer	*konpyuuta(a)*
telephone	*denwa*
fax machine	*fakkusuki*
book shelf	*hondana*
file cabinet	*fairu kyabinetto*
file	*fairu*
boss	*jooshi*
colleague	*dooryoo*
employee	*juugyooin*
staff	*shokuin*
company	*kaisha*
business	*gyoomu*
factory	*koojoo*
meeting room	*kaigishitsu*
meeting	*kaigi*
appointment	*yakusoku, yoyaku*
salary	*kyuuryoo*
job	*shigoto*
busy	*isogashii*
to work	*hataraku*
to earn	*kasegu*

LESSON 22

DAI NIJUU NIKA

A. IT COSTS . . .

Kore wa . . . shimasu.	This costs . . .
Kore wa gosen en shimasu.	This costs five thousand yen.
Kono nooto wa gohyaku gojuu en shimasu.	This notebook costs five hundred fifty yen.
Kono booshi wa gosen en shimashita.	This hat cost me five thousand yen.
Kono doresu ni ichi man gosen en haraimashita.	I paid fifteen thousand yen for this dress.
Kono kuruma o sanbyakuman en de kaimashita.	I bought this car for three million yen.
Ichi rittoru nisen en desu.	It's two thousand yen a liter.
Ichi meetoru nihyaku gojuu en desu.	That costs two hundred fifty yen a meter.
Sen nihyaku en shimasu.	The price is twelve hundred yen. It costs twelve hundred yen.
Hitotsu gojuu en desu.	They cost fifty yen a piece.

B. THE TELEPHONE NUMBER IS . . .

Watashi no denwa bangoo wa san yon hachi san no san roku yon hachi ban desu.	My telephone number is 3483-3648.

San san san yon no goo nii[1] san roku ban ni kakete mite kudasai.	Try number 3334-5236.
Denwa bangoo ga kawarimashita. Ima no wa san nii roku yon no nii nii nii yon ban desu.	My telephone number has been changed; it's now 3264-2224.
Denwa wa san kyuu nii nii no san san rei nana ban desu.	Their phone number is 3922-3307.

C. MY ADDRESS IS . . .

Yoyogi juuni-choome juunana banchi ni sunde imasu.	I live at 17, 12-chome (street), Yoyogi.
Yamada-san wa doko ni sunde imasu ka?	Where does Mr. Yamada live? [Where is Mr. Yamada residing?]
Kono machi ni sunde imasu.	He lives in this town.
Asakusa san-choome yon banchi ni sunde imasu.	She lives at 4, 3-chome, Asakusa.
Ikebukuro yon-choome juuni banchi desu.	Our address is 12, 4-chome, Ikebukuro.
Ogikubo go-choome nihyaku rokujuu san banchi ni sunde imasu.	We live at 263, 5-chome, Ogikubo.

[1] When giving phone numbers, numerals with one syllable can be pronounced with long vowels: *goo* and *nii*.

**Heya no bangoo wa   My room number is
  yonjuu ni desu.   42.**

D. SOME DATES

**Sen happyaku kyuu-   It happened in 1891.
  juu ichi nen ni oko-
  rimashita.**

Nyuu Yooku no Sekai   The New York World's
  hakurankai wa sen   Fair took place in
  kyuuhyaku sanjuu   1939.
  kyuu nen ni arimashita.

Sen kyuuhyaku hachijuu   I was born in
  ni nen ni   1982.
  umaremashita.

Korera no koto wa   All of this happened in
  subete sen kyuuhyaku   1999.
  kyuujuu kyuu nen
  ni okorimashita.

Watashi wa nisen roku   I was in Tokyo in
  nen ni wa Tookyoo   2006.
  ni imashita.

Nisen yo nen no   The 2004 Olympic Games
  Orinpikku wa   took place in Athens,
  Girisha no Atene   Greece.
  de kaisaisaremashita.

QUIZ 18

1. *Kore wa gosen en*   a. This costs five thou-
   shimasu.   sand yen.
2. *Denwa bangoo wa*   b. I bought this car for
   san nana nii kyuu   five million yen.
   no san san rei nana
   ban desu.

3. *Kono kuruma o go-*   c. Their phone number
   hyakuman en de   is 3729-3307.
   kaimashita.

4. *Watashi wa nisen*   d. They cost fifty yen
   roku nen ni wa   apiece.
   Tookyoo ni imashita.

5. *Sore wa hitotsu*   e. I was in Tokyo in
   gojuu en desu.   2006.

ANSWERS
1—a; 2—c; 3—b; 4—e; 5—d.

LESSON 23

DAI NIJUU SANKA

A. WHAT TIME IS IT?

Nanji desu ka?	What time is it?
Nanji ka oshiete ku-dasaimasen ka?	Do you have the time, please?
Ichiji desu.	It's one o'clock.
Niji desu.	It's two o'clock.
Sanji desu.	It's three o'clock.
Yoji desu.	It's four o'clock.
Goji desu.	It's five o'clock.
Rokuji desu.	It's six o'clock.
Shichiji desu.	It's seven o'clock.
Hachiji desu.	It's eight o'clock.
Kuji desu.	It's nine o'clock.
Juuji desu.	It's ten o'clock.
Juuichiji desu.	It's eleven o'clock.
Juuniji desu.	It's noon. It's twelve o'clock.

Gogo ichiji desu.	It's 1:00 p.m.
Gogo niji desu.	It's 2:00 p.m.
Gogo sanji desu.	It's 3:00 p.m.
Gogo yoji desu.	It's 4:00 p.m.
Gogo goji desu.	It's 5:00 p.m.
Gogo rokuji desu.	It's 6:00 p.m.
Gogo shichiji desu.	It's 7:00 p.m.
Gogo hachiji desu.	It's 8:00 p.m.
Gogo kuji desu.	It's 9:00 p.m.
Gogo juuji desu.	It's 10:00 p.m.
Gogo juuichiji desu.	It's 11:00 p.m.
Gogo juuniji desu.	It's 12:00 p.m.
Yoru no juuniji desu.	It's midnight.

B.   THE TIME IS NOW . . .

byoo	second
fun, pun	minute
ji	hour
Niji juu gofun desu.	It's two fifteen.
Niji juu gofun sugi desu.	It's a quarter after two.
Niji juu gofun mae desu.	It's a quarter to two.
Sanji yonjuu gofun desu.	It's three forty-five.
Niji-han desu.	It's half-past two.
Niji sanjippun desu.	It's two thirty.
Goji nijippun mae desu.	It's twenty to five.
Kuji sanjuu gofun desu.	It's nine thirty-five.
Shoogo desu.	It's noon.
Juuniji gofun mae desu.	It's five to twelve.

Juuniji gofun sugi desu.	It's five past twelve.
Gozen ichiji desu.	It's one o'clock in the morning.
Goji goro desu.	It's about five.
Shichiji goro desu.	It's about seven.
Juuichiji sukoshi mae desu.	It's almost eleven.
Mada rokuji-han desu.	It's only half-past six.
Goji sugi desu.	It's after five.

C. WHEN WILL YOU COME?

Itsu oide ni narimasu ka?	When will you come *(respect)?* [What time will you come?]
Sanji ni soko e ikimasu.	I'll be there at three o'clock.
Sanji nijuppun mae ni kimashita.	She came at twenty to three.
Gogo niji ni kimasu.	He'll come at 2:00 p.m.
Kuji nijuu gofun goro ni soko e ikimasu.	We'll be there about nine twenty-five.
Konban no juuji-han ni kaette kimasu.	He'll be back at ten thirty this evening.
Hachiji juu gofun goro ni soko de ome ni kakari-mashoo.	I'll see you there about eight fifteen.
Rokuji ni aimasu.	We'll meet at six.
Yoji ni dekakemasu.	I'm going out at four o'clock.
Shichiji to hachiji no aida ni kite kuda-sai.	Come between seven and eight, please.

Yoru no rokuji ni ki-masu.	He'll come at six in the evening.
Konban juuji ni kite kudasai.	Come at ten o'clock tonight, please.
Densha wa shichiji nijuu sanpun ni tsukimasu.	The train arrives at seven twenty-three.
Densha wa kuji yon-jippun ni demasu.	The train leaves at nine forty.

D. IT'S TIME

Jikan desu.	It's time.
Sore o suru jikan desu.	It's time to do it. [(It) is to-do-it time.]
Deru jikan desu.	It's time to leave.
Uchi e kaeru jikan desu.	It's time to go home.
Jikan ga arimasu.	I have time.
Juubun jikan ga ari-masu.	I have enough time.
Jikan ga arimasen.	I don't have the time.
Dono kurai nagaku soko ni iru tsumori desu ka?	How long do you in-tend to stay there?
Dono kurai nagaku koko ni imashita ka?	How long have you been there?
Jikan no muda o shite imasu.	He's wasting his time.
Suru jikan o agete kudasai.	Give her time to do it, please.
Kimono o kigaeru aida dake matte kudasai.	Just give me enough time to change my clothes. [Please wait

just for the duration
that I am changing
clothes.]

Tokidoki kimasu.   He comes from time to
time.

QUIZ 19

1. *Niji-han desu.*

   a. I'll see you there
      about eight fifteen.

2. *Niji juu gofun
   desu.*

   b. The train arrives at
      seven twenty-three.

3. *Jikan desu.*

   c. He's wasting his
      time.

4. *Jikan no muda o
   shite imasu.*

   d. Come at ten o'clock
      this evening, please.

5. *Soko de hachiji juu
   gofun goro ni ome
   ni kakarimasu.*

   e. It's one o'clock in
      the morning.

6. *Densha wa shichiji
   nijuu sanpun ni
   tsukimasu.*

   f. He'll come at 2:00.

7. *Konban juuji ni
   kite kudasai.*

   g. We'll be there about
      nine twenty-five.

8. *Gozen ichiji desu.*

   h. It's two fifteen. It's
      a quarter after two.

9. *Kuji nijuu gofun
   goro ni soko e iki-
   masu.*

   i. It's half-past two.
      It's two thirty.

10. *Niji ni kimasu.*

   j. It's time.

ANSWERS
1—i; 2—h; 3—j; 4—c; 5—a; 6—b; 7—d; 8—e;
9—g; 10—f.

E. Word Study

anpaia	umpire
baatendaa	bartender
dezainaa	designer
konsarutant	consultant
enjinia	engineer
maneejaa	manager
sarariiman	salaried man
seerusuman	salesman
suponsaa	sponsor
taipisuto	typist

LESSON 24

DAI NIJUU YONKA

A. Ago

mae	ago
ichijikan mae	an hour ago
nijikan mae	two hours ago
sanjikan mae	three hours ago
ichinichi mae	a day ago
futsuka mae	two days ago
sanshuukan mae	three weeks ago
gokagetsu mae	five months ago
gonen mae	five years ago
juunen mae	ten years ago
zutto mae	a long time ago
kanari mae	a rather long time ago, quite a long time ago
sukoshi mae	a short time ago

B. MORNING, NOON, AND NIGHT

asa	morning
hiru ⎫ shoogo ⎭	noon
gogo	afternoon
ban	evening
yoru	night
hi	the day
shuu	the week
isshuukan	a week
nishuukan	two weeks
tsuki	month
toshi	year
kinoo	yesterday
kyoo	today
ashita	tomorrow
ototoi	the day before yesterday
tsugi no hi	the next day
asatte	the day after tomorrow
ima	now
sugu	in a moment, soon
kesa	this morning
kinoo no asa	yesterday morning
ashita no asa	tomorrow morning
kyoo no gogo	this afternoon [today's afternoon]
kinoo no gogo	yesterday afternoon
ashita no gogo	tomorrow afternoon
konban	this evening, tonight
kinoo no ban ⎫ sakuban ⎭	yesterday evening
ashita no ban	tomorrow evening

kinoo no yoru	
sakuya	last night
yuube	
ashita no yoru	tomorrow night

C. This Week, Next Month, etc.

konshuu	this week
senshuu	last week
raishuu	next week
saraishuu	in two weeks, the week after next
kongetsu	this month
sengetsu	last month
raigetsu	next month
saraigetsu	the month after next
sensengetsu	two months ago, the month before last
kotoshi	this year
kyonen	last year
sakunen	
rainen	next year
sarainen	in two years, the year after next
issakunen	the year before last
ototoshi	
asa	in the morning
ban	in the evening
hiru goro	around noon
yuushokugo	after dinner (the evening meal)
shuumatsu	at the end of the week
getsumatsu	at the end of the month

konshuu no owari goro ni	toward the end of the week
ichijikan mae	an hour ago
juu gofun inai ni	in a quarter of an hour
sono uchi ni	one of these days
Sono uchi ni ome ni kakarimasu.	See you one of these days.
mainichi	every day
ichinichi juu	all day (long)
hitoban juu	all night (long)
Asa kara ban made hatarakimasu.	He works from morning to night.
Kyoo wa nannichi desu ka?	What's the date today?

D. EXPRESSIONS OF PAST, PRESENT, AND FUTURE

PAST	PRESENT	FUTURE
tsui sakki	**ima**	**sugu ato de**
a moment ago	now	in a moment
kinoo no asa	**kesa**	**ashita no asa**
yesterday morning	this morning	tomorrow morning
kinoo no gogo	**kyoo no gogo**	**ashita no gogo**
yesterday afternoon	this afternoon	tomorrow afternoon
sakuban	**konban**	**ashita no ban**
yesterday evening	this evening	tomorrow evening

sakuya	**kon'ya**	**ashita no yoru**
last night	tonight	tomorrow night
senshuu	**konshuu**	**raishuu**
last week	this week	next week
sengetsu	**kongetsu**	**raigetsu**
last month	this month	next month
sakunen[1]	**kotoshi**	**rainen**
last year (official)	this year	next year

LESSON 25

DAI NIJUU GOKA

A. DAYS OF THE WEEK

Getsuyoobi	Monday
Kayoobi	Tuesday
Suiyoobi	Wednesday
Mokuyoobi	Thursday
Kin'yoobi	Friday
Doyoobi	Saturday
Nichiyoobi	Sunday

B. DAYS OF THE MONTH

In Japanese, each day of the month has a name. These names, with the exception of the word for the first day,

---

[1] *Sakunen* is an official way to say "last year." *Kyonen* is a more colloquial form.

can also be used to count the *number* of days.[1] For example, *futsuka*, "second day," can also mean "two days"; but to count "one day," you must say *ichinichi*.

tsuitachi	first day (of the month)
futsuka	second day
mikka	third day
yokka	fourth day
itsuka	fifth day
muika	sixth day
nanoka, nanuka	seventh day
yooka	eighth day
kokonoka	ninth day
tooka	tenth day
juuichinichi	eleventh day
juuninichi	twelfth day
juusannichi	thirteenth day
juuyokka	fourteenth day
juugonichi	fifteenth day
juurokunichi	sixteenth day
juushichinichi	seventeenth day
juuhachinichi	eighteenth day
juukunichi	nineteenth day
hatsuka	twentieth day
nijuu ichinichi	twenty-first day
nijuu ninichi	twenty-second day
nijuu sannichi	twenty-third day
nijuu yokka	twenty-fourth day
nijuu gonichi	twenty-fifth day

[1] For counters, see Section 11 of the Summary of Japanese Grammar.

nijuu rokunichi	twenty-sixth day
nijuu shichinichi	twenty-seventh day
nijuu hachinichi	twenty-eighth day
nijuu kunichi	twenty-ninth day
sanjuunichi	thirtieth day
sanjuu ichinichi	thirty-first day

C. WHAT'S THE DATE TODAY?

Kyoo wa nannichi desu ka?	What's the date today?
Doyoobi wa nannichi desu ka?	What will the date be on Saturday? [As for Saturday, what is the date?]
Kyoo wa tooka desu.	Today's the tenth.
Kyoo wa hatsuka desu.	Today's the twentieth.
Kyoo wa Kayoobi desu ka? Suiyoobi desu ka?	Is today Tuesday, or is it Wednesday?
Kyoo wa Suiyoobi desu.	Today's Wednesday.
Kyoo wa Getsuyoobi desu.	Today's Monday.
Raishuu no Doyoobi ni kite kudasai.	Come next Saturday, please.
Raishuu no Kayoobi ni tachimasu.	She's leaving next Tuesday.
Senshuu no Getsuyoobi ni tsukimashita.	She arrived last Monday. [She arrived last week's Monday.]

Raishuu no Getsu-yoobi ni tsu-kimasu.	She's arriving next Monday.
Soko ni mikka ima-shita.	I was there three days.
Soko ni ichinichi shika imasen de-shita.	I was there only one day. [(I) wasn't there any more than one day.]

QUIZ 20

1. *ototoi*	a. afternoon
2. *kyoo*	b. day before yester-day
3. *gogo*	c. today
4. *tsui sakki*	d. day after tomorrow
5. *ashita no gogo*	e. a moment ago
6. *kyoo no gogo*	f. tomorrow afternoon
7. *asatte*	g. all night long
8. *Jikan o muda ni shite imasu.*	h. He's wasting his time.
9. *hitoban juu*	i. this afternoon
10. *Dono kurai nagaku koko ni imashita ka?*	j. How long have you been here?
11. *raishuu*	k. the month after next
12. *senshuu*	l. the week before last
13. *sensenshuu*	m. next week
14. *saraigetsu*	n. the year before last
15. *ototoshi*	o. last week
16. *Jikan desu*	p. It's time to go home.
17. *Jikan ga arimasu.*	q. tomorrow night

18. *Uchi e kaeru jikan*   r. this evening
    desu.
19. *ashita no yoru*   s. It's time.
20. *konban*   t. I have time.

ANSWERS
1—b; 2—c; 3—a; 4—e; 5—f; 6—i; 7—d; 8—h;
9—g; 10—j; 11—m; 12—o; 13—l; 14—k; 15—n;
16—s; 17—t; 18—p; 19—q; 20—r.

D. MONTHS OF THE YEAR

Ichigatsu	January
Nigatsu	February
Sangatsu	March
Shigatsu	April
Gogatsu	May
Rokugatsu	June
Shichigatsu	July
Hachigatsu	August
Kugatsu	September
Juugatsu	October
Juuichigatsu	November
Juunigatsu	December

Kyoo wa Rokugatsu tsuitachi desu.	Today is the first of June.
Watashi wa Shigatsu juuninichi ni umaremashita.	I was born on April twelfth.
Imooto wa Gogatsu itsuka ni umaremashita.	My sister was born on May fifth.

Watashi no tan-joobi wa Nigatsu futsuka desu.
My birthday is February second.

Shichigatsu juuyokka ni kimasu.
I'll come on the fourteenth of July.

Gakkoo wa Kugatsu hatsuka ni hajima-rimasu.
School begins on the twentieth of September.

Sangatsu nijuu ninichi ni kaerimasu.
I'll be back on March twenty-second.

Juuichigatsu juuichi-nichi wa yasumi desu.
November eleventh is a holiday.

Shichigatsu mikka ni tachimasu.
She's leaving on July third.

Tegami wa Rokugatsu muika zuke desu.
The letter is dated June sixth.

Gogatsu juuichinichi ni otazune shimasu.
We'll come to see you on May eleventh.

Kyoo wa sen kyuuhyaku kyuujuu ninen Gogatsu itsuka desu.
Today is May fifth, 1992.

E. THE SEASONS

haru	spring
natsu	summer
aki	autumn
fuyu	winter
fuyu ni	in winter
natsu ni	in summer
aki ni	in autumn, in fall
haru ni	in spring

QUIZ 21

1. *Kyoo wa nan' yoobi desu ka?*
2. *Sono uchi ni ome ni kakarimasu.*
3. *ichinichi juu*
4. *natsu ni.*
5. *juugo fun de*
6. *Raishuu no Getsu-yoobi ni tsukimasu.*
7. *Kyoo wa Getsu-yoobi desu.*
8. *Raishuu no Doyoobi ni kite kudasai.*
9. *fuyu*
10. *Nichiyoobi*
11. *Kyoo wa hatsuka desu.*
12. *Doyoobi wa nanni-chi desu ka?*
13. *Shichigatsu no juuyokka ni kimasu.*
14. *Kyoo wa Roku-gatsu no tsuitachi desu.*
15. *Tegami wa Roku-gatsu muika zuke desu.*

a. Sunday
b. in a quarter of an hour
c. See you one of these days.
d. all day
e. What day of the week is today?
f. in the summer
g. winter
h. What's the date on Saturday?
i. Today's the twentieth.
j. Today's Monday.
k. Come next Satur-day, please.
l. He'll arrive next Monday.
m. The letter is dated June sixth.
n. I'll come on the fourteenth of July.
o. Today is the first of June.

ANSWERS

1—e; 2—c; 3—d; 4—f; 5—b; 6—l; 7—j; 8—k; 9—g; 10—a; 11—i; 12—h; 13—n; 14—o; 15—m.

Supplemental Vocabulary List 11: Nature

nature	*shizen*
tree	*ki*
flower	*hana*
forest	*mori*
mountain	*yama*
field	*nohara, soogen, bokusoochi*
river	*kawa*
lake	*mizuumi*
ocean	*umi*
sea	*umi*
beach	*kaigan*
desert	*sabaku*
rock	*iwa*
sand	*suna*
sky	*sora*
sun	*taiyoo*
moon	*tsuki*
star	*hoshi*
water	*mizu*
land	*riku, tochi*
plant	*shokubutsu*
hill	*oka*
pond	*ike*

LESSON 26

DAI NIJUU ROKKA

A. *IKU:* To Go[1]

1. I go, I don't go:

PLAIN	POLITE	
iku	**ikimasu**	I, you, we, they go; he, she goes[1]
itta	**ikimashita**	I went
itte	**itte**	I go and ...
ikanai	**ikimasen**	I don't go
ikitai	**ikitai desu**	I wish to go
ikeba ⎱ **ittara** ⎰		if I go
ikanakereba ⎱ **ikanakattara** ⎰		if I don't go
ittari[2]		sometimes I go
ikoo	**ikimashoo**	I think I'll go. Let's go.
ike		Go! *(sharp command)*

2. Study these phrases with forms of *iku:*

Kodomotachi wa doko e ikimasu ka?   Where are the children going?

---

[1] Remember that in Japanese the same forms are used for first, second, and third persons in both the singular and plural.

[2] See footnote 3, page 155.

Doobutsuen e iki-masu.	They are going to the zoo.
Kinoo wa doko e iki-mashita ka?	Where did you go yesterday?
Umi e ikimashita.	I went to the beach [sea].
Kono densha wa doko made ikimasu ka?	How far does this train go?
Koobe made ikimasu.	It goes as far as Kobe.

3. Some common expressions with *iku:*

Itte kudasai!	Please go!
Ikanaide kudasai.	Please don't go.
Yukkuri itte kudasai.	Go slowly, please.
Itte sagashite kudasai.	Go look for it, please. [Go and look for (it), please.]
Soko e ikanakereba narimasen.	We have to go there. [If (I) don't go, (it) won't do.]
Itte wa ikemasen.	You must not go.
Ikanakute mo ii desu.	We don't have to go. [Even if (we) don't go, (it) will be all right.]
Itte mo ikanakute mo ii desu.	It doesn't matter whether we go or not. [Even if (we) go, even if we don't go, (it) will be all right.]
Itte mo ii desu.	You may go. You have my permission to go. [Even if (you) go, (it) will be all right.]
Ikitai desu ga iku koto ga dekimasen.	I want to go, but I can't [go].

Itta koto ga arimasu.	I have been there.
Itta koto wa arimasen.	I have never been there.
Iku koto ga arimasu.	I sometimes go.

4. Verb particles with *iku:*

Soko e iku to[1] kau koto ga dekimasu.	If you go there, you can buy (them).
Ashita iku to[2] iimashita.	I said I would go tomorrow.
Itta keredomo[3] au koto ga dekimasen deshita.	I went, but couldn't meet her/him.
Kinoo wa ikimashita ga[4] kyoo wa ikimasen.	I went yesterday, but I am not going today.
Takushii de itta kara[5] ma ni aimashita.	I went by taxi and so I was able to make it.
Tookyoo e itte kara[6] Kyooto e ikimashita.	I went to Tokyo and then [after that] I went to Kyoto. After I went to Tokyo, I went to Kyoto.
Ame ga futta node[7] ikimasen deshita.	It rained and so [because of that fact] I didn't go.

---

[1] *to* = if, when.
[2] *to* marks the end of something being quoted.
[3] *keredomo* = but.
[4] *ga* (particle) = but.
[5] *kara* (when it follows a sentence-ending form) = and so, and therefore, because of that.
[6] *kara* (when it follows a *-te* form) = and after that, and subsequently.
[7] *node* = and because of that fact, the situation being what it is.

Hiroshima e ikimashita shi[1] Nagasaki e mo ikimashita.	I went to Hiroshima and, in addition [not only that], I even went to Nagasaki.
Hanashinagara[2] ikimashoo.	Let's go as we talk.
Nichiyoobi ni wa Enoshima e ittari Hakone e ittari[3] shimasu.	On Sundays I sometimes go to Enoshima, and sometimes [go] to Hakone.

B.   A Few Action Phrases

Abunai!	Watch out! [(It) is dangerous!]
Ki o tsukete kudasai!	Be careful! Pay attention!
Hayaku itte kudasai.	Please go fast.
Motto hayaku itte kudasai.	Please go faster.
Sonna ni hayaku ikanaide kudasai.	Don't go so fast, please.
Anmari hayaku ikanaide kudasai.	Don't go too fast, please.
Motto yukkuri itte kudasai.	Go slower, please.
Motto hayaku kite kudasai.	Please come sooner.
Motto osoku kite kudasai.	Please come later.
Isoide kudasai.	Please hurry up.

[1] *shi* = and not only that, and in addition to that.
[2] *-nagara* = as, while (denotes simultaneous actions by the same subject).
[3] *-tari . . . -tari* when followed by *suru* = sometimes do A, sometimes do B; do such things as A and B.

Isoganaide kudasai.	Please don't hurry.
Isoide imasu.	I'm in a hurry.
Isoide imasen.	I'm not in a hurry.
Doozo goyukkuri.	Take your time.
Chotto matte kudasai.	Just a minute!
Sugu mairimasu.[1]	I'm coming right away.

C. WORD STUDY

biiru	beer
juusu	juice
kakuteru	cocktail
kokoa	cocoa
koohii	coffee
miruku	milk
shanpen	champagne
sooda	soda
uisukii	whiskey
yooguruto	yogurt

D. *SHINBUN URIBA DE*

Kyaku: **Japan Taimuzu o kudasai. Komakai okane o motte inai n desu ga, sen en de totte moraemasu ka?**

Ten'in: **Ashita de kekkoo desu.**

Kyaku: **Demo kon'ya kuruma ka nan ka ni hikarete shinde shimattara doo shimasu?**

Ten'in: **Kamaimasen. Taishita koto ja arimasen kara.**

AT THE NEWSSTAND

Customer: Give me the *Japan Times,* please. However, I don't have any small change. Can you give me change for one thousand yen?

---

[1] *mairu* (humble verb) = come, go.

Dealer: Pay me tomorrow.

Customer: But suppose I get run over by a car or something tonight?

Dealer: So what! It wouldn't be a great loss.

NOTE

totte moraemasu ka = can I have you take it (from)?

Ashita de kekkoo desu. = Tomorrow will do.

hikarete shinde shimattara: hikareru is a passive form of *hiku* [run over]; *shinde shimau* = (and) die [end up in death]; *-tara* = if, suppose.

kara = and so, and therefore (when used after a sentence-ending form of a verb or an adjective).

LESSON 27

DAI NIJUU NANAKA

A. THEY SAY THAT . . .

-soo desu	They say that . . . It's said that . . . People say that . . . I hear that . . . I heard that . . .
Soko wa taihen kirei da soo desu.[1]	They say that the place is very pretty.
Sore wa hontoo da soo desu.	They say that it is true.
Yamada-san no piano wa taihen yokatta soo desu.	People say that Mr. Yamada played the piano very well.

[1] Notice that the predicate appearing before *soo desu* is in the plain form.

[Talking about Mr. Yamada's piano (-playing), it was very good, so I hear.]

Tanaka-san wa kinoo Yokohama ni tsuita soo desu. I heard that Ms. Tanaka arrived in Yokohama yesterday.

Tanaka-san wa kinoo konakatta soo desu. I heard that Ms. Tanaka did not come yesterday.

Tanaka-san wa ima Tookyoo ni inai soo desu. I hear that Ms. Tanaka is not in Tokyo now.

Takeda-san wa rainen Amerika e iku soo desu. I hear that Mr. Takeda will be going to America next year.

B. I HAVE TO, I MUST . . .

Gohan o tabena- kereba narimasen. I must eat my meal.

Kisoku o yoku oboenakereba narimasen. You have to remember the regulations well.

Isoganakereba narimasen. I have to hurry.

Yukkuri arukanakereba narimasen. You must walk slowly.

Nihongo de hanasanakereba narimasen. You have to speak in Japanese.

Nihon de kawanakereba narimasen. I have to buy it in Japan.

Yamada-san ni awanakereba narimasen.	I have to see Mr. Yamada.
Yamada-san ni denwa o kakenakereba narimasen.	I have to telephone Mr. Yamada.
Keikan ni kikanakereba narimasen.	I have to ask a police-man.
Tookyoo e kuruma de ikanakereba narimasen deshita.	I had to go to Tokyo by car.
Eki de Yamada-san ni awanakereba narimasen deshita.	I had to see Mr. Yamada at the station.
Eki kara Yamada-san ni denwa o kakenakereba narimasen deshita.	I had to phone Mr. Yamada from the station.
Beru o narashite hito ga dete kuru no o matanakereba narimasen deshita.	I had to ring the bell and wait for some-one to answer.
Doa ga shimatte ita node soko ni tatte matte inakereba narimasen deshita.	The door was closed, so I had to stand there and wait.
Okane o motte inakatta node karinakereba narimasen deshita.	I had no money, (and) so I had to borrow (some).

C.   SOMETHING TO DRINK

Mizu ga hoshii desu.	I want some water. [Water is wanted.]

Mizu ga hoshii desu ka?	Do you want some water? [Is water wanted?]
Mizu wa hoshiku arimasen.	I don't want any water.
Ocha wa ikaga desu ka?	How about some (Japanese) tea?
Koohii wa ikaga desu ka?	How about some coffee?
Kuriimu wa ikaga desu ka?	How about some cream?
Osatoo wa ikaga desu ka?	How about some sugar?
Kuriimu wa dono kurai iremashoo ka?	How much cream should I put in?
Osatoo wa dono kurai iremashoo ka?	How much sugar should I put in?
Ocha wa dono kurai kaimashoo ka?	How much (Japanese) tea should I buy?
Koohii wa dono kurai kaimashoo ka?	How much coffee should I buy?
Donna ocha o kaimashoo ka?	What kind of (Japanese) tea should we buy?
Donna koohii o kaimashoo ka?	What kind of coffee should we buy?
Dono koohii o kaimashoo ka?	Which coffee should we buy?
Dono koohii ga hoshii desu ka?	Which coffee do you want?
Donna koohii ga suki desu ka?	What kind of coffee do you like?
Dono koohii ga ichiban suki desu ka?	Which coffee do you like best?
Dono koohii ga ichiban hoshii desu ka?	Which coffee do you want most?

QUIZ 22

1. *Tookyoo e kuruma de ikanakereba narimasen deshita.*
2. *Ocha wa ikaga desu ka?*
3. *Isoganakereba narimasen.*
4. *Yukkuri arukanakereba narimasen.*
5. *To ga shimatte ita node, soko ni tatte matte inakereba narimasen deshita.*
6. *Yamada-san ni denwa o kakenakereba narimasen.*
7. *Okane ga nakatta node, karinakereba narimasen deshita.*
8. *Gohan o tabenakereba narimasen.*
9. *Keikan ni kikanakereba narimasen deshita.*
10. *Eki de Yamada-san ni awanakereba narimasen deshita.*

a. I have to hurry.
b. You have to walk slowly.
c. I had to go to Tokyo by car.
d. How about some (Japanese) tea?
e. I have to phone Mr. Yamada.
f. The door was closed, so I had to stand there and wait.
g. I must eat the meal.
h. I had no money, so I had to borrow some.
i. I had to see Mr. Yamada at the station.
j. I had to ask a policeman.

ANSWERS
1—c; 2—d; 3—a; 4—b; 5—f; 6—e; 7—h; 8—g; 9—j; 10—i.

D.   Word Study

firutaa	filter
fookasu	focus
fuirumu	film
furasshu ranpu	flash lamp
kamera	camera
nega	negative
renzu	lens
serufu taimaa	self-timer
shattaa	shutter
suraido	slide

Supplemental Vocabulary List 12: In The Kitchen

in the kitchen	*daidokoro ni, daidokoro de*
refrigerator	*reizooko*
(kitchen) sink	(*daidokoro no*) *nagashi*
counter	*kauntaa*
stove	*konro, renji*
oven	*oobun*
microwave	*denshirenji*
cupboard	*shokkidana, todana*
drawer	*hikidashi*
plate	*sara*
cup	*kappu*
bowl	*booru, donburi, hachi*
glass	*koppu, gurasu*
spoon	*supuun*
knife	*naifu*
can	*kan*
box	*hako*
bottle	*bin*
carton	*kaaton*

coffee maker	*koohii meekaa*
tea kettle	*yakan*
blender	*mikisaa*
iron	*airon*
ironing board	*airondai*
broom	*hooki*
dishwasher	*saraaraiki*
washing machine	*sentakuki*
dryer	*kansooki, doraiyaa*
to cook	*ryoorisuru*
to do the dishes	*shokki o arau*
to do the laundry	*sentakusuru*
dishwashing detergent	*daidokoroyoo senzai*
laundry detergent	*sentakuyoo senzai*
Bleach	*hyoohakuzai*
clean / dirty	*kirei / kitanai*

LESSON 28

DAI NIJUU HACHIKA

A. A LITTLE AND A LOT

Sukoshi.	A little.
Sukoshi desu ka? **Takusan desu ka?**	A lot or a little? [Is (it) a little, or is (it) a lot?]
Honno sukoshi.	Just a little.
Sukoshi zutsu.	Little by little.
Moo sukoshi kudasai.	A little bit more, please. [Give (me) a little bit more, please.]

Sukoshi shika hanashimasen.	He doesn't talk much. [(He) doesn't talk except a little.]
Sukoshi hoshii desu ka? Takusan hoshii desu ka?	Do you want a little or a lot of it?
Sukoshi koko de yasunde ikimashoo.	Let's rest here a little and (then) go.
Sukoshi kudasai.	Give me a little of it, please.
Sukoshi mizu o kudasai.	Give me a little water, please.
Honno sukoshi dake desu.	It's only a very little bit.
Nihongo wa sukoshi shika dekimasen.	I speak very little Japanese. [(I) can't speak Japanese except a little.]
takusan	a lot, much
Okane wa takusan arimasen.	I don't have a lot of money.
Jikan wa takusan arimasen.	I don't have much time.

B. Too Much/Not Too Much

amari	too
amari takusan	too much
Amari takusan taberu to	if you eat too much
Amari oosugiru to	if too much/many
Amari takusan ja arimasen.	It's not too much.
Amari atsuku arimasen.	It's not so hot.
Amari samuku arimasen.	It's not so cold.
Amari mizu ga ooku arimasen.	There is not so much water.

C. MORE OR LESS

tashoo	more or less
ookute mo	at the most
sukunakute mo	at the least
motto motto	more and more
motto motto suku-naku	less and less
moo rokubai	six times more
motto hayaku	earlier *(adv.)*
motto osoku ⎱ *motto ato de* ⎰	later *(adv.)*
motto atsuku	hotter
Motto atsuku shite kudasai.	Please make it hotter.
motto takaku	more expensive
Motto takaku nari-mashita.	It became more expensive.
Moo arimasen.	There is no more of it. There is no more of it left.
Sore ijoo desu.	It's more than that.
Sore ika desu.	It's less than that.
Ichiban omoshiroi hon desu.	This is the most interesting book.
Ano hito wa oniisan yori se ga takai desu.	He is taller than his older brother.
Watashi hodo se ga takaku arimasen.	She isn't as tall as I am.
Watashi yori hikui desu.	She is shorter than I am.

D. ENOUGH AND SOME MORE

juubun	enough
Juubun desu ka?	Is it enough?

Juubun desu.	It's enough.
Juubun ja arimasen.	It's not enough.
Juubun ookii desu.	It's large enough.
Okane wa juubun motte imasu ka?	Do you have enough money?
motto	some more
Motto desu ka?	(Do you want) some more?
moo sukoshi	a little more
Mizu o moo ippai kudasai.	Give me another glass of water, please.
Pan o moo sukoshi kudasai.	Please give me some/a little more bread.
Niku o moo sukoshi kudasai.	Please give me some/a little more meat.
motto motto	much more, lots more
Moo ichido kite kudasai.	Come again [visit us once more], please.
Moo ichido itte kudasai.	Say it again [once more], please.
Moo ichido kurikaeshite kudasai.	Please repeat it [Repeat it once more . . .].

QUIZ 23

1. *Sukoshi hoshii desu ka? Takusan hoshii desu ka?*

   a. I can speak little English.

2. *Eigo wa sukoshi shika hanasemasen.*

   b. It became more expensive.

3. *Amari atsuku arimasen.*

   c. She is not as tall as I am.

4. *Amari mizu ga ooku arimasen.*

   d. He doesn't talk much.

5. *Motto takaku nari-mashita.*
    e. I don't have a lot of money.

6. *Watashi hodo se ga takaku arimasen.*
    f. There is not so much water.

7. *Okane wa juubun motte imasu ka?*
    g. Do you want a little, or do you want a lot?

8. *Moo ichido itte kudasai.*
    h. It's not so hot.

9. *Okane wa takusan arimasen.*
    i. Do you have enough money?

10. *Sukoshi shika hanashimasen.*
    j. Say it again, please.

ANSWERS
1—g; 2—a; 3—h; 4—f; 5—b; 6—c; 7—i; 8—j; 9—e; 10—d.

LESSON 29

DAI NIJUU KYUUKA

A. I WANT TO . . .

When you want to *have* something you say *ga hoshii desu*. When you want to *do* something, you use *o* (for the object), plus a pre-*masu* form, plus *tai desu*.

The combination of a pre-*masu* plus *tai* acts exactly like an *i*-adjective. The item involved in the action that you want to perform is normally marked by *o*, but the use of *ga* is acceptable in limited cases. Usually, *ga* can be used with daily actions, such as "eat" or "drink."

Nomitai desu.	I want to drink it.
Tabetai desu.	I want to eat it.
Kaitai desu.	I want to buy it.
Mitai desu.	I want to see it.
Nomitaku arimasen.	I don't want to drink it.
Tabetaku arimasen.	I don't want to eat it.
Kaitaku arimasen.	I don't want to buy it.
Mitaku arimasen.	I don't want to see it.
Koohii o nomitai desu.	I'd like some coffee. [(I) want to drink coffee.]
Kudamono o tabetai desu.	I'd like some fruit. [(I) want to eat fruit.]
Kutsu o kaitai desu.	I want to buy (a pair of) shoes.
Eiga o mitai desu.	I want to see a movie.
Koohii o nomitaku narimashita.	I want to drink coffee now (though I didn't before). [(I) became desirous of drinking coffee.]
Kudamono o tabetaku narimashita.	I want to eat fruit now. [I became desirous of eating fruit.]
Kutsu o kaitaku narimashita.	I want to buy shoes now. [I became desirous of buying shoes.]
Eiga o mitaku narimashita.	I want to see a movie now. [I became desirous of seeing a movie.]

B. I INTEND TO . . .

Iku tsumori desu.	I intend to go.
Ryokoo suru tsumori desu.	I intend to travel.

Benkyoo suru tsumori desu.	I intend to study.
Kekkon suru tsumori desu.	I intend to marry.
Iku tsumori desu ka?	Do you intend to go?
Iku tsumori deshita ka?	Did you intend to go?
Iku tsumori ja arimasen ka?	Don't you intend to go?
Iku tsumori ja arimasen deshita ka?	Didn't you intend to go?
Ryokoo suru tsumori deshita ga shimasen deshita.	I (had) intended to travel, but didn't.
Ryokoo suru tsumori deshita ga dekimasen deshita.	I (had) intended to travel, but couldn't.
Ryokoo suru tsumori deshita ga akiramemashita.	I (had) intended to travel, but I gave it [the idea] up.
Ryokoo suru tsumori deshita ga dekiru ka doo ka wakarimasen.	I (had) intended to travel, but I can't tell (now) if I can or not.

C. IT IS SUPPOSED TO . . .

Kuru hazu desu.	It is supposed to come.
Tegami ga kuru hazu desu.	A letter is supposed to come.
Tomodachi ga kuru hazu desu.	A friend of mine is supposed to come.
Denwa ga aru hazu desu.	There is supposed to be a telephone. He is supposed to have a telephone.

Shiranai hazu desu.	He is not supposed to know it.
Kita hazu desu.	It is supposed to have come.
Tegami o uketotta hazu desu.	He is supposed to have received a letter.
Tomodachi ga shiraseta hazu desu.	My friend is supposed to have notified (him about it).
Tomodachi kara denwa ga atta hazu desu.	There is supposed to have been a phone call from a friend of mine.
Minna yonda hazu desu.	He is supposed to have read all of it.
Minna dekite iru hazu desu.	Everything is supposed to have been done.

D. SOMETHING, EVERYTHING, NOTHING

nani = what
nani ka[1] = something
nan demo (used with affirmative) = everything, anything at all
nani mo (used with negative) = nothing, not anything

Nani ka kaimashita ka?	Did you buy something?
Dare ka kimashita ka?	Did someone come?
Itsu ka ikimashoo.	Let's go sometime.
Doko ka de kikimashita.	I heard it somewhere.
Nan demo kaimashita.	I bought everything.

[1] See Section 23 of the Summary of Japanese Grammar for uses of question words with particles.

Dare demo hairemasu.
Anybody can enter.

Itsu demo ikimasu.
I go anytime.

Doko demo kaemasu.
You can buy it at any place.

Nani mo kaimasen deshita.
I didn't buy anything.

Dare mo kimasen deshita.
Nobody came.

Itsu mo imasen deshita.
He wasn't there at any time. He was always absent.

Doko mo mimasen deshita.
I didn't see any place.

Nani ka tsumetai mono o nomimashoo.
Let's drink something cold.

Dare ka Nihongo no yoku dekiru hito ni kikimashoo.
Let's ask someone who can speak Japanese well.

Itsu ka anmari isogashiku nai toki ni ikimashoo.
Let's go there sometime when we are not too busy.

Doko ka motto shizuka na tokoro e ikimashoo.
Let's go somewhere quieter.

Nani o mite mo kaitaku narimasu.[1]
Whatever I see, I [get to] want to buy.

Dare ga kite mo kyoo wa au koto ga dekimasen.
No matter who comes [Whoever may come], I can't meet him/her today.

---

[1] Note the construction: The interrogative, plus the *-te* form, plus *mo* = "-ever" plus the verb.

Itsu itte mo ano hito wa jimusho ni imasen deshita.

No matter when I went to his office, he wasn't there. [Whenever (I) went, he wasn't at his office.]

Doko e itte mo Eigo no dekiru hito ga imashita.

Wherever I went, there was someone who could speak English.

QUIZ 24

1. *Kaitai desu.*

a. Everything is supposed to have been done.

2. *Iku tsumori desu.*

b. I didn't buy anything.

3. *Kuru hazu desu.*

c. Let's drink something cold.

4. *Nani ka kaimashita ka?*

d. Nobody came.

5. *Kaitaku arimasen.*

e. I didn't intend to travel.

6. *Ryokoo suru tsumori desu.*

f. Anybody can enter.

7. *Doko ka de kikimashita.*

g. Let's ask someone who can speak Japanese well.

8. *Kita hazu desu.*

h. Did you buy something?

9. *Dare demo hairemasu.*

i. It is supposed to come.

10. *Dare ka Nihongo no yoku dekiru hito ni kikimashoo.*

j. I intend to travel.

11. *Ryokoo suru tsu-mori ja arimasen deshita.*

k. I don't want to buy it.

12. *Nani mo kaimasen deshita.*

l. I intend to go.

13. *Minna dekite iru hazu desu.*

m. I want to buy it.

14. *Dare mo kimasen deshita.*

n. I heard it some-where.

15. *Nani ka tsumetai mono o nomi-mashoo.*

o. It is supposed to have come.

ANSWERS

1—m; 2—l; 3—i; 4—h; 5—k; 6—j; 7—n; 8—o; 9—f; 10—g; 11—e; 12—b; 13—a; 14—d; 15—c.

E. WORD STUDY

kuraimakkusu	climax
kyasuto	cast
rabushiin	love scene
rokeishon	location
shiin	scene
shinario	scenario
sukuriin	screen
sutaa	star
sutajio	studio
taitoru	title

LESSON 30

DAI SANJUKKA

A. OF COURSE! IT'S A PITY! IT DOESN'T MATTER!

Mochiron desu.	Of course. Certainly.
Shoochi itashimashita.	Fine! [(I) have understood.]
Soo desu ka?	Indeed? Is that so?
Soo omoimasu.	I think so.
Soo omoimasen.	I don't think so.
Tanaka-san desu ka?	Are you Ms. Tanaka?
Hai, soo desu.	Yes, I am. [Am so.]
tabun	perhaps, probably
Tabun soo deshoo.	I suppose so. Probably it is so.
Tabun soo ja nai deshoo.	I suppose not. Probably it is not so.
Soo da to ii to omoimasu.	I hope so. [If (it) is so, it would be good that way (I) think.]
Soo ja nai to ii to omoimasu.	I hope not. [If (it) is not so, it would be good that way (I) think.]
Tashika ni soo desu.	Certainly. [Certainly (it) is so.]
Tashika ni soo ja arimasen.	Certainly not. [Certainly (it) is not so.]
Okinodoku desu.	It's a pity! It's a shame! She has my sympathy.
Sore wa baai ni yorimasu.	That depends [on the occasion].

Kamaimasen.

That's nothing. That's not important. That doesn't matter. [(I) don't mind.]

Zenzen kamaimasen.

That doesn't matter at all.

Gotsugoo ga yoroshi kereba.

If you have no objections. If it doesn't inconvenience you. [If (it) is convenient.]

Dochira de mo kekkoo desu.

I don't care. It's all the same to me. [Either will do.]

QUIZ 25

1. *Soo omoimasu.*
2. *Mochiron desu.*
3. *Tabun soo deshoo.*
4. *Shoochi itashimashita.*
5. *Soo da to ii to omoimasu.*
6. *Tabun soo ja nai to omoimasu.*
7. *Tashika ni soo desu.*
8. *Okinodoku desu.*
9. *Gotsugoo ga yoroshikereba.*
10. *Dochira de mo kekkoo desu.*

a. It's a pity.
b. I suppose not.
c. I hope so.
d. If you have no objections.
e. I don't care. Either will do.
f. Certainly it is so.
g. I think so.
h. Agreed!
i. Of course.
j. I suppose so.

ANSWERS
1—g; 2—i; 3—j; 4—h; 5—c; 6—b; 7—f; 8—a; 9—d; 10—e.

B. The Same

onaji	same
Onaji mono desu.	It's the same thing (*a tangible article*).
Onaji koto desu.	It's the same thing (*abstract*).
Kore wa onaji ja arimasen.	This isn't the same. These aren't the same.
dooji ni onaji toki ni }	at the same time
onaji shunkan ni	at the same moment
onaji machi ni	in the same town

C. Already

moo	already
moo mukoo ni itte imasu.	He is already there. [(He) is already in the state of having gone there.]
Moo shite shimai-mashita.	He has already done that. [(He) has already done that, and (it) is all finished.]
Moo dashite shimai-mashita ka?	Has he sent it already?
Moo sumasete shimai-mashita ka?	Have you finished already?

D. Word Study

abunoomaru	abnormal
chaamingu	charming
derikeeto	delicate

ereganto	elegant
kurashikku	classic
modan	modern
noomaru	normal
riberaru	liberal
senchimentaru	sentimental
yuniiku	unique

LESSON 31

DAI SANJUU IKKA

A. I LIKE IT, IT'S GOOD

Suki desu.	I like it. [That's (my) favorite.]
Nihon ryoori ga suki desu.	I like Japanese cooking.
Kodomo ga suki desu.	I like children.
Hon o yomu koto ga suki desu.	I like reading books.
Oyogu koto ga suki desu.	I like swimming.
Kekkoo desu.	It's good. It's fine.
Kono wain wa kekkoo desu.	This wine is good.
Kono niku wa kekkoo desu.	This meat is good.
Kekkoo na otenki desu ne.	The weather is fine, isn't it?
Motto ikaga desu ka?	How about some more?
Moo kekkoo desu.	No, thanks, I'm fully satisfied.
Taihen kekkoo desu.	It's very good.

Subarashii desu.	It's wonderful.
Migoto desu.	It's admirable.
Kanzen desu.	It's perfect.
Taihen ki ni iri-mashita.	I'm very pleased with it. I like it very much.
Taihen ii hito desu.	He's very nice. [(He) is a very good person.]
Taihen kanji no ii hito desu.	He's very pleasant.
Doomo goshinsetsu ni.	You're very kind. That's very kind of you.

B.   I Don't Like It, It's Bad

Suki ja arimasen.	I don't like it. It's not good. [That's not (my) favorite.]
Sakana wa suki ja arimasen.	I don't like fish. [Fish is not (my) favorite.]
Kirai desu.	I dislike it.
Sakana wa kirai desu.	I dislike fish.
Yamada-san wa kirai desu.[1]	I dislike Mr. Yamada.
Yoku nai desu.	It's not good.
Amari yoku arimasen.	It's not very good.
Warui desu.	It's bad.
Mazui desu.	It tastes bad.
Kanshin dekimasen.	It's not good. [I can't admire it.]
Hon o yomu koto wa suki ja arimasen.	I don't like reading books.
Hon o yomu koto wa kirai desu.	I dislike reading books.

[1] Note that this same sentence can also mean "Mr. Yamada dislikes it."

QUIZ 26

1. *Taihen kekkoo desu.* — a. He's very nice.
2. *Kanshin dekimasen.* — b. It's perfect.
3. *Subarashii desu.* — c. I'm very pleased with it.
4. *Kanzen desu.* — d. I dislike fish.
5. *Taihen ki ni irimashita.* — e. He's very pleasant.
6. *Sakana wa kirai desu.* — f. It tastes bad.
7. *Doomo goshinsetsu ni.* — g. You're very kind.
8. *Mazui desu.* — h. It's wonderful.
9. *Taihen kanji no ii hito desu.* — i. It's very good.
10. *Taihen ii hito desu.* — j. It's not good.

ANSWERS

1—i; 2—j; 3—h; 4—b; 5—c; 6—d; 7—g; 8—f; 9—e; 10—a.

REVIEW QUIZ 3

1. *San tasu ni wa* _____ (five) *desu.*
   a. *go*
   b. *roku*
   c. *hachi*

2. _____ (Last week) *kaerimashita.*
   a. *Sengetsu*
   b. *Senshuu*
   c. *Sakuban*

3. *Kyoo wa* _____ (Monday) *desu.*
   a. *Getsuyoobi*
   b. *Doyoobi*
   c. *Suiyoobi*

4. _____ (Must hurry) *narimasen.*
   a. *Ikanakereba*
   b. *Isoganakereba*
   c. *Oboenakereba*

5. *Koohii ga* _____ (want) *desu.*
   a. *hoshii*
   b. *suki*
   c. *yoku nai*

6. Ginkoo e _____ (am going).
   a. *haraimasu*
   b. *kashimasu*
   c. *ikimasu*

7. _____ (Sugar) *wa ikaga desu ka?*
   a. *Osatoo*
   b. *Ocha*
   c. *Mizu*

8. *Okane o* _____ (a little) *kashite kudasai.*
   a. *sukoshi*
   b. *takusan*
   c. *nisen en*

9. *Okane o* _____ (much) *motte imasu.*
   a. *sukoshi*
   b. *takusan*
   c. *sukoshi mo*

10. _____ (More) *arimasu.*
    a. *Sukoshi*
    b. *Motto*
    c. *Moo sukoshi*

11. _____ (Enough) *arimasen.*
    a. *Nani mo*
    b. *Takusan*
    c. *Juubun*

12. _____ (Expensive) *desu.*
    a. *Yasui*
    b. *Takai*
    c. *Hikui*

13. *Sore wa kore* _____ (as) *oishiku arimasen.*
    a. *wa*
    b. *hodo*
    c. *mo*

14. _____ (All) *yonde shimaimashita.*
    a. *Hanbun*
    b. *Sukoshi*
    c. *Minna*

15. _____ (Anybody) *hairemasu.*
    a. *Dare demo*
    b. *Dare ga*
    c. *Dare ka*

16. *Soo* _____ (don't think).
    a. *hurimasen*
    b. *omoimasen*
    c. *kaimasen*

17. *Iku* _____ (intend to) *desu*.
    a. *hazu*
    b. *tsumori*
    c. *yoo*

18. _____ (Nothing) *kaimasen deshita.*
    a. *Dare mo*
    b. *Nani mo*
    c. *Dore mo*

19. *Dore demo* _____ (same).
    a. *onaji desu*
    b. *chigaimasu*
    c. *hoshii desu*

20. _____ (Already) *sumasete shimaimashita ka?*
    a. *Motto motto*
    b. *Motto*
    c. *Moo*

ANSWERS
1—a; 2—b; 3—a; 4—b; 5—a; 6—c; 7—a; 8—a;
9—b; 10—b; 11—c; 12—b; 13—b; 14—c; 15—a;
16—b; 17—b; 18—b; 19—a; 20—c.

C. WORD STUDY

bakkumiraa	rearview mirror
banpaa	bumper
bureeki	brake
enjin	engine
gasorin	gasoline
giya	gear
handoru	handle (of a tool), steering wheel
heddoraito	headlight

kuratchi	clutch
taiya	tire

D. WARAIBANASHI

Tanaka-san to Yamada-san ga resutoran e itte bifuteki o chuumon shimashita. Shibaraku tatte bifuteki ga kimashita. Hitokire wa ookikute hitotsu wa chiisakatta no desu. Tanaka-san wa sugu ookii hoo o torimashita. Sore o mite Yamada-san wa okorimashita. Soshite "Nan to reigi no nai hito daroo. Hito yori saki ni toru toki wa chiisai hoo o toru mon da" to iimashita.

Kore o kiite Tanaka-san wa: "Anata ga watashi dattara doo shimasu ka?" to tazunemashita.

"Mochiron chiisai hoo o torimasu yo!" to Yamada-san wa kotaemashita.

Tanaka-san wa: "Sore gorannasai, monku wa nai hazu ja arimasen ka? Chiisai hoo o anata ga, moratta n da kara," to iimashita.

A FUNNY STORY

Tanaka and Yamada went to a restaurant and ordered steak. A few minutes later the steaks arrived. One piece was large and one piece was small. Tanaka immediately took the large piece. Yamada saw it, became furious, and said to him: "What bad manners you have! Don't you know that since you were the first to help yourself, you should have taken the smaller piece?"

Tanaka heard this and asked: "If you were in my place, which piece would you have taken?"

"The smaller one, of course," said Yamada.

"Well, then," Tanaka answered, "what are you complaining about? You got it, didn't you?"

NOTE

waraibanashi: "a story to laugh"

chuumon shimashita: ordered

shibaraku tatte: after a short while

okorimashita: became furious

soshite: and

Nan to . . . daroo: What a . . . !

reigi: manners

shiranai: (negative of *shiru*): don't know

. . . mono da: that's what one should do; that's an accepted way to do

dattara: if (you) were

torimasu yo: yo is an emphatic particle corresponding to an exclamation mark.

monku: complaint

nai hazu desu: there is supposed to be not; there isn't supposed to be

Supplemental Vocabulary List 13: Entertainment

entertainment	*goraku*
movie / film	*eiga*
to go to the movies	*eiga ni iku*
to see a movie	*eiga o miru*
theater	*gekijoo*
to see a play	*shibai* (*engeki*) *o miru*
opera	*kageki, opera*
concert	*konsaato*
club	*kurabu*
circus	*saakasu*
ticket	*ken, kippu, chiketto*
museum	*hakubutsukan, bijutsukan*
gallery	*garoo, bijutsukan, gyararii*

painting	*e, kaiga*
sculpture	*chookoku*
television program	*terebibangumi*
to watch television	*terebi o miru*
comedy	*kigeki, komedii*
documentary	*dokyumentarii*
drama	*dorama*
book	*hon*
magazine	*zasshi*
to read a book	*hon o yomu*
to read a magazine	*zasshi o yomu*
to listen to music	*ongaku o kiku*
song	*uta*
band	*bando*
the news	*nyuusu*
talk show	*tookushoo*
to flip channels	*channeru o kaeru*
to have fun	*tanoshimu*
to be bored	*taikutsusuru*
funny	*okashii, omoshiroi*
interesting	*kyoomibukai, omoshiroi*
exciting	*kakkitekina, shigekitekina, wakuwakusaseru*
scary	*osoroshii*
party	*paatii*
restaurant	*resutoran*
to go to a party	*paatii ni iku*
to have a party	*paatii o suru*
to dance	*odoru, dansusuru*

LESSON 32

DAI SANJUU NIKA

A. WHO? WHAT? WHEN? ETC.

dono	which . . . ?
Dono hon desu ka?	Which book is it?
Dono tegami desu ka?	Which letter is it?
dore	which one?
itsu	when?
dare	who?
nani, nan	what?
naze, dooshite	why?
doko	where?
ikura	how much?
doo, dooshite	how?

1. *Nani, Nan:* What?

Nani o shite imasu ka?	What are you doing?
Nani ga hoshii desu ka?	What do you want? What would you like?
Kore kara nani o shitai desu ka?	What do you want to do now?
Nani o sagashite imasu ka?	What are you looking for?

Nan is used instead of *nani* when the word that follows it is *desu, to* (with a verb *iu* [say], etc.), *no,* or a counter.

Onamae wa nan desu ka?	What's your name?

Kono machi no namae wa nan desu ka?	What's the name of this town?
Kono toori no namae wa nan desu ka?	What's the name of this street?
Nan to iimashoo ka?	What will we say?
Nan to osshaimashita ka?	What did she say *(extra polite)?*
Nan to iu machi desu ka?	What is the name of the town? [What is the town called?]
Nan no hon desu ka?	What book is it?
Kore wa nan no e desu ka?	What picture is this?
Kyoo wa nannichi desu ka?	What's the date today?
Nangatsu desu ka?	What month is it?
Nanji desu ka?	What time? [What hour is it?]

2. *Dore:* Which one?

Dore desu ka?	Which one is it?
Dore ga anata no hon desu ka?	Which is your book?
Watakushi no wa dore desu ka?	Which is mine?
Dore ga ii hoo desu ka?	Which is the better one?
Dore ga hoshii desu ka?	Which one do you want?
Dore ga tadashii desu ka?	Which one is right?

3. *Itsu:* When?

Itsu desu ka?	When is it?
Itsu made desu ka?	Until when is (it)?

Itsu kimasu ka?	When are you coming?
Itsu oide ni narimasu ka?	When are you coming *(respect)?*
Itsu tachimasu ka?	When are you leaving?
Itsu otachi ni narimasu ka?	When are you leaving *(respect)?*

4. *Dare:* Who?

Dare desu ka?	{ Who is it? { Who are you?
Donata desu ka?	Who are you *(respect)?*
Dare ga sore o shitte imasu ka?	Who knows that?
Dare no desu ka?	Whose is it?
Dare no tame desu ka?	Who is it for? [For whose sake is it?]
Dare ni hanashite imasu ka?	Who are you talking to?
Dare no koto o hanashite imasu ka?	Who are you speaking about? [About whose matters are you speaking?]
Dare to kimasu ka?	Who are you coming with?
Dare ni aitai desu ka?	Who do you want to see?
Donata ni oai ni naritai desu ka?	Who do you want to see *(respect)?*
Dare o sagashite imasu ka?	Who are you looking for?
Donata o sagashite irasshaimasu ka?	Who are you looking for *(respect)?*

5. *Naze, dooshite:* Why?

Naze desu ka?	Why is it?
Dooshite desu ka?	Why is it?
Dooshite dame desu ka?	Why not? [Why is it no good?]
Naze sonna koto o iu no desu ka?	Why do you say that [such a thing]?
Dooshite sonna koto o shita no desu ka?	Why did he do such a thing?

6. *Doo, dooshite:* How?

Doo desu ka?	How is it?
Doo shimasu ka?	How do you do it?
Doo iu imi desu ka?	What do you mean?
Nihongo de kono kotoba wa doo kakimasu ka?	How do you write this word in Japanese?
Sore wa Eigo de doo iimasu ka?	How do you say that in English?
"Thanks" wa Nihongo de doo iimasu ka?	How do you say "thanks" in Japanese?
Doo shita n desu ka?	How did it happen?
Doo shitara ii n desu ka?	What shall I do?
Doo sureba ii n desu ka?	What shall I do?
Sore wa doo shite tsukurimasu ka?	How's it made? [Acting how do you make (it)?]
Sore wa dooshite tsukurimashita ka?	How did you make it?
Soko e wa doo ikimasu ka?	How do you go there?

Doo shimashoo ka?

What's to be done?
What can one do?
[How shall we do?]

**Sono futatsu wa doo
    chigaimasu ka?**

What is the difference
between the two?
[As for the two, how
do they differ?]

QUIZ 27

1. *Dono hon desu ka?*

2. *Nan to iimashita
   ka?*

3. *Nani o sagashite
   imasu ka?*

4. *Dono tegami desu
   ka?*

5. *Onamae wa nan
   desu ka?*

6. *Nani o shite imasu
   ka?*

7. *Kyoo wa nannichi
   desu ka?*

8. *Nani ga hoshii
   desu ka?*

9. *Nangatsu desu ka?*

10. *Kono toori no namae
    wa nan desu ka?*

11. *Kore kara nani o
    shitai desu ka?*

12. *Nanji desu ka?*

a. How is it?

b. What is the differ-
   ence between the
   two?

c. Why did he do
   such a thing?

d. Who are you look-
   ing for?

e. Why is it?

f. How do you go
   there?

g. Until when?

h. Which one do you
   want?

i. What is the name
   of the street?

j. What do you want
   to do now?

k. What time is it?

l. What do you want/
   would you like?

13. *Sono futatsu wa doo chigaimasu ka?*   m. What month is it?

14. *Dooshite desu ka?*   n. Which letter?

15. *Dore ga hoshii desu ka?*   o. What is your name?

16. *Itsu made desu ka?*   p. What are you looking for?

17. *Donata o sagashite irasshaimasu ka?*   q. What's the date today?

18. *Dooshite sonna koto o shita no desu ka?*   r. What are you doing?

19. *Doo desu ka?*   s. Which book is it?

20. *Soko e wa doo ikimasu ka?*   t. What did you say?

ANSWERS

1—s; 2—t; 3—p; 4—n; 5—o; 6—r; 7—q; 8—l; 9—m; 10—i; 11—j; 12—k; 13—b; 14—e; 15—h; 16—g; 17—d; 18—c; 19—a; 20—f.

B. Word Study

akademikku	academic
ekizochikku	exotic
gurotesuku	grotesque
nooburu	noble
pedanchikku	pedantic
romanchikku	romantic
senseeshonaru	sensational

C. How Much?

Nedan wa?	The price? How much is this?
Nedan wa ikura desu ka?	What's the price?
Ikura?	How much?
Ikura desu ka?	How much is it? How much do you want for it?
Zenbu de ikura desu ka?	How much for everything? How much does it all cost?
Hitotsu ikura desu ka?	How much each?

D. How Many?

Ikutsu?	How many?
Ikutsu nokotte imasu ka?	How many are left?
Ikutsu motte imasu ka?	How many of them do you have?
Nannin desu ka?	How many persons?
Nanjikan?	How many hours?
Nando?	How many times?
Dono kurai desu ka?	How much time?
Dono kurai nagai desu ka?	How long?
Soko e iku ni wa dono kurai jikan ga kakarimasu ka?	How long [how much time] does it take to get there?

QUIZ 28

1. *Ikutsu arimasu ka?*
2. *Ikura desu ka?*

a. How many persons?
b. How much for everything?

3. *Ikutsu nokotte imasu ka?*
4. *Nedan wa ikura desu ka?*
5. *Dono kurai nagai desu ka?*
6. *Zenbu de ikura desu ka?*
7. *Nannin desu ka?*
8. *Ikutsu motte imasu ka?*
9. *Hitotsu ikura desu ka?*
10. *Soko e iku ni wa dono kurai jikan ga kakarimasu ka?*

c. How long does it take to get there?
d. How much each?
e. What's the price?
f. How much is it?
g. How many are left?
h. How long is it?
i. How many of them do you have?
j. How many are there?

ANSWERS
1—j; 2—f; 3—g; 4—e; 5—h; 6—b; 7—a; 8—i; 9—d; 10—c.

LESSON 33

DAI SANJUU SANKA

A. SOME, SOMEONE, SOMETHING[1]

ikura ka no   some *(an indeterminate amount of)*

ikutsu ka no   some *(an indeterminate number of)*

[1] See Lesson 29-F and Section 23 of the Summary of Japanese Grammar for more information.

ikura ka no okane	some money
ikura ka no hiyoo	some expense
ikura ka no jikan	some time
Ikura ka no jikan ga kakarimasu.	It takes some time.
Ikura ka no okane ga irimasu.	We need some money.
Ikutsu ka no kotoba o shitte imasu.	I know some words.
nannin ka no	some *(an indeterminate number of persons)*
Nannin ka no hito ni kikimashita.	I have asked some/several people.
Nannin ka kite imasu.	Several people are here.
nani ka	something, anything *(not a specific thing)*
nani ka atarashii mono	something new, anything new
nani ka kaitai mono	something you want to buy, anything you want to buy
Nani ka kaitai mono ga arimasu ka?	Do you have anything you want to buy?
Nani ka kikitai koto ga arimasu ka?	Do you have anything you want to ask?
Nani ka kudasai.	Give me something, please.
Nani ka kaku mono o kudasai.	Give me something to write with, please.
Nani ka ochimashita.	Something fell down.
Nani ka kaimashita.	She bought something.
Nani ka shirimasen.	I don't know what it is.
dare ka	someone
Dare ka sore no dekiru hito ga imasu ka?	Is there anyone who can do it?

Dare ka Eigo no yoku dekiru hito ga imasu ka?	Is there anyone who can speak English well?
aru hito	someone
Aru hito ga hoshii to itte imasu.	Someone (a certain person who shall be nameless) says that she wants to have it.
aru tokoro	someplace
Aru tokoro e iki-mashita.	He went someplace.
itsu ka	sometime
Itsu ka kite kudasai.	Please come sometime.
Itsu ka ikimashoo.	Let's go there some-time.
tokidoki	sometimes, occasion-ally
Sono hito ni tokidoki aimasu.	I see him sometimes.
Soko de tokidoki go-han o tabemasu.	I eat [my meal] there sometimes.

B. ONCE, TWICE

-do, -kai	a time
ichido, ikkai	once, one time
nido, nikai	twice, two times
maido, maikai	every time, each time
kondo	this time, this coming time
dai ikkai	the first time
Dai ikkai wa sen kyuuhyaku kyuujuu deshita.	The first time was (in) 1990.
hajimete	for the first time

Hajimete ikimashita.	I went there for the first time.
tsugi	the next time, the next item, the next number, etc.
kono mae	last time
betsu no toki	another time, another occasion
mata	again
moo ichido	once more

C. Up to

made	up to
ima made	up to now
soko made	up to there
owari made	(up) to the end
eki made	up to the station
konban made	up to this evening
ashita made	up till tomorrow
Getsuyoobi made	up to Monday

D. I Need It, It's Necessary

Irimasu.	I need it.
Kore wa irimasen.	She doesn't need this one.
Nani ka irimasu ka?	Do you need anything?
Nani mo irimasen.	I don't need anything.
Zenzen irimasen.	I don't need it at all.
Zehi oai shinakereba narimasen.	It's absolutely necessary that I see you.
Ano hito ni hanasanakereba narimasen.	I have to tell him.

Hayaku uchi e kaette konakereba narimasen.	I must come home early.
Hontoo da to iu koto o mitomenakereba narimasen.	One must admit that it is true.

E. I FEEL LIKE[1]

Hoshii desu.	I'd like to have it. I feel like having it. I want to have it.
Ikitaku arimasen.	I don't feel like going there. I don't want to go.
Ano hon ga hoshii.	I want that book.
Aisukuriimu ga hoshii desu.	I feel like having some ice cream.
Aisukuriimu ga tabetai desu.	I feel like eating some ice cream.
Kono eiga wa mitai desu ka?	Would you like to see this movie?

F. AT THE HOME OF

The choice of the particle *de* or *ni* depends on the verb that follows it.

... **otaku de** ⎫ ... **otaku ni** ⎭	at the home of (someone else)
uchi de ⎫ **uchi ni** ⎭	at my home

[1] See Lesson 29 for "I want to."

Sensei no otaku ni We were at the home
imashita.[1] of our teacher.
Yamada-san no otaku I'll see you at the Ya-
de aimashoo.[2] madas' house.
Genkin wa uchi ni There is no cash at
arimasen. home.
Uchi de paatii o We had a party at my
shimashita. home.

QUIZ 29

1. *Ikura ka no okane*   a. To the end
2. *Ichido*   b. I need that.
3. *Owari made*   c. Please come
                               sometime.
4. *Irimasu.*   d. Some money
5. *Itsu ka kite kudasai.* e. Once

ANSWERS
1—d; 2—e; 3—a; 4—b; 5—c.

REVIEW QUIZ 4

1. *Kono machi no namae wa* _____ (what) *desu ka?*
   a. *dare*
   b. *nan*
   c. *doko*

2. *Ano kata wa* _____ (who) *desu ka?*
   a. *donata*
   b. *donna*
   c. *dotchi*

---

[1] Notice that *ni* is used here because it appears in conjunction with
a form of the verb *imasu.*
[2] Notice that *de* is used here because it appears in conjunction with
a form of the verb *au.*

3. _____ (When) *kimasu ka?*
   a. *Ikutsu*
   b. *Itsu*
   c. *Ikura*

4. _____ (Why) *sonna koto o iu no desu ka?*
   a. *Donna*
   b. *Doo*
   c. *Dooshite*

5. *Dai* _____ (twelfth) *kai.*
   a. *juuni*
   b. *nijuu*
   c. *nijuuni*

6. *Kono booshi wa* _____ (two thousand) *en shimashita.*
   a. *niman*
   b. *nihyaku*
   c. *nisen*

7. *Ni-choome* _____ (seventeen) *banchi ni sunde
   imasu.*
   a. *shichijuu*
   b. *juushichi*
   c. *juuhachi*

8. _____ (Noon) *desu.*
   a. *Hiru*
   b. *Yoru*
   c. *Asa*

9. _____ (Six) *ji ni aimashoo.*
   a. *San*
   b. *Ku*
   c. *Roku*

10. *Sore o suru* _____ (time) *desu.*
    a. *hito*
    b. *jikan*
    c. *tokoro*

11. *Kyoo wa* _____ (Wednesday) *desu.*
    a. *Kayoobi*
    b. *Suiyoobi*
    c. *Getsuyoobi*

12. *Raishuu no* _____ (Tuesday) *ni demasu.*
    a. *Kayoobi*
    b. *Mokuyoobi*
    c. *Nichiyoobi*

13. *Kyoo wa* _____ (June) *no tsuitachi desu.*
    a. *Rokugatsu*
    b. *Shichigatsu*
    c. *Hachigatsu*

14. *Kore wa* _____ (doesn't need).
    a. *ikimasen*
    b. *irimasen*
    c. *arimasen*

15. *Kono kotoba wa Nihongo de* _____ (how) *kakimasu ka?*
    a. *dore*
    b. *doo*
    c. *dare*

16. *Watakushi wa Shigatsu* _____ (eleventh) *ni umaremashita.*
    a. *juuyokka*
    b. *nijuuninichi*
    c. *juuichinichi*

17. _____ (How many) *nokotte imasu ka?*
   a. *Ikutsu*
   b. *Kokonotsu*
   c. *Mittsu*

18. _____ (Intend to go) *desu.*
   a. *Iku hazu*
   b. *Iku tsumori*
   c. *Iku jikan*

19. *Ashita* _____ (I must go).
   a. *ikanakereba narimasen*
   b. *ikanakute mo ii desu*
   c. *itte mo ii desu*

20. *Yamada-san wa sono koto o* _____ (is supposed to know).
   a. *shitte imasen deshita*
   b. *shitte iru hazu desu*
   c. *shiritai deshoo*

ANSWERS
1—b; 2—a; 3—b; 4—c; 5—a; 6—c; 7—b; 8—a;
9—c; 10—b; 11—b; 12—a; 13—a; 14—b; 15—b;
16—c; 17—a; 18—b; 19—a; 20—b.

SUPPLEMENTAL VOCABULARY LIST 14:
   AT HOME

at home	*uchi ni, uchi de*
house	*ie, uchi*
apartment	*apaato*
room	*heya*
living room	*ima, ribinguruumu*
dining room	*shokudoo, daininguruumu*

kitchen	*daidokoro, kicchin*
bedroom	*shinshitsu*
bathroom	*yokushitsu*
hall	*hiroma, hooru*
closet	*shuunooshitsu, todana, oshiire, monooki*
window	*mado*
door	*to, doa*
table	*teeburu, chabudai*
chair	*isu*
sofa, couch	*sofaa, nagaisu*
curtain	*kaaten*
carpet	*juutan, kaapetto*
television	*terebi*
CD player	*cd pureeyaa*
lamp	*ranpu*
DVD player	*dvd pureeyaa*
sound system	*onkyoo sisutemu*
painting, picture	*e, kaiga*
shelf	*tana*
stairs	*kaidan*
ceiling	*tenjoo*
wall	*kabe*
floor	*yuka*
big / small	*ookii / chiisai*
new / old	*atarashii / furui*
wood / wooden	*ki / mokusei no*
plastic / made from plastic	*purasuchikku / purasuchikkusei no*

LESSON 34

DAI SANJUU YONKA

A. ON THE ROAD

Chotto ukagaimasu ga, kono machi no namae wa nan deshoo ka?	Excuse me, but what is the name of this town?
Tookyoo made dono kurai arimasu ka?	How far is it to [as far as] Tokyo?
Koko kara Tookyoo made nan kiro arimasu ka?	How many kilometers from here to Tokyo?
Koko kara jukkiro desu.	It's ten kilometers from here.
Koko kara nijukkiro desu.	That's twenty kilometers from here.
Koko kara Tookyoo made doo ikimasu ka?	How do I get to Tokyo from here?
Kono michi o ikimasu.	Follow this road.
Kono banchi e doo iku no ka oshiete kudasai.	Can you tell me how I can get to this address?
Koko e doo iku no ka oshiete kudasai.	Can you tell me how I can get to this place?
Kono toori no namae wa nan to iimasu ka?	What is the name of this street?
. . . wa doko desu ka?	Where is . . . ?
Ginza Doori wa doko desu ka?[1]	Where is Ginza Doori?

[1] Note that *doko desu ka?* is the same as *doko ni arimasu ka?*

Koko kara tooi desu ka?	Is it far from here?
Koko kara chikai desu ka?	Is it near here?
Kono michi o ikimasu.	Go this way.
Massugu ikimasu.	Go straight ahead.
Kado made itte hidari ni magarimasu.	Go to the corner and turn left.
Migi ni magarimasu.	Turn right.
Gareeji wa doko ni arimasu ka?	Where is the garage?
Keisatsusho wa doko desu ka?	Where is the police station?
Shiyakusho wa doko desu ka?	Where is City Hall?

B. Bus, Train, Subway, Taxi

Kono basu wa doko kara kimasu ka?	Where does this bus come from?
Shinjuku kara kimasu.	It comes from Shinjuku.
Basutei wa doko desu ka?	Where is the bus stop?
Chuushingai ni iku basu wa dore desu ka?	Which bus goes to the center of town?
Dono eki de orimasu ka?	What station do I get off at?
Doko de orimasu ka?	Where do I get off?
Chikatetsu no eki wa doko desu ka?	Where's the subway station?
Densha no eki wa doko ni arimasu ka?	Where is the train station?

Tookyoo yuki no densha ni wa doko kara norimasu ka?	Where do I get the train for Tokyo?
Niban sen desu.	On track two.
Densha wa ima demashita.	The train just left.
Tsugi no densha wa nanji ni demasu ka?	What time does the next train leave?
Kyooto yuki no oofukukippu o kudasai.	May I have a round-trip ticket for Kyoto?
Ikura desu ka?	How much is that?
Nisen gohyaku gojuu en desu.	Two thousand five hundred and fifty yen.
Jikan wa dono kurai kakarimasu ka?	How long does it take to get there?
Kujikan to chotto desu.	A little over nine hours.

C. WRITING AND MAILING LETTERS, E-MAILS, AND FAXES

Tegami o kakitai n desu ga . . .	I'd like to write a letter, but (would you mind if I did?)
Enpitsu o motte imasu ka?	Do you have a pencil?
Pen o motte imasu ka?	Do you have a pen?
Fuutoo o motte imasu ka?	Do you have an envelope?
Kitte o motte imasu ka?	Do you have a postage stamp?
Kitte wa doko de kaemasu ka?	Where can I buy a postage stamp?

Kookuubin no kitte o motte imasu ka?
Do you have an airmail stamp?

Yuubinkyoku wa doko desu ka?
Where is the post office?

Kono tegami o dashitai n desu ga . . .
I'd like to mail this letter.

Kitte wa nanmai irimasu ka?
How many stamps do I need on this letter?

Hoteru ni konpyuutaa wa arimasu ka?
Does the hotel have a computer?

Ikutsuka denshi-meeru (ii-meeru) o okuranakute wa ikenai no desu ga.
I need to send a few e-mails.

Tenpu fairu o okutte mo ii desu ka?
May I send an attachment?

(Karaa de) yon peeji insatsu shinakute wa ikenai no desu ga.
I need to print four pages (in color).

Insatsudai wa ichipeeji atari ikura desu ka?
How much it cost to print each page?

Intaanetto no setsuzoku wa nani o tsukatte imasu ka?
What kind of internet connection is it?

Intaanetto no shiyooryoo wa ichijikan ikura desu ka?
How much does it cost to use the internet for one hour?

Fakkusu o okuritai no desu ga . . . Doko de okuremasu ka?
I'd like to send a fax. Where can I send it?

Kono jimusho de okuremasu.
You can send it in (from) this office.

Soko e tsuku no ni dono kurai kakarimasu ka?
How long will it take to get there?

D. TELEPHONING

Koko ni denwa ga arimasu ka?	Is there a phone here?
Doko de denwa ga kakeraremasu ka?	Where can I phone?
Denwa wa doko ni arimasu ka?	Where is the telephone?
Denwa bokkusu wa doko ni arimasu ka?	Where is the phone booth?
Tabakoya ni arimasu.	In the cigar store [tobacco shop].
Keitai denwa o motte imasu ka?	Do you have a cell phone?
Keitai (denwa) no bangoo wa nan(ban) desu ka?	What is your cell phone number?
Denwa o kashite kudasai.	May I use your phone? [Please lend me your phone.]
Doozo otsukai kudasai.	Go ahead! [Please use (it).]
Chookyori denwa o onegai shimasu.	May I have long distance, please?
Tookyoo e no tsuuwa wa ikura desu ka?	How much is a call to Tokyo?
Goo roku kyuu rei no ichi ichi ichi ni ban o onegai shimasu.	5690-1112, please.
Chotto omachi kudasai.	One moment, please.
Ohanashichuu desu.	The line's busy.
Moshi moshi, chigau bangoo ni kakarimashita.	[Hello, hello,] Operator, you gave me the wrong number.
Ohenji ga gozaimasen.	There is no answer *(extra polite)*.

Yamada-san o onegai shimasu.	May I speak to Mr. Yamada, please?
Watakushi desu.	Speaking.
Kochira wa Taitasu desu.	This is Titus speaking. [This side (it) is Titus.]

E. WORD STUDY

anaunsaa	announcer
antena	antenna
daiyaru	dial
nyuusu	news
puroduusaa	producer
puroguramu	program
rajio	radio
saikuru	cycle
suitchi	switch
terebi	television

SUPPLEMENTAL VOCABULARY LIST 15:
COMPUTERS AND THE INTERNET

computers and the internet	*konpyuuta(a) to intaanetto*
computer	*konpyuuta(a)*
keyboard	*kiiboodo*
monitor / screen	*monitaa / sukuriin*
mouse	*mausu*
modem	*modemu*
memory	*memorii*
CD-ROM	*cd romu*

CD-ROM drive	*cd romu doraibu*
file	*fairu*
document	*bunsho, dokyumento*
cable	*keeburu*
internet	*intaanetto*
website	*uebusaito*
webpage	*uebupeiji*
e-mail	*denshimeeru, iimeeru*
chatroom	*chattoruumu*
web log (blog)	*ueburogu*
instant message	*insutanto messeeji*
attachment	*tenpu, atacchimento*
to compose	*messeeji no sakusei*
to print	*insatsu*
printer	*purintaa*
to send an e-mail	*denshimeeru (iimeeru) o sooshinsuru*
to send a file	*fairu o okuru, fairu o sooshinsuru*
to forward	*tensoosuru*
to reply	*henshinsuru*
to delete	*sakujosuru*
to save a document	*bunsho o hozonsuru*
to open a file	*fairu o hiraku*
to close a file	*fairu o tojiru*
to attach a file	*fairu o tenpusuru*
folder	*foruda*
inbox	*jushinbako, jushintorei*
sent (items)	*sooshinzumi aitemu*
deleted (items)	*sakujozumi aitemu*
draft	*shitagaki*
to cut	*kiritori*
to copy	*kopii*
to paste	*haritsuke*
spell check	*superuchekku*

address book	*adoresuchoo*
encoding	*enkoodo*
tool	*tsuuru*
help	*herupu*
sender	*sooshinsha*
subject	*kenmei*
date received	*jushinnichiji*

LESSON 35

DAI SANJUU GOKA

A. What's Your Name?

Onamae wa nan to osshaimasu ka?	What is your name?
Yamada Yoshio to mooshimasu.[1]	My name is Yoshio Yamada.
Ano hito no namae wa nan to iimasu ka?	What is his name?
Ano hito no namae wa Tanaka Makoto desu.	His name is Makoto Tanaka.
Ano hito no namae wa nan to iimasu ka?	What is her name?
Ano hito wa Satoo Michiko to iimasu.	Her name is Michiko Sato.
Ano hitotachi no namae wa nan to iimasu ka?	What are their names?

---

[1] *moosu* = call, say (humble verb).

Ano otoko no hito no namae wa Shimada Yukio de, ano onna no hito no namae wa Takahashi Noriko desu.	His name is Yukio Shimada and hers is Noriko Takahashi.
Ano hito no namae wa nan to iimasu ka?	What's his first name?
Ano hito no namae wa Nobuo desu.	His first name is Nobuo.
Ano hito no namae wa nan to iimasu ka?	What is his last name?
Ano hito no myooji wa Yasuda to iimasu.	His last name is Yasuda.

B. WHERE ARE YOU FROM? HOW OLD ARE YOU?

Okuni wa dochira desu ka?	Where are you from?
Tookyoo desu.	I'm from Tokyo.
Anata wa doko de umaremashita ka?	Where were you born?
Nagoya de umaremashita.	I was born in Nagoya.
Otoshi wa ikutsu desu ka?	How old are you?
Hatachi[1] desu.	I'm twenty.
Kugatsu de nijuu ichi ni narimasu.	I'll be twenty-one in September.

[1] *hatachi* = twenty years old.

Watashi wa sen kyuuhyaku nanajuu nen no Hachigatsu juuku nichi ni umaremashita.	I was born on August 19, 1970.
Anata no otanjoobi wa itsu desu ka?	When is your birthday?
Watashi no tan-joobi wa nishuukan saki no Ichigatsu nijuu sannichi desu.	My birthday is in two weeks—January twenty-third.
Otoko no kyoodai wa nannin imasu ka?	How many brothers do you have?
Ani ga hitori to otooto ga hitori imasu.	I have one older brother and one younger brother.
Ani wa nijuu go sai desu.	My older brother is twenty-five.
Sono ani wa daigaku ni itte imasu.	He attends the university.
Otooto wa juushichi desu.	My younger brother is seventeen.
Otooto wa kookoo no sannensei desu.	My younger brother is in the third year of senior high school.
Oniisan ya imooto san wa nannin desu ka?	How many older and younger sisters do you have?
Imooto ga hitori iru dake desu.	I have just one younger sister.
Imooto wa juugo desu.	She's fifteen.
Imooto wa chuugakkoo no sannensei desu.	She is in the third year of junior high school.

C. Professions

Donna oshigoto o shiteirasshaimasu ka?	What do you do?
Otoosan no oshigoto wa nan desu ka?	What does your father do?
Okaasan no oshigoto wa nan desu ka?	What does your mother do?
Chichi wa bengoshi desu.	He's [Father is] a lawyer.
Chichi wa kenchikuka desu.	He's an architect.
Kyooshi desu.	He's a teacher.
Daigaku kyooju desu.	He's a university professor.
Okaasan no oshigoto wa nan desu ka?	What does your mother do?
Isha desu.	She's a doctor.
Kaishain desu.	She's a company employee.
Orimonogaisha o yatte imasu.	She's in the textile business.
Hyakushoo desu.	She's a farmer.
Koomuin desu.	She's a government employee.
Jidoosha koojoo de hataraite imasu.	He works in an automobile factory.

D. Family Matters

Koko ni goshinseki ga oari desu ka?	Do you have any relatives here?
Gokazoku wa minna koko ni sunde irasshaimasu ka?	Does your whole family live here?

Sofubo no hoka wa kazoku wa minna koko ni sunde imasu.	All my family except my grandparents live here.
Sofubo wa Nagoya ni sunde imasu.	They live in Nagoya.
Anata wa Taketomi-san no goshinseki desu ka?	Are you related to Mr. Taketomi?
Watashi no oji desu.	He's my uncle.
Ano hito wa watashi no itoko desu.	He's my cousin.
Anata wa Sakata-san no goshinseki desu ka?	Are you related to Ms. Sakata?
Watashi no oba desu.	She's my aunt.
Watashi no itoko desu.	She's my cousin.

REVIEW QUIZ 5

1. _____ (This) *machi no namae wa nan to iimasu ka?*
   a. *Koko*
   b. *Kore*
   c. *Kono*

2. *Koko kara Tookyoo made* _____ (how) *ikimasu ka?*
   a. *doko*
   b. *doo*
   c. *dore*

3. *Kono toori no namae wa* _____ (what) *to iimasu ka?*
   a. *dore*
   b. *naze*
   c. *nan*

4. *Ginza Doori wa* _____ (where) *desu ka?*
   a. *doko*
   b. *nan*
   c. *dore*

5. _____ (Post office) *wa doko desu ka?*
   a. *Yuubinkyoku*
   b. *Shiyakusho*
   c. *Basutei*

6. *Kado made itte* _____ (left) *ni magarimasu.*
   a. *hidari*
   b. *migi*
   c. *higashi*

7. _____ (How much) *desu ka?*
   a. *Ikutsu*
   b. *Ikura*
   c. *Itsu*

8. *Tegami o* _____ (would like to write) *n desu ga.*
   a. *dashitai*
   b. *kakitai*
   c. *mitai*

9. _____ (Postage stamp) *wa doko de kaemasu ka?*
   a. *kitte*
   b. *zasshi*
   c. *shinbun*

10. _____ (Corner) *ni arimasu.*
   a. *Kado*
   b. *Tonari*
   c. *Asoko*

11. _____ (Here) *ni denwa ga arimasu ka?*
   a. *Koko*
   b. *Soko*
   c. *Asoko*

12. _____ (Wrong) *bangoo ni kakarimashita.*
   a. *Chigau*
   b. *Hoshii*
   c. *Byooin no*

13. *Ano hito no* _____ (first name) *wa nan to iimasu ka?*
   a. *namae*
   b. *myooji*
   c. *jimusho*

14. *Anata wa doko de* _____ (was born) *ka?*
   a. *kaimashita*
   b. *umaremashita*
   c. *aimashita*

15. *Otooto wa* _____ (seventeen) *desu.*
   a. *juushichi*
   b. *juuichi*
   c. *juuhachi*

16. *Chichi wa* _____ (lawyer) *desu.*
   a. *noojookeieisha*
   b. *bengoshi*
   c. *isha*

17. _____ (Government employee) *desu.*
    a. *Koomuin*
    b. *Kyooshi*
    c. *Kaishain*

18. *Anata wa Taketomi-san no* _____ (relative)
desu ka?
    a. *goshinseki*
    b. *tomodachi*
    c. *bengoshi*

19. _____ (Birthday) *wa itsu desu ka?*
    a. *Goryokoo*
    b. *Tanjoobi*
    c. *Gokekkon*

20. *Koko kara* _____ (far) *desu ka?*
    a. *tooi*
    b. *chikai*
    c. *nan kiro*

21. *Niban* _____ (track) *desu.*
    a. *sen*
    b. *me*
    c. *ressha*

22. _____ (Next) *densha wa nanji ni demasu ka?*
    a. *Tsugi no*
    b. *Asa no*
    c. *Gogo no*

23. _____ (Envelope) *o motte imasu ka?*
    a. *Fuutoo*
    b. *Enpitsu*
    c. *Kitte*

24. _____ (Line's busy) *desu*.
    a. *Ohanashichuu*
    b. *Chigau bangoo*
    c. *Tashika*

25. *Sofubo* _____ (except) *kazoku wa minna koko ni sunde imasu*.
    a. *no hoka*
    b. *to issho ni*
    c. *to*

ANSWERS
1—c; 2—b; 3—c; 4—a; 5—a; 6—a; 7—b; 8—b;
9—a; 10—a; 11—a; 12—a; 13—a; 14—b; 15—a;
16—b; 17—a; 18—a; 19—b; 20—a; 21—a; 22—a;
23—a; 24—a; 25—a.

SUPPLEMENTAL VOCABULARY LIST 16: JOBS

jobs	*shigoto*
policeman / policewoman	*keikan / fujinkeikan*
lawyer	*bengoshi*
doctor	*isha, ishi*
engineer	*gishi, enjinia*
businessperson	*jitsugyooka*
salesperson	*ten'in, gaikooin, seerusuman, seerusuuuman* (women only), *joten'in* (women only), *joseigaikooin* (women only)
teacher	*sensei, kyooshi*
professor	*kyooju*
banker	*ginkooka, ginkooin*
architect	*kenchikuka*
veterinarian	*juui*
dentist	*haisha, shikai*

stay-at-home parent	*shufu*
carpenter	*daiku*
construction worker	*kensetsusagyooin*
taxi driver	*takushii no untenshu*
artist	*geijutsuka*
writer	*sakka*
plumber	*haikankoo*
electrician	*denkigishi, denkikoo*
journalist	*kisha, jaanarisuto*
actor / actress	*haiyuu / joyuu*
musician	*ongakuka*
farmer	*noojookeieisha, noofu*
secretary / assistant	*hisho / asisutanto*
unemployed	*shitsugyoosha*
retired	*taishokushita, intaishita*
full-time	*jookin no, sennin no*
part-time	*hijookin no, paato taimu no*
steady job	*teishoku*
summer job	*natsu no shigoto, natsu no arubaito*

LESSON 36

DAI SANJUU ROKKA

A. *KAIMONO:* SHOPPING

Study the notes at the end of this section for greater comprehension.

1. **Ikura desu ka?**
   How much is it?

2. **Sen en desu.**
   One thousand yen.

3. **Chotto takasugimasu ga, hoka ni arimasen ka?**
   It's [a little] too expensive. Don't you have anything else?

4. **Onaji shurui no desu ka?**
   Of the same kind?

5. **Onaji shurui no ka nita no ga hoshii n desu ga.**
   I want the same kind or something similar.

6. **Koo yuu no ga gozaimasu.**
   We have this (kind).

7. **Moo hoka ni wa arimasen ka?**
   Don't you have anything else (to show me)?

8. **Motto oyasui no desu ka?**
   Less expensive [one]? [Cheaper one?]

9. **Moshi attara.**
   If possible. [If there is.]

10. **Kore wa ikaga desu ka?**
    Would you like this? [How about this one?]

11. **Sore wa nedan ni yorimasu ne.**
    That depends on the price. [(I think it is all right) depending on the price.]

12. **Kore wa hassen en desu.**
    This is eight thousand yen.

13. **Kore wa doo desu ka? Mae no yori yasui n desu ka, takai n desu ka?**

How about this? Is it cheaper or more expensive
(than the former one)?

14. **Motto takai desu.**
More expensive.

15. **Hoka ni arimasen ka nee?**
Don't you have anything else?

16. **Ima wa gozaimasen ga, atarashii kata no ga
chikajika kuru hazu desu ga . . .**
Not at the moment, but I'm expecting some new
styles soon. [. . . new style ones are supposed to
come soon.]

17. **Itsu goro desu ka?**
When? [About when?]

18. **Moo jiki da to omoimasu ga. Konshuu matsu
goro otachiyori kudasai mase.**
Any day now. Drop in toward the end of the
week. [I think it'll be very soon . . .]

19. **Ja soo shimasu. Tokoro de kore wa ikura desu
ka?**
I'll do that. By the way, how much is this?

20. **Issoku sanbyaku en desu.**
Three hundred yen a pair.

21. **Ichi daasu kudasai.**
Let me have a dozen. [Give me a dozen, please.]

22. **Omochi ni narimasu ka?**
Will you take (them with you)?

23. **Iie, haitatsu shite kudasai.**
No. Please deliver them.

24. **Gojuusho wa onaji desu ne?**
At the same address? [The address is the same, isn't it?]

25. **Onaji desu.**
It's still the same.

26. **Maido arigatoo gozaimasu.**
Thank you very much. [Thank you (for your patronage) each time (you come).]

27. **Sayonara.**
Good-bye.

28. **Sayonara.**
Good-bye.

NOTE

Title: *Kaimono* = Shopping

4. *Shurui no:* same as *shurui no mono* = one(s) of the same kind. See also #13 for similar construction.

5. *Nita no ga* = one (that) resembles (it).

6. *Gozaimasu:* an extra-polite form of *arimasu* which would be used by the shopkeeper to the customer.

8. *Oyasui:* an extra-polite form of *yasui* or *yasui desu* containing the "honorific" prefix o-. Nearly all adjectives can take this prefix "honoring" the person to whom or about whom you are speaking. However, an adjective that itself begins with *o* cannot add the honorific prefix *o*. For instance, *omoshiroi* [It is interesting] cannot become *oomoshiroi*.

10. *Ikaga* is extra-polite for *doo*.

11. *Ni yorimasu* = depending on.

13. *Mae no:* same as *mae no mono* = one(s) of the previous time.

16. *Chikajika* = soon, shortly.

Kuru hazu desu ga: When the particle *ga* is used to terminate a clause, it signifies "but" or "and," but does not have quite the same force. It serves to make the sentence less sharp or less pointed, and is commonly used in extra-polite speech.

Otachiyori kudasai (respect): same as *tachiyotte kudasai*.

Note the construction: *O* plus the pre-*masu* form plus *kudasai.*

For example: *okaki kudasai = kaite kudasai; otabe kudasai = tabete kudasai.*

19. *Ja:* same as *dewa* = well, then.
Tokoro de = by the way.

20. *Soku* = a counter for socks, stockings, shoes.

22. *Omochi ni narimasu ka* (respect): same as *mochimasu ka* or *motte ikimasu ka.* Notice the construction: *o* plus the pre-*masu* form plus *ni narimasu.* This method for the construction of the respect form of a verb can be used for almost any plain verb (i.e., a verb that is not already respect). Further examples: *okaki ni narimasu = kakimasu; otabe ni narimasu = tabemasu; okai ni narimashita = kaimashita.*

24. *Gojuusho* (respect): same as *juusho. Gojuusho* and all other respect words of expressions introduced here cannot be used for things or actions pertaining to the speaker or persons identified with the speaker.

26. *Maido arigatoo gozaimasu:* The usual expression used by shopkeepers.

QUIZ 30

1. _____ (How much) *desu ka?*
   a. *Ikura*
   b. *Ikaga*
   c. *Ikutsu*

2. *Onaji* _____ (kind) *no desu ka?*
   a. *shurui*
   b. *nedan*
   c. *tokoro*

3. *Onaji shurui no* _____ (or) *nita no ga hoshii n desu ga . . .*
   a. *ga*
   b. *ka*
   c. *to*

4. _____ (This type) *ga gozaimasu ga . . .*
   a. *Doo yuu no*
   b. *Soo yuu no*
   c. *Koo yuu no*

5. _____ (Less) *oyasui no desu ka?*
   a. *Sukoshi*
   b. *Motto*
   c. *Taihen*

6. _____ (That) *wa nedan ni yorimasu ne.*
   a. *Sore*
   b. *Kore*
   c. *Dore*

7. *Ima wa gozaimasen* _____ (but) *atarashii kata no ga chikajika kuru hazu desu ga . . .*
   a. *kara*
   b. *ga*
   c. *noni*

8. _____ (Around when) *desu ka?*
   a. *Itsu*
   b. *Nanji gurai*
   c. *Itsu goro*

9. _____ (One dozen) *kudasai*.
   a. *Ichi mai*
   b. *Ichi daasu*
   c. *Issatsu*

10. _____ (Deliver) *shite kudasai*.
    a. *Haitatsu*
    b. *Benkyoo*
    c. *Kekkon*

ANSWERS
1—a; 2—a; 3—b; 4—c; 5—b; 6—a; 7—b; 8—c;
9—b; 10—a.

B. WORD STUDY

baketsu	bucket
booru	bowl
fooku	fork
furaipan	frying pan
gasu	gas
mikisaa	mixer
napukin	napkin
naifu	knife
supuun	spoon
toosutaa	toaster

SUPPLEMENTAL VOCABULARY LIST
17: CLOTHING

clothing	*irui, ifuku*
shirt	*shatsu*
pants	*zubon*
jeans	*jiipan, jiinzu*

tee shirt	*tiishatsu*
shoe(s)	*kutsu*
sock(s)	*kutsushita, sokkusu*
belt	*beruto*
sneaker /	*undoogutsu, suniikaa,*
tennis shoe	*tenisu shuuzu*
dress	*doresu, wanpiisu, ifuku*
skirt	*sukaato*
blouse	*burausu*
suit	*suutsu*
hat	*booshi*
glove(s)	*tebukuro*
scarf	*sukaafu*
winter scarf	*mafuraa*
jacket	*uwagi, jaketto*
coat	*kooto*
earring	*iyaringu, mimikazari*
bracelet	*buresuretto, udewa*
necklace	*nekkuresu, kubikazari*
eyeglasses	*megane*
sunglasses	*sangurasu*
watch	*tokei*
ring	*yubiwa*
underpants	*pantsu, zubonshita*
undershirt	*hadagi, shatsu*
bathing trunks	*suieipantsu*
bathing suit	*mizugi*
pajamas	*pajama, nemaki*
cotton	*men, kotton*
leather	*kawa, rezaa*
silk	*kinu, siruku*
size	*saizu, ookisa*
to wear	*kiru*

LESSON 37

DAI SANJUU NANA KA

A. *ASAGOHAN:* **BREAKFAST**

Study the notes at the end of this section for greater comprehension.

1. Mr. Y:[1] **Onaka ga suita daroo.**
   Mr. Y: You must be hungry.

2. Mrs. Y: **Ee, nani ka itadakitai wa.**
   Mrs. Y: Yes, (I) would like to have something.

3. Mr. Y: **Kono hoteru ni wa ii resutoran ga aru to yuu kara soko e itte miyoo.**
   Mr. Y: They say there is a good restaurant in this hotel. Let's go there.

4. Mrs. Y: **Sore ga ii wa. Soo shimashoo.**
   Mrs. Y: That's a good idea. Let's do so.

5. Mr. Y: **Chotto sumimasen!**
   Mr. Y: Hello! [Excuse me.]

6. W: **Oyobi de gozaimasu ka?**
   W: Yes? [(You) called, (sir)?]

7. Mr. Y: **Asagohan o tabetai n desu ga . . .**
   Mr. Y: We'd like some breakfast.

8. Mrs. Y: **Nani ga itadakemasu no?**
   Mrs. Y: What can we have?

[1] *Mr. Y* stands for "Mr. Yamada," *Mrs. Y* for "Mrs. Yamada," *W* for "Waiter."

9. W: **Koohii, koocha, mata wa hotto choko-reeto. Onomimono wa nani ni nasaimasu ka?**
   W: Coffee, black tea, or hot chocolate. What would you like to have?

10. Mrs. Y: **Hoka no mono wa?**
    Mrs. Y: What else?

11. W: **Rooru pan ni toosuto, sore kara hotto keeki mo dekimasu.**
    W: Rolls, toast, and hotcakes, too.

12. Mrs. Y: **Bataa wa tsukanai n desu ka?**
    Mrs. Y: No butter?

13. W: **Mochiron tsukimasu. Hoka ni jamu mo otsuke shimasu.**
    W: Of course, butter and jelly. [Of course, (we) will serve (it). (We) will serve jelly also.]

14. Mrs. Y: **Dewa watakushi wa koohii to toosuto dake ni shimasu.**
    Mrs. Y: I'd like to have just some coffee and toast.

15. Mr. Y: **Kochira mo sore to onaji ni shite, sono hoka ni hanjuku tamago o tsukete kudasai.**
    Mr. Y: The same for me, and a soft-boiled egg, as well.

16. W: **Kashikomarimashita. Hoka ni nani ka?**
    W: Certainly, sir. Would you like anything else?

17. Mr. Y: **Iya, sore de takusan.**
    Mr. Y: No, that'll be all.

18. Mrs. Y: **Napukin o motte kite kudasaimasu ka?**
    Mrs. Y: May I have a napkin, please?

19. Mr. Y: **Sore kara fooku mo. Koko ni wa fooku ga nai yoo dakara.**
    Mr. Y: Would you also get a fork, please? I don't have one. [(It) seems (it) is not here.]

20. Mrs. Y: **Osatoo mo onegai shimasu.**
    Mrs. Y: And some sugar, too, please.

21. W: **Omatase itashimashita.**
    W: Here you are, madam. [Sorry to have kept you waiting.]

22. Mrs. Y: **Kono koohii wa sukkari tsumetaku natte iru wa. Atsui no to torikaete kudasaimasu ka?**
    Mrs. Y: My coffee is cold. Please bring me another cup.

23. W: **Kashikomarimashita.**
    W: Gladly.

24. Mr. Y: **Denpyoo o motte kite kudasai.**
    Mr. Y: May I have the check?

25. W: **Omatase itashimashita.**
    W: Here you are, sir. [Sorry to have kept you waiting.]

26. Mr. Y: **Ja kore de totte kudasai. Otsuri wa ii desu.**
    Mr. Y: Here, keep the change.

27. W: **Maido arigatoo gozaimasu.**
    W: Thank you very much, sir.

28. Mr. Y: **Ja sayonara.**
    Mr. Y: Good-bye.

NOTE

Title: *Asagohan* = Breakfast

1. The conversation here is first carried on between husband and wife; later it is continued between the couple and their waiter. Notice how freely the plain forms instead of the usual *-masu* or *-desu* forms of verbs and adjectives are used in such a conversation.

   Onaka ga suita daroo (from *onaka ga suku* = get hungry [The stomach gets empty]. *-daroo* [must be, probably]) is the plain form of *-deshoo*. *-daroo* at the end of a sentence is used exclusively by men in casual conversation.

2. *Itadakitai* (extra polite, humble)[1] (from *itadaku*) = want to eat, drink, receive.

   Wa: a particle used exclusively by women in casual conversation. It appears at the end of a sentence and adds a feminine touch.

8. *No:* another particle used almost exclusively by women which takes the place of *no desu* or *n desu* at the end of a sentence. With a rising intonation, it is, like the particle *ka,* a spoken question mark.

12. *Tsukanai* (from *tsuku*) = does not go with; is not served with.

13. *Otsuke shimasu: otsuke* comes from *tsukeru* = serve something with. It is a transitive verb to be paired with *tsuku* (see #12, above). The construction employed here, that is, *o* plus the pre-*masu* form, plus *suru,* is the one used in respectful speech when the speaker discusses doing something for the person with whom or about whom he/she is talking.

---

[1] *Humble,* as opposed to *respect,* is a word form that demotes the status of the speaker. Usually it is the speaker who humbles him- or herself.

14. *Ni shimasu* = one makes (his/her choice or decision) to be; one decides on (taking).

15. *Kochira* = this side, this way; sometimes used in place of *watakushi* [I]. Similarly, *sochira* or *sochira sama* can be used for "you," "he," "she," or "they."

18. *-kudasaimasu ka:* one type of a request form. It is softer than *-kudasai*.

20. *Onegai shimasu:* an idiom used when the speaker requests that someone do something.

22. *Tsumetaku natte iru* = is cold, is chilled [is in the state of having become cold].

26. *Ja:* a variant of *dewa* = Well, then, if that is the case, when used at the beginning of a sentence. *Kore de totte kudasai* = Using this (money), please take (what I owe you). *Otsuri wa ii desu* = Keep the change. [As for the change (it) will be all right (for you to keep it).]

B. A Sample Menu

KONDATE	MENU
Osuimono	Clear soup
sayori	snipe fish
warabi	brackens
namayuba	fresh bean curd skin
Sashimi	Sashimi (sliced raw fish)
maguro	tuna
Sunomono	A dish consisting in part of vinegar
sazae	turbo
karashisumiso	dressed with vinegar, mustard, and bean paste
Yasai no nimono	Cooked vegetables
kuwai	arrowhead bulbs
sayaendoo	snow peas

takenoko	bamboo shoots
udo	udo (Japanese asparagus)
Yakizakana	Broiled fish
koi-teriyaki	broiled carp
tsukeawase	served with fancy relish
Kobachi	Small bowl
tsukushi-	omelet with horsetails
tamago-toji	(vegetable)
Gohan	Rice
kuri-gohan	rice cooked with chestnuts
Misoshiru	Soybean paste soup
toofu	tofu
negi	green onions
Tsukemono	Pickles
takuan	pickled white radish
narazuke	pickles seasoned with sake
kabura	turnips

REVIEW QUIZ 6

1. *Onaka ga* _____ (must be hungry).
   a. *tsuita daroo*
   b. *suita daroo*
   c. *kaita daroo*

2. _____ (Something) *itadakitai wa.*
   a. *Nani mo*
   b. *Nani ka*
   c. *Nan de mo*

3. *Kono hoteru ni wa ii resutoran ga* _____ (there is).
   a. *arimasu*
   b. *imasu*
   c. *shimasu*

4. *Kono koohii wa* _____ (cold) *natte iru wa.*
   a. *waruku*
   b. *samuku*
   c. *tsumetaku*

5. *Kochira mo sore to* _____ (the same) *ni shite kudasai.*
   a. *nita*
   b. *onaji*
   c. *chigau*

6. _____ (Sugar) *o motte kite kudasaimasu ka?*
   a. *Osatoo*
   b. *Ocha*
   c. *Tamago*

7. *Sore kara fooku* _____ (also).
   a. *moo*
   b. *to*
   c. *mo*

8. _____ (Check) *o motte kite kudasai.*
   a. *Denpyoo*
   b. *Kippu*
   c. *Tanjoobi*

9. *Fooku ga* _____ (missing) *yoo da.*
   a. *nai*
   b. *inai*
   c. *ikanai*

10. _____ (Change) *wa ii desu.*
    a. *Denpyoo*
    b. *Okane*
    c. *Otsuri*

ANSWERS
1—b; 2—b; 3—a; 4—c; 5—b; 6—a; 7—c; 8—a;
9—a; 10—c.

LESSON 38

DAI SANJUU HACHI KA

A. IN, ON, UNDER

1. *Ni, de, e, no:* In, into

Sore wa jisho ni arimasu.	That's in the dictionary.
Poketto ni iremashita.	He put it in his pocket.
Kare no heya ni arimasu.	You'll find it in his room. [It is in his room.]
Hikidashi ni irete kudasai.	Put it into the drawer, please.
Me ni nani ka hairi-mashita.	I have something in my eye. [Something got into my eyes.]
Tookyoo de kaima-shita.	I bought it in Tokyo.
Tookyoo no hakubutsukan de mimashita.	I saw it in the museum in Tokyo.

2. *No naka ni (. . . de, . . . e, . . . no, . . . o):* Inside

Sono kaban no naka o mite kudasai.	Please look in that briefcase. [Please look in the within of that briefcase.]

Gakkoo no naka no shokudoo de gohan o tabemashita.

We ate [had our meal] in the dining room of [in the within of] the school.

Yamada-san to issho ni tatemono no naka e hairimashita.

Together with Mr. Yamada, we entered the inside of the building.

Kusuriya wa sono tatemono no naka ni arimasu.

The drugstore is in [inside] that building.

3. *No ue ni (. . . de, . . . no, . . . e):* On

Kono tegami o, kare no tsukue no ue ni oite kudasai.

Please put this letter on his desk.

Oka no ue de asonde imasu.

They are playing on the hill.

Fuutoo no ue ni kaite kudasai.

Please write it on the envelope.

4. *No shita ni (. . . de, . . . no, . . . e):* Under

Isu no shita ni arimasu.

It's under the chair.

Sono hon wa hoka no hon no shita ni arimasu.

You'll find the book under the others.

Beddo no shita ni okimashita.

She put it under the bed.

Hashi no shita de hiroimashita.

I picked it up under the bridge.

5. *Naka:* Place inside

Naka wa samui desu.	It is cold inside.
Naka o minaide kudasai.	Please do not look inside.

6. *Ue:* Top, surface

Ue ni oite kudasai.	Put it on top, please.
Ue o mite kudasai.	Look on the top, please.

7. *Shita:* Bottom, place under, place below

Sore o shita ni oite kudasai.	Please put that underneath.
Kono shita o mite kudasai.	Please look under here.

B. IF, WHEN

1. *Moshi*[1] *. . . -ba; -nara:* If

Notice that the *-(r)eba* ending form of a verb, the *-kereba* ending form of an *i*-adjective, and the *nara* form of a copula express the idea "if (something) happens," or "if (something) is the case."[2]

These forms are called the "provisional" and are used *only* for a present or future hypothetical condition.

moshi dekireba	if I can
moshi juubun okane ga areba	if I have enough money

---

[1] The word *moshi* is optional.
[2] Use *-eba* with consonant verbs; use *-reba* with vowel verbs. For further discussion of the formation of *-ba* form, see Section 36 of the Summary of Japanese Grammar.

Soko e ikeba minna ni aemasu.	If you go there, you can meet everybody.
Samukereba sugu kaerimasu.	If it is cold, I will come back right away.
Yasukereba kau tsumori desu.	If it is inexpensive, I intend to buy it.
Tenisu ga joozu nara ii n desu ga . . .	I hope she is good at tennis. [If she is good at tennis, it is good . . .]
Sashimi nara nan demo kekkoo desu.	If it is raw fish, anything is fine.

2. *-Tara:* If, when

Notice that the *-tara* form is made by adding *-ra* to the *-ta* form. It is used to express a condition of the past, present, or future. The *-tara* form is called the "conditional."

Ashita ame ga futtara ikimasen.	If it rains tomorrow, I won't go.
Ashita atsukattara ikimasen.	If it's hot tomorrow, I won't go.
Okane ga nakattara kaemasen.	If you don't have the money, you can't buy it.
Takasugiru to ittara yasuku shimashita.	When I said it was too expensive, he lowered the price [he made it cheap].
Tabetakattara tabete mo ii desu.	If you want to eat it, you can [eat it].
Takakattara honmono desu.	If it is expensive, it is [a] genuine [thing].

Sono kusuri o nondara sugu yoku narimashita.	When I took [drank] that medicine, I got well right away.

3. *To:* If, when, whenever

Notice that *to* is used only when what follows it is a natural consequence of what is stated in the clause that precedes it. *To* is always preceded by the present form of a verb, an adjective, or the copula; it cannot be used when the terminal clause ends in *-te kudasai.*

Kono michi o massugu iku to bijutsukan no mae ni demasu.	If you follow [go] this road straight ahead, you will come to the front of the Fine Arts Museum.
Basu de iku to gojikan kakarimasu.	If you go by bus, it takes five hours.
Wakaranai koto ga aru to Yamada-san ni kikimasu.	When there are things that I don't understand, I ask Mr. Yamada.
Ame ga furu to kuru hito ga sukunaku narimasu.	When it rains, fewer people come [persons who come get fewer].
Mainichi kaku to joozu ni narimasu.	When you write it every day, you become more skillful [in it].

C. WITHOUT

1. *Nashi ni:* Without

okane nashi ni	without money
nani mo nashi ni	without anything

machigai nashi ni	without fail
konnan nashi ni	without difficulty
Konnan nashi ni dekimasu.	You can do it without any difficulty.

2. *-Nai de:* Without

Asagohan o tabenai de dekakemashita.	I went out without having breakfast.
Benkyoo shinai de shiken o ukemashita.	Without studying, I took a test.

QUIZ 31

1. *Sore o shita ni oite kudasai.*
2. *Poketto ni iremashita.*
3. *Sore wa jisho ni arimasu.*
4. *Fuutoo no ue ni kaite kudasai.*
5. *Oka no ue de asonde imasu.*
6. *Ue o mite kudasai.*

7. *yasukereba*

8. *moshi juubun okane ga areba*
9. *takasugiru to ittara*
10. *machigai nashi ni*
11. *konnan nashi ni*

a. It's in the dictionary.
b. Please put that underneath.
c. He put it in his pocket.
d. They are playing on the hill.
e. Write it on the envelope, please.
f. You will find the book under the others.
g. Put it on top, please.
h. Look on the top, please.
i. if it is cold
j. if it is inexpensive
k. if I have enough money

12. *okane nashi ni*   l. when I said it was
                                 too expensive
13. *samukereba*   m. without money
14. *Ue ni oite kudasai*   n. without fail
15. *Sono hon wa hoka*   o. without difficulty
    no hon no shita ni
    arimasu.

ANSWERS
1—b; 2—c; 3—a; 4—e; 5—d; 6—h; 7—j; 8—k;
9—l; 10—n; 11—o; 12—m; 13—i; 14—g; 15—f.

REVIEW QUIZ 7

1. _____ (That one) *ga hoshii desu.*
   a. *Asoko*
   b. *Are*
   c. *Anna*

2. _____ (This) *wa ikaga desu ka?*
   a. *Kore*
   b. *Kono*
   c. *Koko*

3. *Nihongo de* _____ (how) *iimasu ka?*
   a. *dore*
   b. *donna*
   c. *doo*

4. *Soko e itta* _____ (never).
   a. *tsumori desu*
   b. *koto ga arimasen*
   c. *hazu desu*

5. _____ (Nothing) *kaimasen deshita.*
   a. *Nan de mo*
   b. *Nani ka*
   c. *Nani mo*

6. *Kono hon wa* _____ (her) *desu.*
   a. *dono hito no*
   b. *sono otoko no hito no*
   c. *kanojo no*

7. *Watashi no* _____ (aunt) *desu.*
   a. *oba*
   b. *oji*
   c. *itoko*

8. _____ (One week) *kakarimasu.*
   a. *Ikkagetsu*
   b. *Isshuukan*
   c. *Ichinen*

9. _____ (Next) *basu de ikimashoo.*
   a. *Ashita no*
   b. *Tsugi no*
   c. *Asatte no*

10. *Doomo* _____ (thanks).
    a. *wakarimasen*
    b. *arigatoo gozaimasu*
    c. *dekimasen*

11. *Ni san* _____ (days) *shitara denwa o kakete kudasai.*
    a. *jikan*
    b. *nichi*
    c. *nen*

12. *Kono kata o* _____ (know) *ka?*
    a. *gozonji desu*
    b. *sagashite imasu*
    c. *goshookai itashimasu*

13. *Iie, soo* _____ (don't think).
    a. *ikimasen*
    b. *omoimasen*
    c. *kimasen*

14. *Kyooto de* _____ (bought).
    a. *tsukurimashita*
    b. *kikimashita*
    c. *kaimashita*

15. *Sono tegami wa* _____ (wrote) *ka?*
    a. *mimashita*
    b. *kakimashita*
    c. *uketorimashita*

16. *Watakushi wa* _____ (morning) *wa koohii o nomimasu.*
    a. *hiru*
    b. *yoru*
    c. *asa*

17. *Eki de tomodachi ni* _____ (met).
    a. *hanashimashita*
    b. *aimashita*
    c. *kikimashita*

18. *Anata no denwa bangoo o* _____ (give me).
    a. *shitte imasu*
    b. *kudasai*
    c. *agemashoo*

19. *Sore wa taihen* _____ (good) *desu.*
    a. *kekkoo*
    b. *omoshiroi*
    c. *yasui*

20. _____ (Soon) *kimasu.*
    a. *Sugu*
    b. *Ashita*
    c. *Ato de*

ANSWERS
1—b; 2—a; 3—c; 4—b; 5—c; 6—c; 7—a; 8—b;
9—b; 10—b; 11—b; 12—a; 13—b; 14—c; 15—b;
16—c; 17—b; 18—b; 19—a; 20—a.

D. *Shakuya Sagashi:* House Hunting

Study the notes at the end of this section for greater comprehension.

1. **Kashiya ga aru soo desu ga.**
I hear you have a house to rent.

2. **Dochira deshoo ka? Futatsu aru n desu ga.**
Which one? We have two.

3. **Shinbun no kookoku o mite shitta no desu ga.**
It's the one I saw advertised in the paper.

4. **Hai, wakarimashita.**
Oh, that one.

5. **Donna ie ka sukoshi setsumei shite morae-masen ka?**
Can you describe them?

6. **Ookii hoo wa go-eru-dii-kee desu.**
The larger of the two is 5LDK.

7. **Chiisai hoo wa doo desu ka?**
How about the smaller one?

8. **Yon-eru-dii-kee desu.**
   (It) is 4LDK.

9. **Ookii hoo wa gareeji ga tsuite imasu ka?**
   Does the larger house have a garage?

10. **Hai, tsuite imasu.**
    Yes, it does.

11. **Niwa ga arimasu ka?**
    Is there a garden there?

12. **Hai, gozaimasu. Nihonshiki no rippa na niwa desu.**
    Yes, there is. It's a fine, Japanese-style garden.

13. **Chiisai hoo wa?**
    How about the smaller house?

14. **Niwa to iu hodo no niwa wa gozaimasen ga miharashi no ii takadai ni gozaimasu.**
    There isn't any garden to speak of, but the house is situated on top of a hill and has a nice view. [(It)'s not much of a garden that there is . . .]

15. **Shizuka na tokoro desu ka?**
    Is it in a quiet neighborhood?

16. **Hai, oodoori kara hanarete imasu kara taihen shizuka desu.**
    Yes, it is away from big streets, and it's very quiet there.

17. **Yachin wa dono kurai desu ka?**
    What's the rent?

18. **Ookii hoo wa tsuki nijuuman en desu.**
The rent for the larger house is two hundred thousand yen per month.

19. **Chiisai hoo wa?**
And the smaller house?

20. **Tsuki juugoman en desu.**
One hundred and fifty thousand yen per month.

21. **Kagu zoosaku wa doo nan desu ka?**
What about furniture and other equipment?

22. **Mina tsuite orimasu. Tatami mo harikaeta bakari desu.**
(It)'s well furnished. The floor mats have been completely repaired.

23. **Reizooko nado wa nai deshoo ne?**
I suppose a refrigerator is not included?

24. **Iie, saishinshiki no reizooko ga tsuite orimasu.**
There is a late-model refrigerator. [There is a refrigerator of the latest style.]

25. **Ichinen no keiyaku de karitai to omotte iru n desu ga, sore de ii desu ka?**
I would like to get a lease for a year. Do you think that's possible [agreeable]?

26. **Sono ten wa yanushi to gosoodan itadakitai to omoimasu.**
You'd have to see the owner for that.

27. **Shikikin wa iru n desu ka?**
Do I have to pay a security deposit? [Is a security deposit necessary?]

28. **Hai, sankagetsubun itadaku koto ni natte orimasu.**
Yes, we ask three months' rent (for it).

29. **Hoka ni wa?**
Nothing else?

30. **Hoshoonin ga irimasu.**
You have to have references.

31. **Tsuide ni okiki shimasu ga denwa wa tsuite imasu ka?**
Is there a telephone already installed?

32. **Ainiku tsuite orimasen.**
No, there isn't. [Sorry, but it isn't installed.]

33. **Aa soo desu ka.**
I see.

34. **Chikatetsu ya JR no eki ni mo chikakute taihen benri na tokoro desu.**
The house is located not too far from the subway and the JR-line station. So it's quite convenient.

35. **Aa soo desu ka. Soko kara Marunouchi made wa dono kurai kakarimasu ka?**
I see. How much time does it take from there to Marunouchi?

36. **Yaku nijuppun gurai desu.**
I would say about twenty minutes.

37. **Basu mo chikaku o tootte imasu ka?**
Is there any bus line running nearby?

38. **Hai, Tookyoo-eki yuki ga kado hitotsu saki o tootte imasu.**
Yes, there is one a block away. The bus goes to Tokyo Station.

39. **Sono uchi wa ima itte miraremasu ka?**
May we see the house now?

40. **Sumimasen ga gozen-chuu shika ome ni kakerarenai n desu ga.**
I'm sorry, but it is open for inspection only in the morning.

41. **Aa soo desu ka. Sore ja ashita no asa kimasu. Iroiro osewasama deshita.**
I see. I'll come tomorrow morning. Thanks a lot.

42. **Doo itashimashite. Kochira koso shitsurei itashimashita.**
Not at all. Glad to be able to help you.

NOTE

Title: *Shakuya Sagashi* = Searching (for) a House to Rent

1. *Aru soo desu* = I understood that there is.
2. *Dochira* = which (of the two).
3. *Kookoku* = advertisement.
5. *Setsumei shite moraemasen ka* = Can't I have you explain the details for me?
6. *Go-eru-dii-kee* = 5LDK (5 rooms, L = living room, DK = dining kitchen).
9. *Tsuite imasu* = are attached; are equipped.
14. *Niwa to iu hodo no niwa* = a garden (worthy of) calling it a garden; (there isn't any) garden to speak of.

Miharashi = view.

Takadai = top of a hill (within a city area).

16. *Hanarete imasu* = is away from.
17. *Yachin* = house rent.
18. *Tsuki* = per month.
21. *Kagu zoosaku* = furniture and other equipment.
22. *Tatami* = Japanese-style floor mat.

    Harikaeta bakari desu = We have just replaced the mat covers with new ones (the *-ta* form of a verb plus *bakari desu* = just finished doing . . .).
23. *Reizooko nado* = a refrigerator and things like that.
24. *Iie* = no. Notice that this is used where "yes" would be used in English, for the thought is, "No, what you have mentioned is not correct." *Saishinshiki no reizooko* = latest-model refrigerator.

    Orimasu: humble (polite) form of *imasu*.
25. *Keiyaku* = contract; lease.
26. *Yanushi* = landlord.

    Gosoodan itadakitai = I would like to have you consult.
27. *Shikikin* = key money, security deposit.
28. *Sankagetsubun* = the equivalent of three months' (rent). (*-bun* = the portion for)

    Koto ni natte orimasu = It is arranged that, it is fixed that (we receive).
30. *Hoshoonin* = reference (i.e., one who guarantees).
34. *Chikatetsu* = subway.
35. *Marunouchi* = the heart of the business section in Tokyo.
38. *Tookyoo-eki yuki* = bound for Tokyo: *yuki* = bound for, when used after a place-name.
39. *Miraremasu* = can see. The same form—made by adding *-(r)areru* to the base—is used for both the passive voice and respect expressions.

40. *Ome ni kakerarenai* = can't show (you); *kake-rarenai:* a negative form of *kakerareru,* which is a potential form made from *kakeru* by adding *-rareru* to the base.

41. *Osewasama deshita* = thanks: a common way of expressing thanks for services rendered.

QUIZ 32

1. _____ (Quiet) *na tokoro desu ka?*
    a. *Rippa*
    b. *Shizuka*
    c. *Benri*

2. *Oodoori kara* _____ (away from) *imasu.*
    a. *hanarete*
    b. *hanashite*
    c. *tooi*

3. _____ (Rent) *wa dono kurai desu ka?*
    a. *Yachin*
    b. *Nedan*
    c. *Shikikin*

4. *Sankagetsubun* _____ (receive) *koto ni natte orimasu.*
    a. *harau*
    b. *itadaku*
    c. *tazuneru*

5. _____ (Furniture) *wa tsuite imasu ka?*
    a. *Tatami*
    b. *Reizooko*
    c. *Kagu zoosaku*

6. *Yaku* _____ (twenty minutes) *gurai desu.*
   a. *nijuppun*
   b. *juunifun*
   c. *nijuufun*

7. _____ (Garden) *ga arimasu ka?*
   a. *Heya*
   b. *Niwa*
   c. *Takadai*

8. *Gozenchuu* _____ (only) *ome ni kake-raremasen.*
   a. *demo*
   b. *hoka*
   c. *shika*

9. _____ (Tomorrow) *no asa kimasu.*
   a. *Kinoo*
   b. *Ashita*
   c. *Asatte*

10. *Iroiro* _____ (thanks for your service) *deshita.*
    a. *omachidoosama*
    b. *ohanashichuu*
    c. *osewasama*

ANSWERS
1—b; 2—a; 3—a; 4—b; 5—c; 6—a; 7—b; 8—c;
9—b; 10—c.

SUPPLEMENTAL VOCABULARY LIST 18:
    IN THE BATHROOM

in the bathroom   *yokushitu ni, yokushitsu de*
toilet   *otearai, tearaijo, toire*

sink (wash basin)	*senmendai*
bath tub	*yokusoo*
shower	*shawaa*
mirror	*kagami*
medicine cabinet	*kusuribako*, *kyuukyuubako*
towel	*taoru*
toilet paper	*toirettopeepaa*
shampoo	*shanpuu*
soap	*sekken*
bath gel	*nyuuyokuyoo jeru*
shaving cream	*higesoriyoo kuriimu*
razor	*kamisori*
to wash oneself	*karada o arau*
to take a shower / to take a bath	*shawaa o abiru* / *ofuro ni hairu*
to shave	*soru*
cologne	*koron*
perfume	*koosui*
deodorant	*deodoranto*
bandage	*hootai*
powder	*kona*, *paudaa*

LESSON 39

DAI SANJUU KYUU KA

A. *KURU:* TO COME

Kimasu.	I (you, . . .) come.
Kite kudasai.	Please come!
Koko e kite kudasai.	Come here, please.
Watakushi to issho ni kite kudasai.	Come with me, please.

Mata kite kudasai.	Come again, please.
Uchi made kite kudasai.	Come to the house, please.
Itsu ka yoru kite kudasai.	Come some night, please.
Konaide kudasai.	Please don't come.
Doko kara kimasu ka?	Where are you coming from?
Tookyoo kara kimasu.	I am coming from Tokyo.
Gekijoo kara kimasu.	I am coming from the theater.
Sugu kimasu.	I am coming right away.

-ta bakari desu = to have just completed an action

Amerika kara kita bakari desu.	I have just come from the United States.
Sono tegami wa ima kita bakari desu.	That letter has just arrived.

-te kuru = to have just started to, to have started doing something and continued up to the present

Ame ga futte kimashita.	The rain has started to fall.
Nihongo ga wakatte kimashita.	I have started to understand Japanese. [Japanese has begun to be clear to me.]
Nihongo o rokkagetsu benkyoo shite kimashita.	I have been studying Japanese for six months.

Nihongo no hon bakari yonde ki- mashita.   I have been reading nothing but books in Japanese.

B. *IU (YUU):* TO SAY

Iimasu.   I (you, . . .) say.

to iu = to say that . . .

Ikanai to iimashita.   I said that I wouldn't go. [(I) said, "(I) will not go."]

Ikanai ka to ii- mashita.   I said, "Aren't you going?" He said, "Aren't you go- ing?"

to ka iu = to say something to the effect that, to say something like

Ikanai ka to ka ii- mashita.   He said something like, "Aren't you go- ing?" (but I am not exactly sure what he said).

Hitori de itta to ka iimashita.   He said something to the effect that he went alone.

Iinikui desu.   It's hard to say.

Itte kudasai.   Say (it)! Tell (it), please.

Moo ichido itte kuda- sai.   Say it again, please.

Nihongo de itte kuda-sai.	Say it in Japanese, please.
Yukkuri itte kudasai.	Say it slowly, please.
Iwanaide kudasai.	Don't say that, please.
Kare ni itte ku-dasai.	Tell (it) to him, please.

yoo ni iu = to tell someone to

Kuru yoo ni itte ku-dasai.	Tell him to come, please.
Konai yoo ni itte ku-dasai.	Please tell him not to come.
Kau yoo ni itte kuda-sai.	Please tell him to buy (it).
Kawanai yoo ni itte kudasai.	Please tell him not to buy (it).
Kare ni iwanaide kudasai.	Don't tell him, please.
Kare ni nani mo iwanaide kudasai.	Don't tell him any-thing, please.
Dare ni mo iwanaide kudasai.	Please don't tell that to anybody.
Nan to iimashita ka?	What did you say?
Nan to osshaimashita ka?	What did you say *(re-spect)*?
Nani mo iimasen deshita.	She hasn't said any-thing.

QUIZ 33

1. *Gekijoo kara ki-masu.*	a. Come with me, please.
2. *Hitori de itta to ka iimashita.*	b. Where are you com-ing from?

3. *Sugu kimasu.*	c. Come some night, please.
4. *Doko kara kimasu ka?*	d. I'm coming right away.
5. *Itte kudasai.*	e. I'm coming from the theater.
6. *Nihongo de itte kudasai.*	f. Say it in Japanese, please.
7. *Ame ga futte ki-mashita.*	g. I have just come from the United States.
8. *Itsu ka yoru kite kudasai.*	h. The rain has started to fall.
9. *Watakushi to issho ni kite kudasai.*	i. He said something to the effect that he went alone.
10. *Amerika kara kita bakari desu.*	j. Tell me, please.

ANSWERS
1—e; 2—i; 3—d; 4—b; 5—j; 6—f; 7—h; 8—c; 9—a; 10—g.

C. *SURU:* TO DO

Shimasu.	I (you, . . .) do.
Shite imasu.	I'm doing it.
Nani o shite imasu ka?	What are you doing?
Doo shimasu ka?	How do you do that?
Nani o shite imashita ka?	What have you been doing?
Shinaide kudasai.	Please don't do it!
Moo shinaide kudasai.	Please don't do it anymore.

Shinakereba narimasen.	You must do it.
Shite wa ikemasen.	You mustn't do it.
Moo shite wa ikemasen.	You mustn't do it anymore.
Shite shimaimashita.	It's done. [(I)'ve finished doing (it).]
Nani mo shite imasen.	I'm not doing anything.
Nani mo shinaide kudasai.	Don't do anything, please.
Moo ichido shite kudasai.	Please do it once more.
Hayaku shite kudasai.	Do it quickly, please!
Chuui shite kudasai.	Pay attention, please!
Benkyoo shite kudasai.	Please study it.
Ima shita bakari desu.	I've just done it now.
Moo oai shimashita.	I've already met her *(respect)*.
Doo shimashoo ka?	{ What's to be done? What shall we do? What can be done? [How shall we do?]
Dare ga shimashita ka?	Who did that?
Doo shitara ii ka wakarimasen.	I don't know what to do.
Ookiku shimashita.	We enlarged (it).
Iku koto ni shimashita.	We've decided to go. [(We)'ve acted on (our) going.]

QUIZ 34

1. *Doo shimasu ka?*
2. *Shinaide kudasai.*

a. You mustn't do it.
b. Do it quickly, please.

3. *Shite shimaimashi-ta.*
    c. What are you do-ing?

4. *Doo shimashoo ka?*
    d. How do you do that?

5. *Chuui shite kuda-sai.*
    e. Please don't do it.

6. *Ookiku shimashita.*
    f. It's done.

7. *Moo ichido shite kudasai.*
    g. You must do it.

8. *Dare ga shimashita ka?*
    h. What's to be done?

9. *Ima shita bakari desu.*
    i. What have you been doing?

10. *Iku koto ni shi-mashita.*
    j. Do it once more, please.

11. *Shinakereba ike-masen.*
    k. Pay attention, please.

12. *Shite wa ikemasen.*
    l. We've decided to go.

13. *Nani o shite imasu ka?*
    m. I've just done it now.

14. *Hayaku shite kuda-sai.*
    n. We made it large.

15. *Nani o shite ima-shita ka?*
    o. Who did that?

ANSWERS

1—d; 2—e; 3—f; 4—h; 5—k; 6—n; 7—j; 8—o; 9—m; 10—l; 11—g; 12—a; 13—c; 14—b; 15—i.

REVIEW QUIZ 8

1. *Sugu* _____ (I'm coming).
    a. *kite imasu*
    b. *kimasu*
    c. *kimashita*

2. _____ (Hard to say) *desu.*
   a. *Inikui*
   b. *Ikinikui*
   c. *Iinikui*

3. *Nani o* _____ (do) *imasu ka?*
   a. *shitte*
   b. *shite*
   c. *shiite*

4. *Doo* _____ (do) *ii ka wakarimasen.*
   a. *ittara*
   b. *mitara*
   c. *shitara*

5. *Ano hito wa rippa na uchi o* _____ (have).
   a. *tsukutte imasu*
   b. *motte imasu*
   c. *sagashite imasu*

6. _____ (Don't take) *kudasai.*
   a. *Toranaide*
   b. *Minaide*
   c. *Nomanaide*

7. *Sugu* _____ (stop) *kudasai.*
   a. *tomatte*
   b. *tatte*
   c. *tabete*

8. *Ashita wa ii otenki ni nareba ii to* _____
   (think).
   a. *iimasu*
   b. *omoimasu*
   c. *kakimashita*

9. *Watashi wa* _____ (did not see).
   a. *ma ni aimasen deshita*
   b. *mairimasen deshita*
   c. *mimasen deshita*

10. *Moo ichido* _____ (see) *kudasai.*
    a. *mite*
    b. *nite*
    c. *shite*

11. *Ano hito no banchi wa* _____ (do not know).
    a. *arimasen*
    b. *shirimasen*
    c. *chigaimasu*

12. *Sono koto wa mae kara yoku* _____ (know).
    a. *shite imasu*
    b. *shitte orimasu*
    c. *benkyoo shite orimasu*

13. *Ima denwa de* _____ (is talking).
    a. *kotaete imasu*
    b. *kiite imasu*
    c. *hanashite imasu*

14. *Ima sugu iku* _____ (can).
    a. *tsumori desu*
    b. *koto ga dekimasu*
    c. *hazu desu*

15. *Ano hito wa watakushi no iu koto ga yoku*
    _____ (understands).
    a. *dekimasu*
    b. *wakarimasu*
    c. *kikoemasu*

16. *Booshi o* _____ (please buy).
    a. *totte kudasai*
    b. *katte kudasai*
    c. *motte kudasai*

17. *Kono machi ni* _____ (person I know) *wa dare
mo orimasen.*
    a. *yonde iru hito*
    b. *shite iru hito*
    c. *shitte iru hito*

18. *Moo sukoshi* _____ (want) *desu.*
    a. *hoshikatta*
    b. *hoshiku nai*
    c. *hoshii*

19. *Ikutsu* _____ (left) *imasu ka?*
    a. *nokotte*
    b. *katte*
    c. *motte*

20. *Itsu* _____ (must you go) *ka?*
    a. *ikanakute mo ii desu*
    b. *ikanakereba narimasen*
    c. *itte wa ikemasen*

ANSWERS
1—b; 2—c; 3—b; 4—c; 5—b; 6—a; 7—a; 8—b;
9—c; 10—a; 11—b; 12—b; 13—c; 14—b; 15—b;
16—b; 17—c; 18—c; 19—a; 20—b.

D. I'M A STRANGER HERE

Gomen kudasai.
Hello. [Pardon.]

Aa, Sumisu-san desu ka. Omachi shite orimashita.
Oh, Ms. Smith. I've been waiting for you.

Kyoo wa doo mo oisogashii tokoro o arigatoo goza-imasu.
I certainly appreciate your taking time out for me.
[Thank you (for taking the time for me) when you are
so busy.]

Doo itashimashite. Oyasui goyoo desu. Dewa sugu dekakemashoo.
Don't mention it. It is an easy task. Shall we get going?

Watakushi wa mada migi mo hidari mo wakari-masen kara yoroshiku onegai itashimasu.
I'm a total stranger here. [(I) can't even tell right from
left, and would appreciate (your) taking me around.]

Hai, kashikomarimashita. Yuubinkyoku ni goyoo ga aru to osshaimashita ne.
Surely. You said you wanted to go to the post office,
didn't you?

Ee, soo na n desu.
Yes, that's right.

Dewa kono michi o ikimashoo.
Then let's take this street.

Kono michi no namae wa nan to yuu n desu ka?
What's the name of this street?

Shoowa Doori to iimasu. Omona mise wa taitei koko ni arimasu.
It's Showa Street. Most of the important stores are
here.

Nakanaka nigiyaka na tokoro desu ne.
It's quite busy here, isn't it?

Itsu mo koo desu.
It is always crowded here, day and night.

Aa, ano ookii tatemono wa nan desu ka?
Oh, yes. What's that big building over there?

Aa, are desu ka?
You mean that one?

Ee.
Yes (that one).

Are wa depaato desu.
Oh, a department store.

Asoko ni wa Amerika no shokuryoohin nado mo arimasu ka?
Do they sell any American food?

Ikura ka arimasu.
Not much, but some.

Sore kara ima no depaato no tonari no tatemono wa nan desu ka?
What's that building next to the department store? [And then.. . .]

Shiyakusho desu. Sugu ushiro ni keisatsusho ga arimasu.
That is City Hall. The police station is right in back of it.

Kore wa zuibun ookii kusuriya desu ne.
Isn't that a big drugstore!

Ee, kore wa Amerikan Faamashii to itte Nippon no kusuri mo gaikoku no kusuri mo utte imasu.
Yes, this is called (the) American Pharmacy, and it carries both Japanese and foreign drugs.

Soo desu ka? Kono machi ni wa ii byooin ga arimasu ka?
Is that right? Is there a good hospital in this city?

Hai, ikutsu mo arimasu ga, ma, Daigaku Byooin ga ichiban ii deshoo.
Yes, there are quite a few of them, but—well—perhaps the best is the University Hospital.

Aa, soo desu ka.
Oh, I see.

Daigaku Byooin ni wa Eigo no yoku dekiru isha ga takusan imasu.
There are many doctors there who speak English well.

Soo desu ka? Doko ni aru n desu ka?
Is that right? Where is it?

Daigaku no koonai desu ga, koko o hashitte iru basu de iku to nijuppun gurai desu.
It's on the university campus. If you take the bus from here, you can get there in twenty minutes.

Kore wa rippa na hoteru desu ne.
This is a fine hotel, isn't it?

Soo desu nee. Gaikokujin wa taitei koko ni tomarimasu.
Yes. Foreigners usually stay here.

Haa. Sore kara eki wa doko desu ka?
Is that so? Then where is the railroad station?

Tsugi no kado o migi ni magatte kado hitotsu saki desu.
You turn right at the next corner. It's one block from there.

Aa, densha no jikokuhyoo ga hoshii n desu ga . . .
[Oh, (I remember).] I wanted to get a timetable.

E! Sore nara eki made ikanakute mo te ni hairimasu. Sono kado no hon'ya de utte imasu.
OK, if that's the case, you don't have to go to the station. You can buy [get hold of] (one) at the bookstore on the corner.

Densha no jikokuhyoo wa kau n desu ka?
So you have to pay for it, do you?

Ee, soo na n desu. Kono kuni de wa jikanhyoo wa kawanakereba narimasen.
That's right. In this country you have to buy train timetables.

Soo desu ka. Sore wa shirimasen deshita.
Oh, I see. I didn't know that.

Yuubinkyoku wa sugu soko desu ga, jikokuhyoo o kau no wa ima ni shimasu ka? Soretomo ato ni shimasu ka?
The post office is right there, but do you want to buy the timetable now or [otherwise] later?

Soo desu nee. Ato ni shimasu. Saki ni kakitome o dashite shimaitai desu kara.
Let me see. I'll buy it later. I would like to send registered mail first.

Aa, soo desu ka. Sore ja sugu ikimashoo.
Oh, I see. Then let's go right away.

Onegai itashimasu.
That'll be fine. (Yes, please.)

Kore ga yuubinkyoku desu.
This is the post office.

Zuibun konde imasu ne.
It's quite crowded, isn't it?

Kakitome no madoguchi wa hidari no hoo desu.
The registered mail window [window for registered mail] is to the left.

Aa, wakarimashita. Asoko desu ne.
Oh, yes. I see it. That's it, isn't it?

Soo desu. Watakushi[1] wa koko no benchi de omachi shimasu.
Right. I'll be waiting for you at the bench here.

Soo desu ka. Dewa onegai itashimasu.
Fine! I would appreciate that.

Goyukkuri doozo.
Don't hurry.

QUIZ 35

1. _____ (Don't mention it.)
    a. *Gomen kudasai.*
    b. *Doo itashimashite.*
    c. *Kashiko-marimashita.*

---

[1] Note the use of the formal *watakushi*.

2. _____ (The post office) *ni ikimashoo.*
   a. *Yuubinkyoku*
   b. *Shiyakusho*
   c. *Jimusho*

3. *Migi mo hidari mo* _____ (can't tell).
   a. *miemasen*
   b. *wakarimasen*
   c. *kakimasen*

4. *Kono machi ni wa* _____ (hospital) *ga arimasu ka?*
   a. *byooin*
   b. *byooki*
   c. *biyooin*

5. *Kono* _____ (street) *no namae wa nan to iimasu ka?*
   a. *machi*
   b. *michi*
   c. *uchi*

6. *Ano ookii* _____ (building) *wa nan desu ka?*
   a. *tabemono*
   b. *uchi*
   c. *tatemono*

7. *Depaato no* _____ (next) *ni Shiyakusho ga arimasu.*
   a. *tonari*
   b. *ushiro*
   c. *mae*

8. *Gaikokujin wa taitei kono hoteru ni* _____ (stay).
   a. *sumimasu*
   b. *yasumimasu*
   c. *tomarimasu*

9. _____ (Registered mail) *o dashite shimaitai desu.*
    a. *Denwa*
    b. *Densha*
    c. *Kakitome*

10. _____ (The station) *wa doko desu ka?*
    a. *Eki*
    b. *Densha*
    c. *Shiyakusho*

ANSWERS
1—b; 2—a; 3—b; 4—a; 5—b; 6—c; 7—a; 8—c; 9—c; 10—a.

LESSON 40

DAI YONJUKKA

A. THE MOST COMMON VERB FORMS

1. Plain forms:

	I EAT (VOWEL VERB)	I FINISH (CONSO- NANT VERB)	I COME (IRREGULAR	I DO VERBS)
PRESENT AFFIRMATIVE (DICT. FORM)	*taberu*	*owaru*	*kuru*	*suru*
-ta FORM (PAST)	*tabeta*	*owatta*	*kita*	*shita*
-te FORM (TENTATIVE)	*tabeyoo*	*owaroo*	*koyoo*	*shiyoo*

Verbs ending in *-eru* or *-iru,* with some exceptions, take all the forms listed above for *taberu.* For example:

hareru	the sky clears
atsumeru	gather (something)
hajimeru	start (something)
ochiru	fall

All other verbs, except *kuru* [come] and *suru* [do], which are irregular, are declined like *owaru.* For construction of the *-ta* forms, see Section 17, part 2, of the Summary of Japanese Grammar. For example:

agaru	rise
arau	wash
atsumaru	gather
hakaru	measure

2. Polite forms:

tabemasu	I eat (it). I'll eat (it).
tabemashita	I ate (it).
tabemashoo.	I think I'll eat (it). Let's eat (it).

owarimasu	I finish (it). I'll finish (it).
owarimashita	I finished (it).
owarimashoo	I think I'll finish (it). Let's finish (it).

kimasu	I come. I'll come.
kimashita	I came.
kimashoo.	I think I'll come. Let's come.

shimasu	I do (it). I'll do (it).
shimashita	I did (it).
shimashoo	I think I'll do (it). Let's do (it).

3. Future:

tabemasu	owarimasu	kimasu	shimasu
tabemashoo	owarimashoo	kimashoo	shimashoo
taberu	owaru	kuru	suru
deshoo	deshoo	deshoo	deshoo

Notice that the forms used to express the future vary. If the event under discussion is definite, then you use *-masu,* the same form used for the present. If it is not definite, then you use *-mashoo* or *-(r)u deshoo.* Use *-mashoo* when the speaker determines whether or not the event will take place. (Usually, the event will take place for the sake of the nonspeaker.) Use *-(r)u deshoo* when the determination of whether the event will take place does not depend on you. Compare the following forms:

Tabemasu.
- I shall eat it.
- I will eat it.
- I eat it.
- [Eating takes place definitely, in the present or the future.]

Tabemashoo.
- I think I'll eat it.
- Let's eat it.
- [(It)'s not definite but (I) think (I)'ll eat; (the choice) is up to me (us).]

Taberu deshoo.
- I think he will eat it.
- [(It)'s not definite, but he will probably eat it; it's not up to me.]

Denwa o kakemashoo.	Let's phone.
Kawaku deshoo.	It'll dry, I think.
Juppun de kawaki- **masu.**	It will dry in ten min-utes (definitely).
Koko ni oitara **nakunaru deshoo.**	If you leave it here, it will get lost (I think).
Sugu naoru deshoo.	He'll get well soon.
Tanaka-san ni tano- **mimashoo.**	Let's ask Ms. Tanaka to do it.
Yamada-san ga *tetsudau deshoo.*	Mr. Yamada will prob-ably help you.
Sonna ni hataraitara *tsukareru deshoo.*	If you work so hard, you will probably get tired.
Tsuzukemashoo.	Let's continue it.

4. Past:

tabe- *mashita* (from *taberu*)	*owari-* *mashita* (from *owaru*)	*ki-* *mashita* (from *kuru*)	*shi-* *mashita* (from *suru*)

The -*mashita* form expresses an action or state that is already completed, and in most cases, it is equivalent to the past and present perfect tenses in English. For example:

Tsutsumimashita.	I wrapped it up.
Ugokashimashita.	I moved it.
Ugokimashita.	It moved.
Urimashita.	I sold it.
Utaimashita.	I sang it.
Wakemashita.	I divided it.
Waraimashita.	I laughed.
Warimashita.	I broke it.

Watashimashita.	I handed it.
Yaburimashita.	I tore it.

5. I used to . . .

Tabeta mono deshita. *Tabeta mono desu.*	I used to eat it.
Owaraseta mono deshita. *Owaraseta mono desu.*	I used to finish it.
Kita mono deshita. *Kita mono desu.*	I used to come.
Shita mono deshita. *Shita mono desu.*	I used to do it.

Use the *-ta* form plus *mono deshita* (or *desu*) when referring to an action or state that used to take place but no longer does. For example:

Bikkuri shita mono deshita.	I used to be surprised.
Te de hakonda mono deshita.	I used to carry it by hand.
Maitoshi hikkoshita mono deshita.	I used to move every year.

6. I have . . .
(EXPERIENCE)

Tabeta koto ga arimasu.	I have eaten it.
Yonda koto ga arimasu.	I have read it.
Kita koto ga arimasu.	I have come.
Shita koto ga arimasu.	I have done it.

Most of the ideas expressed in English by the present perfect ("have" plus the past participle) are expressed in Japanese by the use of the *-mashita* form. However, when you intend to say that you have had the experience of doing something one or more times in the past, you must use the -ta form plus *koto ga arimasu,* as seen in the preceding examples, as well as in the following:

Eigo ni yakushita koto ga arimasu.	I [have] once translated it into English.
Eigo ni yakushima-shita.	I [have] translated it into English.
Tabako wa mae ni yameta koto ga ari-masu.	I have once before stopped [discontin-ued] smoking.
Sono koto ni tsuite shirabeta koto ga arimasu.	I have [once] made an investigation con-cerning that matter.

7. I had . . .

Kaite arimashita.	I had written it. [(It) had been written.]
Yonde arimashita.	I had read it. [(It) had been read.]
Kite imashita.	I had come.
Shite arimashita.	I had done it. [(It) had been done.]

In most cases the ideas expressed in English by the past perfect ("had" plus the past participle) can be expressed in Japanese by *-te arimashita* for transitive verbs and *-te imashita* for intransitive verbs. Note that in the case of transitive verbs, however, the object of the verb in Japanese becomes the subject in English. For example:

Kudamono wa katte arimashita.	I had purchased the fruit (when he ar-rived). [The fruit had been purchased . . .]

Hana wa moo chitte imashita.	The flowers had already fallen off (the trees when we went there).
Puroguramu wa moo hajimatte imashita.	The program had already started (when we arrived there).
Zaseki wa totte arimashita.	She had already taken the seats (for us when we arrived).

8. Commands and requests:

Each verb has a form called the "plain imperative," which is very brusque and is used almost exclusively in conversations between or among men. To form the plain imperative, add *-ro* to the base for vowel verbs and *-e* to the base for consonant verbs.

Tabero!	Eat!
Dete ike!	Leave!
Damare!	Shut up!
Koi![1]	Come!
Hayaku shiro![2]	Do it quickly!

Another command expression consists of the pre-*masu* form plus *nasai*. An adult will usually use this form when ordering a child to do something.

Soko e ikinasai.	Go there.
Heya o katazukenasai.	Tidy up the room.
Sugu nenasai.	Go to bed right away.

[1] Irregular: from *kuru*.
[2] Irregular: from *suru*.

Notice that an ordinary polite request ends in -*te kudasai* for the affirmative. An adult will usually use this form when ordering a child to do something.

Yomanaide kudasai.	Please don't read.
Tabenaide kudasai.	Please don't eat.

To construct an even more polite expression of request, you must prefix the pre-*masu* form of the verb with *o-* and add *kudasai* or *ni natte kudasai* for the affirmative. You can form the negative as described in the preceding paragraph.

Otori kudasai.	Take it, please.
Otori ni natte kudasai.	Take it, please (respect).
Otori ni naranaide kudasai.	Please do not take it (respect).
Tetsudatte kudasai.	Please help me! [Give a hand, please.]
Moo sukoshi motte kite kudasai.	Bring me some more, please.
Watakushi no tokoro e motte kite kudasai.	Bring it to me, please. [Bring it to my place, please.]
Tomatte kudasai!	Stop, please!
Sugu tomatte kudasai!	Stop right here, please!
Sono hito o tomete kudasai!	Stop him, please!
Koshikakete kudasai.⎱ *Okoshikake kudasai.*⎰	Sit down./Have a seat, please.
Shinjite kudasai.	Please believe me!
Kiite kudasai.	Please listen.
Watakushi no iu koto o kiite kudasai.	Listen to me. [Listen to what I say, please.]

Kore o kiite kudasai.	Listen to this, please.
Chuui shite kiite kudasai.	Listen carefully, please.
Kare no iu koto o kiite kudasai.	Listen to him, please.
Kare no iu koto o kikanaide kudasai.	Please don't listen to him.
Haitte kudasai.	Please come in! Please enter!
Ohairi kudasai.	Come in. Enter, please.
Kare no tokoro e okutte kudasai.	Send it to him, please.
Watakushi no tokoro e okutte kudasai.	Send them (it) to me, please.
Kare no tokoro e ikuraka okutte kudasai.	Send him some, please.
Watakushi no tokoro e ikuraka okutte kudasai.	Send me some, please.
Tameshite kudasai.	Please try. [Please check!]
Tamesanaide kudasai.	Please don't try (it)!
Tabete mite kudasai.	Please try eating it.
Yonde mite kudasai.	Please try reading it.
Kao o aratte kudasai.	Please wash yourself [wash your face]!
Tatte kudasai.	Please stand up! Please get up!
Otachi kudasai.	Please stand up. Kindly rise.
Yonde kudasai.	Please read that!
Watakushi o soko e tsurete itte kudasai.	Please take me there!
Moo hitotsu otori kudasai.	Please take another one. [Please take one more.]

Densha de itte kudasai.	Please take the train. [Please go by train.]
Densha de oide kudasai.	Please take the train. [Please go by train.] *(respect)*
Takushii de itte kudasai.	Take a taxi, please.
Mite kudasai.	Please look!
Goran ni natte kudasai.	Please look *(respect)!*
Moo ichido mite kudasai.	Please look again!
Koko o mite kudasai.	Please look here!
Watashi o mite kudasai.	Please look at me!
Kore o mite kudasai.	Please look at this!
Minaide kudasai.	Please don't look.
Goran ni naranaide kudasai.	Please don't look *(respect).*
Kaeshite kudasai.	Please return it to me.
Okaeshi ni natte kudasai.	Please return it to me *(respect).*
Soko o agatte kudasai.	Go up there, please.
Misete kudasai.	Please show me!
Misenaide kudasai.	Please don't show it!
Wasurenaide kudasai.	Please don't forget.
Dete itte kudasai.	Please leave!
Sugu dete itte kudasai.	Please leave quickly! Please go right away!
Dete ikanaide kudasai.	Please don't leave!
Kore o asoko e motte itte kudasai.	Carry this over there, please.
Totte kudasai.	Take it, please.
Otori kudasai.	Please take it.
Toranaide kudasai.	Please don't take it.
Otori ni naranaide kudasai.	Please don't take it *(respect).*
Uchi e kaette kudasai.	Please go home!

Hayaku uchi e kaette kudasai.	Please go home early!
Moo ichido itte kudasai.	Please say it again.
Moo ichido osshatte kudasai.	Please say it again *(respect).*
Ite kudasai.	Please stay.
Koko ni ite kudasai.	Please stay here.
Shizuka ni shite kudasai.	Please be quiet.
Ugokanaide kudasai.	Please be still. Please don't move.
Tsuite kite kudasai.	Please follow. Please follow me.
Kare ni tsuite itte kudasai.	Please follow him.
Sawaranaide kudasai.	Please don't touch!
Koohii o tsuide kudasai.	Please pour me some coffee.

B. *KYUUYUU TO NO SAIKAI:* MEETING AN OLD FRIEND

Study the notes at the end of this section for greater comprehension.

1. Y: **Zuibun hisashiburi desu ne? Ogenki desu ka?**
   Y: Well! (Long time no see!) How are you?

2. S: **Okage sama de. Otaku wa?**
   S: Fine, thanks. (And) you and your family?

3. Y: **Arigatoo. Minna genki desu. Nagai goryokoo de otsukare deshoo.**
   Y: Thanks, we're all well. (You're) not too tired from your trip?

4. S: **Iya. Betsu ni.**
   S: Not at all.

5. Y: **A! Kanai o goshookai shimashoo.**
   Y: [Oh, yes.] I'd like you to meet my wife.

6. S: **Doozo.**
   S: I'd be very happy to.

7. Y: **Kochira wa Satoo-san.**
   Y: This is (my friend) Sato.

8. S: **Hajimemashite. Doozo yoroshiku.**
   S: I am very happy to know you.

9. Mrs. Y: **Kochira koso.**
   Mrs. Y: Glad to know you.

10. S: **Yaa. Hisashiburi de yukai desu ne.**
    S: Yes, indeed. It's really good to see you again.

11. Y: **Yaa. Mattaku dookan desu. Tokorode Satoo-san anata wa chitto mo kawarimasen ne.**
    Y: Yes, indeed. By the way, you haven't changed a bit.

12. S: **Iyaa. Sono ten ja anata mo sukoshi mo kawatte imasen yo.**
    S: Neither have you. [No, in that respect you haven't changed a bit.]

13. Mrs. Y: **Okusama wa Amerika no goseikatsu o otanoshimi desu ka?**
    Mrs. Y: How does your wife like the United States?

14. S: **Ee. Hijoo ni tanoshinde orimasu.**
    S: [Yes.] She likes it a lot.

15. Mrs. Y: **Achira wa Tookyoo to wa daibu chigau no deshoo ne?**
    Mrs. Y: It must be very different from Tokyo.

16. S: **Tashika ni chigau tokoro wa arimasu ne.**
    S: There certainly are lots of different things in the United States!

17. Mrs. Y: **Tatoeba doo iu tokoro nan desu no?**
    Mrs. Y: For example?

18. S: **Tatoeba desu ne, soo, kusuriya de shokuji o suru nado to itte mo chotto gosoozoo ni narenai deshoo? Doraggu sutoa dewa omocha to ka, kitte to ka, tabako to ka okashi no yoo na mono made mo utteru n desu.**
    S: For example [so, (here is a good one)], it certainly wouldn't occur to you to have a meal in a pharmacy. You also find many other things in a drugstore: toys, stamps, cigarettes, candy . . .

19. Y: **Hoo . . . ! Kawatte iru n desu ne?**
    Y: Hmm! That's really very funny.

20. S: **Mada sono ue ni hon mo aru, bunboogu mo aru, daidokoro yoohin mo aru, keshoohin mo aru, maa, nani mo ka mo aru to itta katachi desu yo.**
    S: On top of that, books, stationery, cooking utensils, cosmetics, and what have you.

21. Y: **Hmm! Ma, yorozuya to iu wake desu ne.**
    Y: Hmm. [So to speak] it's a general store, then?

22. S: **Ee, demo kusuri wa chan to utteru n desu yo.**
     S: Yes, but it's (still) a pharmacy!

NOTE

Title: *Kyuuyuu to no Saikai* = Meeting an Old Friend
  1. *Hisashiburi desu* = It has been a long time since
      (I saw you last).
  2. *Otaku wa* = your family, you.
  3. *Goryokoo de* = on account of a trip.
      Otsukare deshoo = You must be tired.
  4. *Iya* (same as *iie*) = no.
      Betsu ni = (not) especially.
  7. *Satoo-san:* Note the use of *san* in spite of the fact
      that Sato is Yamada's old friend. Adding a *san* is
      a common practice regardless of the extent of the
      friendship. The first name is not usually men-
      tioned in a situation like this.
 11. *Mattaku dookan desu* = I'm in complete agree-
      ment with you. [The] same here.
      Tokorode = by the way.
      Satoo-san: Notice the use of the surname of the
      person with whom you are speaking.
      Kawarimasen = (you) don't change.
 12. *Kawatte imasen* = You haven't changed. [You
      are not in the state of having changed.]
 13. *Tanoshimu* = enjoy; *otanoshimi desu:* o plus the
      pre-*masu* form plus *desu*, a respect expression.
 17. *Tatoeba* = for instance.
 18. *Desu ne* = a meaningless expression similar to
      the American phrase "you know."
      Gosoozoo ni narenai = You cannot imagine
      (respect); nareru = potential form derived from
      the consonant verb *naru*.
      . . . *to ka* . . . *to ka* . . . *to ka* (comparable to . . .
      ya . . . *ya* . . . *ya*) = and . . . and . . . and (with the
      implication that the listing is incomplete).

19. *Kawatte iru* = is different.
20. *Sono ue ni* = on top of that.
    Nani mo ka mo = and what have you; everything.
21. *To iu wake desu* = it amounts to saying; it means.
    Yorozuya = ten-thousand-variety shop; general store.

QUIZ 36

1. _____ (Long time no see) *desu ne.*
    a. *Omoshiroi*
    b. *Atatakai*
    c. *Hisashiburi*

2. _____ (Fine, thanks) *sama de.*
    a. *Oki no doku*
    b. *Okage*
    c. *Omachidoo*

3. *Nagai goryokoo de* _____ (tired) *deshoo.*
    a. *omoshirokatta*
    b. *otanoshimi*
    c. *otsukare*

4. _____ (Wife) *o goshookai shimashoo.*
    a. *Kanai*
    b. *Kodomo*
    c. *Tomodachi*

5. *Hisashiburi de* _____ (pleasure) *desu ne.*
    a. *arigatai*
    b. *yukai*
    c. *saiwai*

6. _____ (Not at all) *kawarimasen ne.*
    a. *Anmari*
    b. *Sukoshi shika*
    c. *Chitto mo*

ANSWERS
1—c; 2—b; 3—c; 4—a; 5—b; 6—c.

C. THE MOST COMMON VERBS AND VERB PHRASES

1. *Miru:* To see

PLAIN	POLITE[1]	
miru	*mimasu*	I see
mita	*mimashita*	I saw
mite	*mite*	I see (saw) and . . .
miyoo	*mimashoo*	let's see
minai	*mimasen*	I don't see
Mimashoo.		Let's see. Let's take a look.
Mimasen.		I don't see.
Nan de mo mi-masu.		I see every-thing.

Notice that *miru* means "to see" only in the sense of perceiving by the eye. Study the following:

Nikko Tooshooguu o mita koto ga arimasu ka?	Have you ever seen the Nikko Shrine?
Yamada-san ni atta[2] koto ga arimasu ka?	Have you ever seen Mr. Yamada?
Ima atta bakari desu.	I've just seen him.
Watashi wa eiga o mimasen.	I don't go to the mov-ies. [I don't see movies.]

[1] In the verb forms that follow, the plain form is given in the first column, the polite form in the second column.
[2] *au* = see (meet).

Anata no iu koto ga wakarimasen.[1]		I don't see what you mean.
Donata ni oai ni narimasu ka?		Who do you see?
Ima atte itadakemasu ka?		Can you see me now *(humble)?* [Can (I) have (you) see me now?]
Itsu ka yoru asobi ni kite kudasai.[2]		Please come to see us some night.

2. *Shitte iru:* To know
   Shiru: To learn, to get to know

shitte iru	*shitte imasu*	I know
shitte ita	*shitte imashita*	I knew
shitte ite	*shitte ite*	I know (knew) and . . .
shiranai	*shirimasen*	I don't know
shiru	*shirimasu*	I learn
shitta	*shirimashita*	I learned
shitte	*shitte*	I learn (learned) and . . .
shiroo	*shirimashoo*	let's learn
shiranai	*shirimasen*	I don't know

Shitte imasu.	I know it. [I'm in the state of having learned it.]
Shirimasen.	I don't know. [I haven't learned.]
Yoku shitte imasu.	I know it well.

[1] *wakaru* = see (understand).
[2] *asobi ni kuru* = come to see (visit).

Nani mo shirimasen.	He doesn't know anything.
Sono koto ni tsuite wa nani mo shirimasen.	I don't know anything about it.
Koko ni iru koto o shitte imasu.	I know that he is here. [I know the fact that he is here.]
Sore o shitte imasu ka?	Do you know that?
Doko ni iru ka shitte imasu ka?	Do you know where she is?
Sono koto ni tsuite wa kore ijoo shirimasen.	She doesn't know any more [than this] about it.
Sono koto ni tsuite wa anata ga shitte iru yoo ni wa shirimasen.	She doesn't know any more about it than you do [know].
Sono koto wa shinbun de shirimashita.	I learned (of) it through the newspaper.

3. *Motsu:* To hold

motsu	*mochimasu*	I hold
motta	*mochimashita*	I held
motte	*motte*	I hold (held) and . . .
motoo	*mochimashoo*	I think I'll hold, let's hold
motanai	*mochimasen*	I don't hold

Kore o chotto motte kudasai.	Hold this for me a moment, please.
Te ni booshi o motte imasu.	He's holding a hat in his hand.

Ima wa motte imasu.	I have it now.
Shikkari motte kudasai.	Hold firm, please.

Notice that the ideas expressed by the English words "have" and "possess" are expressed in Japanese by using the *-te* form of the verb *motsu* [to hold] plus *imasu*. See Lesson 14, as well. Compare the following:

Okane wa ikura motte imasu ka?	How much money do you have?
Nisen en motte imasu.	I have two thousand yen.
Sore wa omosugimasu kara hitori de motsu koto wa dekimasen.	It's too heavy, [and] so I can't hold it alone.

Notice also that the ideas expressed in English by "take (to)," "bring," and "carry around," are expressed in Japanese by using the *-te* form of the verb *motsu* together with the verb *iku* [go], *kuru* [come], *aruku* [walk]. Compare the following:

Kasa o motte itte kudasai.	Please take your umbrella (with you).
Kasa o motte kite kudasai.	Please bring over (your) umbrella.
Ano hito wa itsu mo kasa o motte arukimasu.	He always carries his umbrella around.

4. *Dekiru:* To be able

dekiru	*dekimasu*	I can
dekita	*dekimashita*	I could
dekite	*dekite*	I can (could) and . . .
dekinai	*dekimasen*	I can't

Oodaa suru koto ga dekimasu.	I can order it.
Kuru koto ga dekimasu ka?	Can you come?
Sono shitsumon ni wa kotaeru koto ga dekimasen.	I can't answer the question.
Soko e iku koto ga dekimasen.	I can't go there.
Itsu deru koto ga dekimasu ka?	When can we leave?
Tetsudatte itadakemasuka?	Can you help me?

The idea "to be able to (do something)" or "can (do something)" can be expressed in several ways. The most common is to use a dictionary form plus *koto ga dekiru*, as demonstrated above. Another way is to use a derived potential verb as follows:

    a. For consonant verbs:
        Drop the final *-u* of the dictionary form and add *-eru*. The resulting form is a vowel verb that means "capable of doing something."

CONSONANT VERB		DERIVED POTENTIAL VERB	
iku	go	*ikeru*	can go
kau	buy	*kaeru*	can buy
hanasu	speak	*hanaseru*	can speak

Ashita ikemasu ka?	Can you go tomorrow?
Seibu de kaemasu ka?	Can you buy it at Seibu's (department store)?

    b. For vowel verbs:
        Drop the final *-eru* or *-iru* and add *-rareru* in its place.

VOWEL VERB	DERIVED POTENTIAL VERB	
taberu	*taberareru*	can eat
miru	*mirareru*	can see
okiru	*okirareru*	can get up

Kore wa nama de tabe- — Can we eat this raw?
raremasu ka?

Nara e iku to furui — If you go to the city of
tatemono ga takusan — Nara, you can see
miraremasu. — many ancient build-
ings.

c. For irregular verbs:

IRREGULAR VERB	DERIVED POTENTIAL VERB	
kuru	*korareru*	can come
suru	*dekiru*	can do

Koko e sugu — Can you come
koraremasu ka? — here right away?

Konnan nashi — You can do it with-
ni dekimasu. — out any difficulty.

5. *Wakaru:* To understand

wakaru	*wakarimasu*	I understand
wakatta	*wakarimashita*	I understood
wakatte	*wakatte*	I understand (understood) and . . .
wakaranai	*wakarimasen*	I don't understand

Ano hito wa kore ga — He doesn't understand
wakarimasen. — this.

Yoku wakarimasu. — I understand very well.

Watashi no iu koto ga wakarimasu ka?	Do you understand me [what (I) say]?
Watashi no iu koto ga wakarimasen ka?	Don't you understand me?
Wakarimasu ka?	Do you understand?
Nihongo ga wakarimasu ka?	Do you understand Japanese?
Eigo ga wakarimasu ka?	Do you understand English?
Ano hito ga anata ni itte iru koto ga minna wakarimasu ka?	Do you understand everything he's saying to you?
Wakarimasen.	I don't understand.
Wakarimashita ka?	Did you understand?
Watashi no iu koto ga wakatte morae-masen.	I can't make myself understood. [(I) can't have what (I) say understood.]
Ano hito wa shoobai no koto wa sukoshi mo wakarimasen.	He doesn't understand [not a bit] about business.
Zenzen wakarimasen. *Kaimoku wakari-masen.* *Sukoshi mo wakari-masen.*	I don't understand it at all. I don't understand anything about it. It's a mystery to me. I'm completely in the dark.

6. *Oku:* To put, to place

oku	*okimasu*	I put
oita	*okimashita*	I put *(past)*
oite	*oite*	I put and . . .
okoo	*okimashoo*	I think I'll put, let's put
okanai	*okimasen*	I don't put

Soko ni oite kudasai.	Put it there, please.
Doko ni okimashita ka?	Where did you put it?
Kare wa jibun de mono o oita tokoro o sugu wasuremasu.	He never knows where he puts (his) things. [He forgets right away the place where he has put (his) things himself.]

You use *oku* when you are talking about "putting" or "placing" a thing somewhere. To express the thought of "putting on" apparel, you may use several different words. For example:

kaburu	to put on one's head; to put a thing over one's head
Booshi o kabutte kudasai.	Put your hat on, please.
kiru	to wear on the body
Nihon no kimono o kimashita.	She wore a Japanese kimono.
haku	to wear on the foot or leg
Kuroi kutsu o haite ikimashita.	He was wearing black shoes (when) he went.

When *oku* follows another verb using the -*te* form, it implies that the action of the verb preceding *oku* takes place in anticipation of some future situation. For example:

Sono koto wa Yamada-san ni denwa de shirasete okimashita.[1]	I [have] notified Mr. Yamada in advance over the telephone.

[1] The statement implies, "I have the intention of explaining it in detail when I see him, but for now . . ."

Konshuu wa Doyoobi ni kaimono ga deki-nai node Suiyoobi ni kaimono o shite oki-mashita.

Since I can't do any shopping on Saturday this week, I did the shopping on Wednesday.

7. *Kuru:* To come

kuru	*kimasu*	I come
kita	*kimashita*	I came
kite	*kite*	I come and . . .
koyoo	*kimashoo*	I think I'll come, let's come
konai	*kimasen*	I don't come

Hitori de kimashita.

I came alone. I came by myself.

Hitori de kuru deshoo.

I think she is coming alone.

Moo kite imasu.

He is already here. [He is in the state of having come already.]

Sanji made ni kona-kattara saki ni iki-mashoo.

If he doesn't come by three, let's go ahead of him.

8. *Matsu:* To wait

matsu	*machimasu*	I wait
matta	*machimashita*	I waited
matte	*matte*	I wait (waited) and . . .
matoo	*machimashoo*	I think I'll wait, let's wait
matanai	*machimasen*	I don't wait

Koko de matte kudasai.	Wait here, please.
Watashi o matte kudasai.	Wait for me, please.
Sukoshi matte kudasai.	Wait a little, please.
Chotto matte kudasai.	Wait a minute, please.
Matanaide kudasai.	Don't wait, please.
Kanojo o matte imasu.	I'm waiting for her.
Hoka no hitotachi o matte iru no desu.	She is waiting for the others.
Dare o matte iru no desu ka?	Who are you waiting for?
Naze matte iru no desu ka?	Why are you waiting?
Matasete[1] *sumimasen deshita.* *Omachidoo sama deshita.*	I'm sorry I kept you waiting. [I caused you to wait; I'm sorry.]

9. *Kiku:* To ask

Asoko de kiite kudasai.	Ask over there, please.
Asoko de kare no koto o kiite kudasai.	Ask about him over there, please.
Nani o kiite iru no desu ka?	What's she asking?
Michi ga wakaranaku nattara hito ni kiite kudasai.	Please ask the way if you get lost.
Kare ni jikan o kiite kudasai.	Ask him the time, please.
Kiite kite kudasai.	Please go and ask him. [Please ask and come back (to this place).]

[1] *matsu* plus *-aseru* (causative ending) = *mataseru:* cause someone to wait, make (have, let) someone wait.

Dare ka watashi no koto o kiitara sugu kaette kuru to itte kudasai.		If someone asks for me [please tell him that], I'll be back in a moment.
Doko ni aru ka kikimashita.		She asked where it is.
Denwa o kakete kiite kudasai.		Call her on the phone [and ask], please.

10. -*Tai*: To want to (do something)

Ikitai.	*Ikitai desu.*	I want to go.
Ikitakatta.	*Ikitakatta desu.*	I wanted to go.
Ikitakute . . .	*Ikitakute . . .*	I want (wanted) to go and . . .
Ikitai daroo.	*Ikitai deshoo.*	I suppose he wants to go.
Ikitaku nai.	*Ikitaku nai desu.*	I don't want to go.

Kaitai desu.	I want to buy it.
Nani mo kaitaku arimasen.	I don't want to buy anything.
Dekiru no desu ga shitaku nai no desu.	He can do it, but he doesn't want to.
Kaeritai no desu ka?	Does she want to return?
Watashitachi to issho ni ikitai[1] desu ka?	Do you want to come with us?

[1] Notice the use of *iku* (going away from where we are now).

Notice that the expression *-tai desu* is used when you want to do something. When you want to have or get something, you instead use *hoshii desu*. For example:

Hoshii desu.	I want it.
Hoshiku nai desu. } *Hoshiku arimasen.* }	I don't want it.
Nani mo hoshiku arimasen.	I don't want anything.
Sukoshi hoshii desu.	I want some.
Nani ga hoshii desu ka?	What do you want?

For *-tai desu* and *hoshii desu,* see Lessons 29 and 33.

11. *-(A)nakereba narimasen:* To have to

PLAIN PRESENT NEGATIVE	→	-BA FORM	→	HAVE TO
ikanai	don't go	*ikanake-reba*		*ikanakereba narimasen*
tabenai	don't eat	*tabenake-reba*		*tabenakereba narimasen*
konai	don't come	*konake-reba*		*konakereba narimasen*
shinai	don't do	*shinake-reba*		*shinakereba narimasen*

See Lessons 27, 33, and Section 28 of the Summary of Japanese Grammar.

Ikanakereba narimasen.	I must go.
Konakereba narimasen.	He should (has to) come.
Koko ni inakereba narimasen.	She should (has to) be here.

Karera wa soko ni inakereba narimasen.	They have to be there.
Soko e ikanakereba narimasen ka?	Do you have to go there?
Watashi wa nani o shinakereba naranai no desu ka?	What do I have to do?
Ikura okaeshi shinakereba naranai no desu ka?	How much do I owe you?
Nani mo harawanakute ii desu.	You don't owe me anything. [You need not pay anything.]
Kyoo wa konakute mo ii desu.	You don't have to come today.

Notice that the idea of "don't have to" or "need not" is expressed by a sequence quite different from that for "have to" or "need to":

PLAIN PRESENT NEGATIVE	→	-TE FORM	→	DON'T HAVE TO
ikanai	don't go	*ikanakute*		*ikanakute mo[1] ii desu*
tabenai	don't eat	*tabenakute*		*tabenakute mo ii desu*
konai	don't come	*konakute*		*konakute mo ii desu*
shinai	don't do	*shinakute*		*shinakute mo ii desu*

[1] The use of *mo* is optional.

12. *Suki desu:* To love, to like (something)

Anata wa ano hito ga suki desu ka?	Do you like him (her)?
Sore wa suki ja arimasen.	I don't like it.
Moo hitotsu no hoo ga suki desu.	I like the other better.
-koto ga suki desu	to love, to like to do (something)
Sanpo suru koto ga suki desu.	I love to [take a] walk.
Gaikokugo o narau koto ga suki desu.	I like to learn foreign languages.
Kuruma de ryokoo suru koto ga suki desu.	I like to travel by car.

For *suki desu,* see Lesson 31, as well.

13. *-(R)areru:*

    a. For the passive (to be, to get plus a past participle)
    b. For the potential (to be able to)
    c. Respect

CONSONANT VERB		→	PASSIVE, POLITE (RESPECT)
kaku	write		*kakareru*
yomu	read		*yomareru*

VOWEL VERB			
tomeru	stop		tomerareru
okiru	get up		okirareru

IRREGULAR VERB			
kuru	come		korareru
suru	do		sareru

For potential verbs, see Section C-4 of Lesson 40.

(1) Passive:

Keikan ni tomerare-mashita.	I was stopped by a policeman.
Watakushi wa Yamada-san ni Tanaka-san to machigaerare-mashita.	I was mistaken by Mr. Yamada for Ms. Tanaka.
Iriguchi de namae o kikaremashita.	I was asked my name at the entrance. [At the entrance, I was asked to state my name.]
Ame ni furaremashita.	We were caught in the rain. [We underwent the falling of the rain.]

Notice that the agent of the action is designated by the particle *-ni,* and the person who is affected by the action of the verb is marked with *wa* or *ga.*

(2) Potential:

Ano hito wa gorufu ga suki de yamerare-masen.	He likes golf and can't stop (playing) it.
Okane ga nai node tsuzukeraremasen.	As I do not have (enough) money, I can't continue it.
Kippu no nai hito wa toosemasen.	We can't admit [pass] persons who have no tickets.

Toshokan ga shimatte   The library is closed,
   iru node shiraberare-   so I can't check it out.
   masen.

Kore wa anmari hidoku   This has been damaged
   kowareta node moo   so badly that we can't
   naosemasen.   repair it any longer.

(3) Respect:

Note that all of the following sentences are spoken very politely.

Sensei wa itsu kaette   When is the teacher
   koraremasu ka?   coming back?

Yamada-sensei[1] wa   Mr. Yamada, the
   Kyooto ni ryokoo   teacher, traveled to
   saremashita.   Kyoto.

Yoshino-san wa   Mr. Yoshino died last
   sakunen nakuna-   year.
   raremashita.

Tanaka-san wa sono   Mr. Tanaka refused
   tanomi o kotowarare   that request.
   mashita.

Satoo-san wa sugu   Mr. Sato phoned Ms.
   Shigeta-san ni denwa   Shigeta right away.
   o kakeraremashita.

14. **-(S)aseru:** To make (have, let, allow, force) one to (do something)—causative

CONSONANT VERB		→	CAUSATIVE
iku	go		*ikaseru*
tobu	fly		*tobaseru*

[1] *sensei:* teacher, sir [one who was born earlier]. *Yamada-sensei:* Mr. Yamada (said with great respect).

VOWEL VERB

taberu	eat	*tabesaseru*
oshieru	teach	*oshiesaseru*

IRREGULAR VERB

kuru	come	*kosaseru*
suru	do	*saseru*

Kodomo ni erabase-mashita.	I had the child choose them.
Musume ni nimotsu o hakobasemashita.	I had my daughter carry the baggage.
Kyoo wa sanji ni uchi e kaerasete kudasai.	Please let me go home at three o'clock.
Sono tegami o watakushi ni yoma-sete kudasai.	Please let me read that letter.
Kono kusuri o yojikan oki ni nomasete ku-dasai.	Please have him take this medicine every four hours.

QUIZ 37

1. *Misete kudasai.*	a. Please look at this.
2. *Ohairi kudasai.*	b. Please look here.
3. *Wasurenaide kuda-sai.*	c. Please take the train.
4. *Moo ichido itte kudasai.*	d. Please take another one.
5. *Matte kudasai.*	e. Please take it.
6. *Otori kudasai.*	f. Please wait.
7. *Densha de itte ku-dasai.*	g. Please don't forget.
8. *Moo hitotsu otori kudasai.*	h. Say it again, please.

9. *Koko o mite ku-*   i. Come in, please.
   dasai.

10. *Kore o mite kuda-*   j. Show me, please.
    sai.

ANSWERS
1—j; 2—i; 3—g; 4—h; 5—f; 6—e; 7—c; 8—d;
9—b; 10—a.

D. Public Notices and Signs

Oshirase	Notice	お知らせ
Dansei, Shinshi	Gentlemen	男性、紳士
Josei, Fujin	Ladies	女性、婦人
Toire, (O)tearai	Restroom	トイレ、(お)手洗い
Dansei(yoo) toire	Men's Room	男性(用)トイレ
Josei(yoo) toire	Ladies' Room	女性(用)トイレ
Kin'en, Otabako wa goenryo kudasai	No Smoking	禁煙 お煙草はご遠慮下さい
Eigyoochuu	Open	営業中
(Honjitsu) heiten	Closed (Today)	(本日)閉店
(Honjitsu) kyuugyoo	Closed (Today)	(本日)休業
Iriguchi	Entrance	入口
Deguchi	Exit	出口
Hijooguchi	Emergency Exit	非常口
Erebeetaa	Elevator	エレベーター
Ikkai	First Floor	一階
Osu	Push	押す

Mawasu	Turn	回す
Beru o narashite kudasai	Please Ring	ベルを鳴らして下さい
Tachiiri kinshi	Keep Out!	立入禁止
Tsuukoo kinshi	No Thoroughfare!	通行禁止
Ohairi kudasai	Come In	お入り下さい
Nokku muyoo	No Need to Knock	ノック無用
Nokku o shinaide ohairi kudasai	Enter Without Knocking	ノックをしないで お入り下さい
Nokku o shite kudasai	Knock	ノックをして下さい
Nokku o shite kara ohairi kudasai	Knock Before Entering	ノックをしてから お入り下さい
Kaisoo ni tsuki Kyuugyoo	Closed for Repair	改装につき休業
Shinsoo kaiten	Under New Management	新装開店
Nyuujoo okotowari	No Admittance	入場お断り
Kinjitsu kaiten	Will Open Soon	近日開店
Shuuya eigyoo	Open All Night	終夜営業
Gamu o sutenaide kudasai	Don't Throw Gum	ガムを捨てないで 下さい
Kutsu o onugi kudasai / *Dosoku genkin* }	Take Your Shoes Off	靴をお脱ぎ下さい / 土足厳禁
Surippa ni ohakikae kudasai	Change to Slippers	スリッパに履き替えて 下さい

Inu o hana- sanaide kudasai	Don't Let Your Dog Run Loose	犬を放さないで下さい
Inu o kusari ni tsunaide kudasai	Leash Your Dog	犬を鎖につないで 下さい
Hokoosha senyoo	Pedestrians Only	歩行者専用
Hokoosha tsuukoo kinshi	Pedestrians Keep Out	歩行者通行禁止
Jitensha senyoo	Bicycles Only	自転車専用
Jitensha tsuukoo kinshi	Bicycles Keep Out	自転車通行禁止
Kujoo soodan Madoguchi	Complaint Department	苦情相談窓口
Uketsuke	Reception Desk	受付
Ryoogaejo	Money Exchange Counter	両替所
Madoguchi de omooshikomi kudasai	Apply at the Window	窓口でお申し込み 下さい
Urimasu	For Sale	売ります
Chintai itashimasu	For Rent	賃貸いたします
Kashi apaato kagu nashi	Unfurnished Apartment For Rent	貸しアパート家具なし
Kashi apaato kagu tsuki	Furnished Apartment For Rent	貸しアパート家具付
Waribiki	Reduced	割引

Tokka	Special	特価
Oouridashi	Big Sale	大売出し
Keitaihin Azukarijo	Check Room, Cloak Room	携帯品預かり所
Yoomuinshitsu	Janitor's Room	用務員室
Kanrininshitsu	Superintendent's Office	管理人室
Ukai	Detour	迂回
Koojichuu	Under Construction	工事中
Kaabu kiken	Dangerous Curve	カーブ危険
Chuusha kinshi	No Parking	駐車禁止
Ippoo tsuukoo	One-Way Street	一方通行
Senro o yokogiranaide kudasai	Don't Cross Tracks	線路を横切らないで下さい
Senro oodan kinshi		線路横断禁止
Fumikiri	Railroad Crossing	踏切
Tetsudo	Railroad	鉄道
Gaado	Underpass/Overpass	ガード
Tomare	Stop!	止まれ！
Chuui	Caution!	注意！
Oodanhodoo	Pedestrian Crossing	横断歩道
Koosaten	Crossroads	交差点
Basu tei	Bus Stop	バス停
Basu teiryuujo	Bus Stop	バス停留所
Harigami kinshi	Post No Bills	張紙禁止

Jisoku sanjuk-kiro ika	Speed Limit 30 K.P.H.	時速30キロ以下
Jokoo	Go Slow	徐行
Gakkoo kuiki jokoo	School—Go Slow	学校区域徐行
Kiken, Abunai	Danger!	危険！危ない！
Penki nuri-tate	Fresh Paint	ペンキ塗りたて
Mado kara kao ya te o dasanaide kudasai	Don't Lean Out of the Window!	窓から顔や手を出さないで下さい
Keihooki	Alarm Signal	警報機
Kooatsusen chuui	High Voltage	高圧線注意
Chikatetsu iriguchi	Subway Entrance	地下鉄入口
Tenimotsu ichiji azukarijo	Baggage Room, Check Room	手荷物一時預り所
Machiaishitsu	Waiting Room	待合室
Ittoo	First Class	一等
Nitoo	Second Class	二等
Santoo	Third Class	三等
Toochaku	Arrival	到着
Hassha	Departure (Trains, Buses)	発車
Purattohoomu, Hoomu	Platform	プラットホーム、ホーム
Annaijo	Information	案内所
Yuubinkyoku	Post Office	郵便局
Posuto	Mailbox	ポスト
Nyuujooken uriba } *Kippu uriba* }	Ticket Office	入場券売場 切符売場

Kasaihoochiki	Fire Alarm Box	火災報知器
Kooritsu tosho-kan	Public Library	公立図書館
Keisatsusho	Police Station	警察署
Gasorin sutando	Gas Station	ガソリンスタンド
Shoten, Hon'ya	Bookstore	書店、本屋
Shiyakusho	City Hall	市役所
Rihatsuten	Barber Shop	理髪店
Biyooin	Beauty Shop	美容院
Ishi	Physician	医師
Iin	Physician's Office	医院
Byooin	Hospital	病院
Shika	Dentistry	歯科
Kutsu shuuri	Shoe Repair	靴修理
Machinee	Matinee	マチネー
Yoru no bu hachiji sanjuppun kaien	Evening Performance at 8:30	夜の部 8時30分開演
Seisoo chakuyoo	Formal Dress	正装着用
Heifukku chakuyoo	Informal Dress	平服着用
Renzoku kooen	Continuous Performance	連続公演
Puroguramu henkoo	Change of Program	プログラム変更
Bangumi henkoo	Change of (TV) Program	番組変更
Enmoku henkoo	Change of Performance	演目変更
Kissaten	Coffee Shop	喫茶店

FINAL REVIEW QUIZ

1. _____ (Fine) *desu ka?*
   a. *Ikura*
   b. *Ogenki*
   c. *Itsu*

2. *Yukkuri* _____ (speak) *kudasai.*
   a. *hanashite*
   b. *kaite*
   c. *tabete*

3. *Tabako ga* _____ (have) *ka?*
   a. *hoshii desu*
   b. *kaitai desu*
   c. *arimasu*

4. *Menyuu o* _____ (show me) *kudasai.*
   a. *misete*
   b. *totte*
   c. *motte kite*

5. *Koohii o ippai* _____ (give me).
   a. *nomimashita*
   b. *kudasai*
   c. *agemashita*

6. _____ (Breakfast) *wa hachiji ni tabemashita.*
   a. *Yuuhan*
   b. *Asagohan*
   c. *Hirugohan*

7. *Supuun o* _____ (bring).
   a. *motte itte kudasai*
   b. *motte kite kudasai*
   c. *motte kudasai*

8. _____ (Station) *wa doko ni arimasu ka?*
   a. *Denwa*
   b. *Eki*
   c. *Yuubinkyoku*

9. _____ (Which way) *desu ka?*
   a. *Sochira*
   b. *Kochira*
   c. *Dochira*

10. *Taihen* _____ (near) *desu.*
    a. *tooi*
    b. *chikai*
    c. *ookii*

11. *Okane o* _____ (does he have) *ka?*
    a. *hoshii desu*
    b. *uketorimashita*
    c. *motte imasu*

12. *Watakushi no tegami ga* _____ (are there) *ka?*
    a. *arimasen*
    b. *arimasu*
    c. *arimashita*

13. _____ (Do you understand) *ka?*
    a. *Shitte imasu*
    b. *Wakarimasu*
    c. *Kiite imasu*

14. *Hajimete* _____ (glad to know you).
    a. *ome ni kakarimasu*
    b. *ryokoo shimashita*
    c. *sore o kikimashita*

15. *Sukoshi hoshii desu ka* _____ (want a lot) *desu ka?*
    a. *sukoshi mo hoshiku nai*
    b. *takusan hoshii*
    c. *anmari hoshiku nai*

16. *Yamada-san ni* _____ (must see).
    a. *hanasanakereba narimasen*
    b. *awanakereba narimasen*
    c. *kikanakereba narimasen*

17. *Sore wa Nihongo de doo* _____ (does one say) *ka?*
    a. *kikimasu*
    b. *iimasu*
    c. *kakimasu*

18. *Denwa wa san rei roku no* _____ (3307) *ban desu.*
    a. *sanjuu san shichi*
    b. *san san rei nana*
    c. *sanzen sanbyaku shichi*

19. _____ (What time) *desu ka?*
    a. *Nan' yoobi*
    b. *Nannichi*
    c. *Nanji*

20. _____ (Tomorrow morning) *kite kudasai.*
    a. *Ashita no yoru*
    b. *Ashita no asa*
    c. *Ashita no gogo*

21. *Itta keredomo* _____ (couldn't meet).
  a. *atta koto ga arimasen deshita*
  b. *au koto ga dekimasen deshita*
  c. *au tsumori ja arimasen deshita*

22. _____ (I want to go) *desu.*
  a. *Ikitai*
  b. *Hoshii*
  c. *Iku koto ga suki*

23. *Tanaka-san wa ima Tookyoo ni inai* _____ (I hear).
  a. *soo desu*
  b. *to omoimasu*
  c. *no deshoo*

24. _____ (Check) *o motte kite kudasai.*
  a. *Otsuri*
  b. *Ocha*
  c. *Denpyoo*

25. *Kyooto e* _____ (I have been to).
  a. *iku koto ga dekimasen*
  b. *itta koto ga arimasu*
  c. *iku koto ga suki desu*

ANSWERS
1—b; 2—a; 3—c; 4—a; 5—b; 6—b; 7—b; 8—b;
9—c; 10—b; 11—c; 12—b; 13—b; 14—a; 15—b;
16—b; 17—b; 18—b; 19—c; 20—b; 21—b; 22—a;
23—a; 24—c; 25—b.

SUMMARY OF JAPANESE GRAMMAR

1. THE ALPHABET AND ROMANIZATION

The sounds of Japanese have been transcribed into the Roman alphabet, and all of the letters in the English language except "l," "q," and "x" are employed. Generally speaking, the *r* sound is close to "l." Note that *c* is used only in the combination *ch*.

There are two major systems of romanization: the Hepburn System and the Japanese National System. The Hepburn System has a longer history and wider acceptance than does the Japanese National System. The National System is more logical, however, and reflects the phonological structure of the language better.

A slightly modified form of the Hepburn System is used here to present Japanese words and sentences. The system has been modified as follows:

a. So-called "long vowels" are written as double vowels instead of with a macron (¯) over the vowel symbol (i.e., *Tookyoo* instead of *Tōkyō*; *kuuki* instead of *kūki*).

b. The syllabic *n* is written as an *n* at all times (instead of as an *m* when it precedes *p*, *b*, or *m*).

The following table illustrates the various ways in which consonants and vowels are combined in the Hepburn System to produce the sounds of Japanese. Chart I aligns *vertically* the five vowel sounds, and shows *horizontally* the basic (mostly voiceless) consonants with which they can be used to create the basic syllables of Japanese. Chart II shows the sounds (mostly the voiced counterparts) into which these consonants can change. The same relationship that exists between Charts I and II also exists between Charts III and IV.

Blank squares occur where particular consonant-vowel combinations would *never* be used.

TABLE I

SYLLABLES OF THE MODIFIED HEPBURN
SYSTEM IN MODERN JAPANESE[1,2]

The differences between the Hepburn and National Systems are limited to the syllables listed below:

			0	1	2	3	4	5	6	7	8	9	10
CHART 1	V	1	a	ka	sa	ta	na	ha[3] (fa)	ma	ya	ra	wa	n
	O	2	i	ki	shi	chi (ti)	ni	hi (fi)	mi		ri		
	W	3	u	ku	su	tsu (tu)	nu	hu	mu	yu	ru		
	E	4	e	ke	se	te (tse)	ne	he (fe)	me		re		
	L S	5	o	ko	so	to	no	ho (fo)	mo	yo	ro	wo (o)	

[1] The *o* in column 9 and the *o* in column 0 are pronounced in the same manner, but are represented by different *hiragana*; see "The Writing System." The *o* in column 9 is used only for the particle *o*.

[2] The syllables in parentheses appear in borrowed words.

[3] Notice that in vertical column 5, the *h* of Chart I is converted to either *b* or *p* in Chart II.

	0	**1**	**2**	**3**	**4**	**5**	**6**	**7**	**8**	**9**	**10**
CHART 1		ga	za	da		ba	pa				(va)
II 2		gi	ji	(di)		bi	pi				(vi)
3		gu	zu	(du)		bu	pu				(vu)
4		ge	ze	de		be	pe				(ve)
5		go	zo	do		bo	po				(vo)

CHART 1	kya	sha	cha	nya	hya	mya		rya		
III 3	kyu	shu	chu	nyu	hyu	myu		ryu		
5	kyo	sho	cho	nyo	hyo	myo		ryo		
		(she)	(che)							

CHART 1	gya	ja			bya	pya				
IV 3	gyu	ju			byu	pyu				
4		(je)								
5	gyo	jo			byo	pyo				

CHART	-kk-	-ss-	-tt-		-pp-					
V		-ssh-	-tch-							
			-tts-							
	-(gg)-	-(zz)-	-(dd)-							
			-(dj)-							

HEPBURN SYSTEM	JAPANESE NATIONAL SYSTEM	HEPBURN SYSTEM	JAPANESE NATIONAL SYSTEM
shi	*si*	*chu*	*tyu*
chi	*ti*	*cho*	*tyo*
tsu	*tu*	*ja*	*zya*
fu	*hu*	*ju*	*zyu*
ji	*zi*	*jo*	*zyo*
sha	*sya*		
shu	*syu*		
sho	*syo*		
cha	*tya*		

TABLE II
SYLLABLES OF THE NATIONAL SYSTEM IN MODERN JAPANESE

The syllables in italics are spelled differently in the Hepburn system. See the list of syllables on page 310 for a comparison.

			0	1	2	3	4	5	6	7	8	9	10
CHART I	V O W E L S	1	a	ka	sa	ta	na	ha	ma	ya	ra	wa	n
		2	i	ki	*si*	*ti*	ni	hi	mi		ri		
		3	u	ku	su	*tu*	nu	*hu*	mu	yu	ru		
		4	e	ke	se	te	ne	he	me		re		
		5	o	ko	so	to	no	ho	mo	yo	ro	wo	

CHART II	1	ga	za	da		ba	pa				va
	2	gi	*zi*	*zi*		bi	pi				vi
	3	gu	zu	zu		bu	pu				vu
	4	ge	ze	de		be	pe				ve
	5	go	zo	do		bo	po				vo

CHART	1		kya	*sya*	*tya*	nya	hya	mya		rya			
III	3		kyu	*syu*	*tyu*	nyu	hyu	myu		ryu			
	5		kyo	*syo*	*tyo*	nyo	hyo	myo		ryo			

CHART	1		gya	*zya*			bya	pya					
IV	3		gyu	*zyu*			byu	pyu					
	5		gyo	*zyo*			byo	pyo					

CHART		-kk-	-ss-	-tt-			-pp-							
V														

2. SIMPLE VOWELS

a   like the "a" in "father," but short and crisp.
i   like the "e" in "keep," but short and crisp.
u   like the "u" in "put," but without rounding the lips.
e   like the "ay" in "may," but without the final *y* sound.
o   like the "o" in "go," but without the final *u* sound.

Remember that *i* and *u* differ from the other vowels in that they tend to become "voiceless" or whispered (1) when they are surrounded by the voiceless consonants *ch, f, h, k, p, s, sh, t, ts,* or (2) when they are preceded by a voiceless consonant and followed by a silence or pause (as at the end of a sentence). This is especially true when the syllable in question is not accented. In the following examples, the vowel with a circle underneath is a devoiced vowel:

arimasu̥   there is
ki̥tte   postage stamp

3. VOWEL CLUSTERS

a. Double vowels:

All simple vowels can appear as double[1] or "long" vowels. A double vowel is always pronounced twice as long as a simple vowel:

aa   pronounced twice as long as a single *a: haato* [heart]
ii   pronounced twice as long as a single *i: riiru* [reel]
uu   pronounced twice as long as a single *u: suugaku* [math]
ee   pronounced twice as long as a single *e: teeburu* [table]
oo   pronounced twice as long as a single *o: Tookyoo* [Tokyo]

b. Other vowel clusters:

All simple vowels can also appear in combination with one or more other simple vowels to form "vowel clusters." In such combinations, each of the vowels has equal weight and is pronounced so that it retains

---

[1] Double vowels can also be indicated by writing the single vowel with a macron over it: e.g., *ā* (for *aa*).

the sound it has as a simple vowel. Vowel clusters should *not* be pronounced like diphthongs, which combine two vowels to make a new sound. For example:

au   *a* and *u* are both pronounced and given equal clarity and length.

ai   *a* and *i* are both pronounced and given equal clarity and length.

4. CONSONANTS AND SEMI-VOWELS

a. The letters *b*, *d*, *j*, *k*, *m*, *p*, *s*, *ts*, *v*, and *y* in Japanese sound almost like the same letters in English. Pronounce the other sounds as follows:

ch   as in "cheese."

f   by forcing the air out from between the lips; similar to English "wh."

g   at the beginning of a word, somewhat like the "g" in the English word "go"; in the middle of a word, it resembles the "ng" in "singer."

h   like the "h" in "hi," when it precedes *a, e, o;* like the "h" in "hue," when it comes before *i* or *y*.

n   as in "name" (but with the tip of the tongue touching the back of the teeth) when it precedes *a, e, o, u;* as in "onion" when it precedes *i* or *y*.

r   by placing the tip of the tongue near the back of the upper teeth and quickly bringing it down; it sometimes sounds like the "r" in a British version of "very" ("veddy").

sh   somewhat like the English "sh" in "sheep."

t   as in the English "to," but with the tip of the tongue touching the back of the upper teeth.

w   like the "w" in "want," but without rounding or protruding the lips; occurs only before *a*.

z   at the beginning of a word, like the *ds* in "beds"; in the middle of a word, like the *z* in "zero" (but some Japanese speakers do not make this distinction; they use the two sounds interchangeably).

b. When a word begins with *ch, h, k, s, t,* or *ts,* and it joins with another word (which then *precedes* it) to make a new compound word, the initial letter or letters may undergo a change:

ch   may become *j,* as it does in the change from *chie* [wisdom] to *warujie* [guile, wiles].

f   and *h* may become *p* or *b,* as *h* does in the change from *hanashi* [story] to *mukashibanashi* [a story of the past].

k   may become *g,* as it does in the change from *ken* (a counter for houses) to *sangen* [three houses].

s   may become *z,* as it does in the change from *sen* [one thousand] to *sanzen* [three thousand].

sh   may become *j,* as it does in the change from *shika* [deer] to *ojika* [male deer].

t   may become *d,* as it does in the change from *to* [door, windows] to *amado* [storm window, Japanese rain window].

ts   may become *z,* as it does in the change from *tsuki* [month] to *tsukizuki* [monthly].

5. DOUBLE CONSONANTS

When a double *p, t, k,* or *s* (*d, z,* or *g* in borrowed words) appears in a word, then the initial consonant of the cluster has one syllable length. This same lengthening takes place when *tch, tts,* or *ssh* (*dj* in borrowed words) appears in a word:

kippu	ticket
mattaku	indeed
nikki	diary
itchi	agreement

6. THE SYLLABIC *N*

The syllabic *n* differs from the ordinary *n* in several ways:

a. It always forms a full syllable by itself (that is, it is always held as long as one full syllable). It *never* joins with a vowel or another consonant to form a syllable. If a vowel follows the syllabic *n*, there is always a syllable boundary between the *n* and the vowel. For example, the word *gen'in* [cause] has four syllables—*ge-n-i-n*—since each of the syllabic *n*'s has the value of a full syllable.

b. The syllabic *n* seldom appears at the beginning of a word.

c. Its sound changes depending on what follows it:

   (1) Before *n, ch, t,* and *d,* it is pronounced like the English "n" in "pen," but the sound is held longer, as in the following examples:

*ko**n**na*	this sort of
*ha**n**choo*	group leader
*cha**n**to*	properly
*ko**n**do*	this time

(2) Before *m*, *p*, or *b*, it is pronounced like the English "m," but the sound is held longer:

SPELLING	PRONUNCIATION	MEANING
sanmai	*sammai*	three sheets
shinpai	*shimpai*	worry, anxiety
kanban	*kamban*	signboard

(3) Before a vowel or a semi-vowel *(w, y)*, the syllabic *n* is pronounced somewhat like the English "ng" in "singer," but without finishing the g sound, and the preceding vowel is often somewhat nasalized. Notice that an apostrophe is used when a vowel or *y* follows the syllabic *n*.

gen'an	original plan
tan'i	unit
hon'ya	bookstore
shinwa	mythology

(4) When the syllabic *n* precedes *k*, *g*, or *s*, or when it appears at the end of a word (that is, when it is followed by a pause), it is pronounced as in (3) above:

sonkei	respect
sangen	three houses
son	loss
kansei	completion

7. CONTRACTIONS

a. The particle *de* [at, by means of] sometimes combines with the particle *wa* [as for] thus: *de* plus *wa = ja*.

Nihon ja yasui desu.   It is cheap in Japan (but not here).

b. The *-te* form of the copula *de* (from *desu*) can also combine with the particle *wa* thus: *de* plus *wa = ja*.

Nihonjin ja arimasen.   She is not Japanese.

c. The *-te* form of a verb sometimes combines with the particle *wa* thus: *-te* plus *wa = cha,* or *-de* plus *wa = ja.*

Itcha ikemasen.   You mustn't go.
Yonja ikemasen.   You mustn't read it.

8. ACCENT

Word accent in Japanese is indicated by lowering the pitch of the voice *after* the accented syllable.

Some words have an accent in Japanese; others do not. Accentless words are spoken with the voice pitch held even on all syllables of the word except the first, where the pitch is slightly lower. This is true regardless of the length of the word.

Certain words lose their accent when they are placed next to an accented word. For this reason, accents within the same sentence may be marked or not marked.

The inclusion or omission of an accent is further determined by various subsidiary rules, not all of which are thoroughly understood at the present time. The student can learn much about the refinements of accentuation by listening to native Japanese speakers.

9. INTONATION

a. In a declarative sentence:
   There is a marked drop in the pitch of the voice on the last voiced syllable.

b. In a direct question:
   There may be a rising intonation on the last voiced syllable. This rise in pitch is optional when the sentence ends with the question particle *ka* or contains a question phrase, such as *doko e* [where to]. When neither a question particle nor question word is used, the rising intonation is used.

c. Suspension:
   The last voiced syllable is spoken in approximately the same level tone as that which precedes it.

10. NOUNS

a. Most nouns in a sentence are accompanied by one or two noun-particles[1] (i.e., *wa, ga, o, mo, no, ni, de, kara*) or by some form of the copula *desu* [it is]. Nouns are not declined.

Nihon ni wa yama ga takusan arimasu.	There are many mountains in Japan.
Fujisan wa takai yama desu.	Mt. Fuji is a high mountain.

b. There are certain words, usually having to do with time, degree, or quantity, which may or may not appear with a particle. These may have the functions not only of nouns, but also of adverbs, and may be used to modify predicates or entire clauses.

---

[1] See the material on page 327 for particles used with nouns.

Kinoo ikimashita. I went there yesterday.
Kinoo wa ikimasen I didn't go there yester-
  deshita. day.

Here is a list of some additional examples of such words:

maiasa	every morning
mainichi	every day
ima	present time, now
moto	former time, previously
sukoshi	a small amount, a little, some
takusan	a large amount, a great deal, plentifully, in a large quantity
hotondo	nearly all, almost completely
mada	as yet, still
zenzen	completely (used with a negative predicate)
nakanaka	quite, considerably

c. Some nouns frequently take on the special function of relating or tying one part of a sentence to another. When this occurs, they assume a role comparable in the English language to that of a preposition, adverb, or conjunction. When thus used, they are always modified by a clause and are sometimes classified as particles rather than as nouns. The list that follows contains some of the most widely used of these functional nouns:

NOUN	NOUN MEANING	FUNCTIONAL WORD MEANING
aida	duration, space; interval	during; as long as; while

ato	site; place behind; time following; condition following	after, subsequent to (usually preceded by the *-ta* form of a verb and followed by *de*)
baai	occasion; situation	in the event that, in case; when; should (something) happen
hazu	notch (of an arrow)	it (something) is "in the cards," it is expected that, it is supposed that (when followed by *desu*); it is not reasonable to expect that, it is hardly possible that (when followed by *wa* or *ga arimasen*)
hodo	approximate degree	to the extent of; not as . . . as . . . (usually followed by a negative predicate):

A wa B hodo yoku arimasen.

A is not as good as B.

Sono sake wa nomeba nomu hodo motto nomitaku narimasu.

The more you drink that sake, the more you want to drink; the more . . . the more . . . (when preceded by a single verb in the present tense or a verb in the provisional form together with the same verb in the present) *hoo*   side, direction, alternative direction   the use of this word denotes that a comparison is being made:

Kono hoo ga yasui desu.   This is cheaper.

Kusuri o nonda hoo ga ii desu.   It would be better (for you) to take some medicine.

ijoo (wa)   the above-mentioned   now that, since, inasmuch as, because of

kagiri   limits, bounds; maximum degree   as far as, so long as, as much as, provided that

kekka   result, outcome, consequence   with the result that, as a result of, because of

kiri   limit   nothing happened after:

Nippon e itta kiri tayori ga arimasen.   There is no news from him since he went to Japan.

koto   fact; thing (abstract)   the act of doing . . . ; the act of having done . . . (makes a noun equivalent out of inflected words; used in many idiomatic expressions):

Hanasu koto wa dekimasen.   Talking is not permitted [possible]. I can't talk.

Hanashita koto wa arimasen.   I've never talked (with him). [The experience of having talked with him does not exist.]

mae   the front; prior time, former time   before, prior to [usually followed by *ni*], ago

mama   will (wish)   as it is (without doing anything further, without

		taking additional action); as it stands; exactly as; according to
mono	thing (tangible); person	the thing which; the one who; it's because (when it is used at the end of a sentence, usually by a female speaker—a use similar to *kara* or *node*); that's the thing to do, you should, it is expected that (when preceded by a verb in the present form and followed by *desu*); used to do (when preceded by the *-ta* form of a verb and followed by *desu*)
nochi	the time after	after (used either with or without *ni* following it); subsequent to having done . . . (when it is preceded by the *-ta* form of a verb)
tabi	occasion, time	every time that
tame	sake	for the sake of; for the purpose of; because of
toki	time	(at the time) when
tokoro	place	just when, in the act of (when followed by *ni* or *de*); even if, no matter who, no matter what (when followed by *de*); to be on the point of

		(when preceded by the present form of a verb and followed by *desu*); to have just finished doing . . . (when preceded by the -*ta* form of a verb and followed by *desu*)
toori	the way, avenue	exactly as
tsumori	idea in mind	intend to, plan to (when preceded by the present tense of a verb and followed by *desu*); (my) notion [recollection] about it is that (something) was the case (when preceded by the -*ta* form of a verb and followed by *desu*)
uchi	the inside [the within]	while, during the time when
ue	top, surface, place over	on top of doing, having done (something), upon doing . . . , besides (doing) . . . ; upon finishing, after (doing something; when followed by *de*)
wake	reason, meaning, logic	that's the background of it, that's the story of it, that's what it is (when followed by *desu*); it is

hardly believable that
(something) should
happen (or should have
happened; when fol-
lowed by *ga arimasen*).

d. Some nouns are converted into verbs when used
with *suru*. The resultant combination means "do
the action of (something)." For instance:

shookai	introduction
shookai suru	to introduce
ryokoo	travel
ryokoo suru	to travel

e. The pre-*masu* form can function as a noun:

yomu	to read
yomi	reading; pronunciation
tsuru	to fish
tsuri	fishing

f. The stem of an adjective (i.e., the plain present
affirmative, minus the final *i*) can function as a
noun:

akai red   *aka* the color red

The stem of an adjective can also function as a
noun when *sa* or *mi* is added:

akai red	*akasa* redness
fukai deep	{ *fukasa* depth (as a measure)
	{ *fukami* depth (of thought)

g. Particles[1] used with nouns:

Following is a list of particles used with nouns, as well as their respective functions:

ga marks an emphatic grammatical subject (see *mo*, below).

wa marks a sentence topic that may be either the subject or object of the sentence, or a modifier.

no links a noun to another noun. It is most frequently used to indicate the possessive ("of").

ni links a noun or noun equivalent (such as the pre-*masu* form of a verb) to a verb, adjective, or copula.

o marks the thing acted upon (see *mo*, below).

mo can be used instead of *ga* or *o* (see above) but carries the additional meaning of "that thing/person also."

e links a noun to a verb and marks the direction toward which an action is performed.

to does one of two things: (i) it links nouns together in a complete list (see also *ya*, below) or (ii) it marks the partner with whom the action is being performed.

ya links nouns together in an incomplete list (see also *to*, above).

yori marks a noun or noun equivalent as the standard against which a comparison is made.

kara marks a starting point in time or space.

made marks an ending point in time or space.

de marks the means, way, place, or manner in which an action is performed.

[1] Note that Japanese has many of these so-called "particles," which show the grammatical relationship of one word to another within a sentence; see also Lesson 11. Mastery of these particles is key to rapidly learning Japanese. See "Particles Used with Verbs," Section 18, of the Summary of Japanese Grammar.

bakari has one of two functions: (i) it can be used in place of (or sometimes together with) *ga* or *o* to carry the additional meaning of "nothing else," or (ii) if it follows a number, it signifies that the number is only approximate.

dake can be used in place of or together with *ga* or *o* to carry the additional meaning of "that was the limit."

hodo can be used (i) to mark a thing against which a comparison is made, and which is about the same in degree or extent as the thing compared, or (ii) to mark a number that is only approximate.

kurai (or *gurai*) marks the approximate quantity, quality, or degree, and can often be used interchangeably with *hodo* (see above).

ka (i) shows that a statement is a question, or (ii) has the meaning of "either . . . or."

11. COUNTERS

Counters form a subclass of nouns often used adverbially to mean "to the extent of." There are several types:

a. Unit counters:

(1) Unit counters name specifically that which is being counted. The following unit counters are used with primary numbers—*ichi, ni, san* [one, two, three], etc.—and are suffixed to these numbers. Where an exception to the general rule occurs, it is shown.

COUNTER	MEANING	EXCEPTIONS
-jikan	hours	*yojikan* = four hours

-ji	o'clock	*yoji* = four o'clock
-fun (or *-pun*)	minutes	See also Section 4-b of the Summary of Japanese Grammar for change of sound
-byoo	seconds	
-nichi	days	See also Lesson 25 for variations
-shuukan	weeks	
-kagetsu	months	
-gatsu	name of the month	
-nen	years	*yonen* = four years
-en	yen (Japanese currency)	
-sento	cent (U.S. currency)	
-doru	dollar (U.S. currency)	
-shiringu	shillings (British currency)	
-pondo	pounds (unit of weight or of British currency)	
-meetoru	meters	
-kiro	kilometers, kilograms	
-kiroguramu	kilograms	
-kiromeetoru	kilometers	

-mairu	miles
-inchi	inches
-do	times
-peeji	pages; page number
-gyoo	lines; line number
-wari	one-tenth
-paasento	percent
-kai	story (of a building)

(2) The following unit counters are used with secondary numbers (*hito-, futa-, mi-,* etc.). They are usually used to count amounts less than four.

-ban	nights
-heya	room
-ma	room

b. Class counters:

(1) Class counters are used in a general rather than a specific sense. The following class counters are used with primary numerals (*ichi, ni, san . . .*):

COUNTER	MEANING	EXCEPTIONS
-hiki (or *-biki*, or *-piki*)	animals, fish, insects	*ippiki, sanbiki, roppiki, juppiki*
-too	large animals (such as horses, cows)	
-wa (or *-ba*, or *-pa*)	birds	*sanba, roppa, juppa*
-satsu	bound volumes (of books	

	and maga-zines)	
-mai	flat, thin things (such as sheets, news-papers, hand-kerchiefs)	
-hon (or *-pon*, or *-bon*)	thin, long things (such as pencils, tubes, sticks, matches, cig-arettes)	*ippon, sanbon, roppon, juppon*
-ken (or *-gen*)	houses	*sangen*
-tsuu	documents, letters, tele-grams	
-dai	vehicles (such as cars, wag-ons), ma-chines (such as typewrit-ers, sewing machines)	
-ki	planes and other aircraft	
-chaku	suits of clothes	
-soku (or *-zoku*)	pairs of things worn on the feet or legs (such as shoes, socks, stockings)	*sanzoku*
-ko	lumps (such as apples,	

	stones, candy)
-hai (or *-pai,* or *-bai*)	something in containers (such as water, coffee)

(2) The following class counters are used with secondary numerals (*hito-, futa-, mi-,* etc.):

-fukuro	bagful (of)
-hako	boxful (of)
-kumi	set, group, couple (of people)
-soroi	set, group
-iro	kind, variety
-kire	slices
-tsumami	pinch

12. PRONOUNS

All of the Japanese words that correspond to English pronouns are nouns. They take the same particles as other nouns and are modified by the same type of words, phrases, and clauses that are used to modify other nouns. Note that in Japanese, there are more varieties of words that correspond to personal pronouns than there are in English.

A list of Japanese equivalents of personal pronouns and instructions for using them follows:

a. I, we:

SINGULAR	PLURAL	MEANING AND USAGE
watakushi	*watakushitachi*	I, we (formal)

watashi	*watashitachi*	I, we (slightly less formal than *watakushi* and used most widely)
boku	*bokutachi*	I, we (used by males only: informal)
ore	*oretachi*	I, we (used by males, but not in refined speech)

b. You:

Avoid using any definite word for "you" as long as the sentence meaning is clear without it. If you cannot avoid such a reference, use the name (usually the surname) of the person you are addressing, and add *-san* with the appropriate particle. If you are speaking to a small child, use the child's given name with *-kun* (for male) or *-chan* (for female). If you are speaking to a teacher, doctor, or someone in a similar position, use *sensei* either preceded by or without the surname of the person you are addressing. If you must employ the pronoun instead of the name, use *anata* [you (sing.)], *anata-gata* [you (pl.)], *minasan* [you (pl.)], or *minasama* [you (pl., very formal)]. Many of the sentence examples in this course contain *anata* or *anata-gata*, but these should be replaced in actual conversation by the name of the person to whom you are speaking whenever possible.

c. He, she, they:[1]

SINGULAR	PLURAL	MEANING AND USAGE
ano kata	ano katagata	he, she, they (*respect*)
ano hito	ano hitotachi	he, she, they (*respect*)
ano otoko no kata	ano otoko no katagata	he, they (*respect:* used only when it is necessary to indicate specifically "he [that man]" or "they [those men]")
ano otoko no hito	ano otoko no hitotachi	he, they (*neutral:* same as above)
ano onna no kata	ano onna no katagata	she, they (*respect:* used only when there is need to indicate specifically "she" or "they" [those women])
ano onna no hito	ano onna no hitotachi	she, they (*neutral:* same as above)

[1] Note that the appropriate variants of these pronouns are often context-dependent. Please refer to the "Meaning and Usage" column for explanations about where they are likely to appear.

| *kare* | *karera* | he, they (these are relatively direct trans lations and thus tend to be less context-dependent than other pronouns; but they are also less common and less accepted in writing) |
| *kanojo* | *kanojora* | she, they |

d. Possessives:

There are no expressly possessive pronouns in Japanese. To form the possessive, combine a noun (used for the person referred to) with *no* [things of], as in the following examples:

watashi no	my, mine
anato no (or the name of the person) plus *no*	your, yours
kare no/kanojo no	his, hers
watashitachi no	our, ours
anatagata no ⎱ *minasan no* ⎰	your, yours *(pl.)*
karera no	their, theirs

13. DEMONSTRATIVES

Demonstratives—words such as *kono* [this] or *konna* [this kind of]—precede a noun and modify its meaning. No particle is used to separate the demonstrative and noun. Demonstratives do not change their forms.

kono	this
sono	that
ano	that over there
dono	which?
konna	this kind of
sonna	that kind of
anna	that kind of
donna	what kind of?

14. *Ko-So-A-Do* WORDS

Some Japanese nouns and demonstratives come in sets of four words that are usually pronounced alike, except for the first syllable. These sets of words are called "ko-so-a-do words" because the first syllable is always one of the following four: *ko-*, *so-*, *a-*, or *do-*. Note that the word in such a group that begins with *do* is always a question word.

a. *Ko-so-a-do* nouns:[1]

kore	this one
sore	that one
are	that one over there
dore	which one?

[1] See Lesson 17.

koko	this place
soko	that place
asoko[1]	that place over there
doko	which place? where?
kochira, kotchi	this way, this one (of two)
sochira, sotchi	that way, that one (of two)
achira, atchi	that way, that one (of two)
dochira, dotchi	which way, which (of two)?

b. *Ko-so-a-do* demonstratives:

kono	this
sono	that
ano	that over there
dono	which?
konna	this sort of
sonna	that sort of (for something not far removed in feeling or time)
anna	that sort of (for something more remote in feeling or time)
donna	what sort of?

15. ADJECTIVES

a. *I*-adjectives:

I-adjectives can end in *-ai, -ii, -ui,* or *-oi,* but never in *-ei*.

akai	(is) red
utsukushii	(is) beautiful
samui	(is) cold
kuroi	(is) black

[1] An irregular form.

I-adjectives are conjugated as follows:

(1) Plain forms:

PRESENT	*takai*	it is high
PAST	*takakatta*	it was high
TENTATIVE PRESENT	*takai daroo*	it is probably high
TENTATIVE PAST	*takakatta daroo*	it was probably high

(2) Polite forms:

PRESENT	*takai desu*	it is high
PAST	*takakatta desu*	it was high
TENTATIVE PRESENT	*takai deshoo*	it is probably high
TENTATIVE PAST	*takakatta de-shoo*	it was probably high

(3) Other forms:

-*TE* FORM	*takakute*	it is (was) high, and . . .
-*KU* FORM	*takaku*	it is (was) high, and . . . highly
-*BA* FORM	*takakereba*	if it is high
-*TARA* FORM	*takakattara*	if (when) it is (was) high

b. *Na*-adjectives:

(1) Plain forms:

PRESENT	*shizuka da*	it is quiet
PAST	*shizuka datta*	it was quiet
TENTATIVE PRESENT	*shizuka daroo*	it is probably quiet
TENTATIVE PAST	*shizuka datta daroo*	it was probably quiet

(2) Polite forms:

PRESENT	*shizuka desu*	it is quiet
PAST	*shizuka deshita*	it was quiet
TENTATIVE PRESENT	*shizuka deshoo*	it is probably quiet
TENTATIVE PAST	*shizuka datta deshoo*	it was probably quiet

(3) Other forms:

-TE FORMS	*shizuka de*	it is (was) quiet and . . .
-NI FORMS	*shizuka ni*	quietly
-TARA FORMS	*shizuka dattara*	if (when) it is (was) quiet and . . .

16. COMPARISONS

There are several ways to show comparison:

a. Use *no hoo* [the side of] to show what is being compared:

Kyooto no hoo ga suki desu.	I like Kyoto better.
Tookyoo no hoo ga samui desu.	Tokyo is colder [in climate].
Kuruma de iku hoo ga ii desu.	It is better to go by car.

Notice that when a verb comes before *hoo*, *no* is omitted.

b. Use *yori* [than] to mark the standard against which a comparison is made:

| *Kyooto yori samui desu.* | It is colder than Kyoto. |
| *Kore wa sore yori ta-kai desu.* | This is more expensive than that. |

c. Use both *no hoo* and *yori* in the same sentence to show that a comparison is being made:

| *Tookyoo no hoo ga Kyooto yori samui desu.* | Tokyo is colder than Kyoto. |
| *Yomu hoo ga hanasu yori muzukashii desu.* | Reading is more diffi-cult than speaking. |

d. Use *zutto* [by far the more] either with or without *no hoo* or *yori*:

| *Sono densha no hoo ga kono densha yori zutto hayai desu.* *Sono densha ga zutto hayai desu.* | That train is much faster (than this train). |
| *Kore wa zutto yasashii desu.* | This is much easier. |

e. Use *motto* [still more] either with or without *no hoo* or *yori:*

Sore wa motto takai desu.	That is still more expensive (than this one).
Sore wa kore yori motto takai desu.	
Motto yukkuri hanashite kudasai.	Please speak more slowly.

f. Use *ichiban* [number one, most of all] or *mottomo* [the most] when comparing more than two things. (*Mottomo* is more formal than *ichiban*.)

Kare ga ichiban se ga takai desu.	He is the tallest.
Kare ga mottomo se ga takai desu.	
Ichiban ii no o kudasai.	Give me the best kind, please.

g. Use *dochira* or *dotchi* [which of the two], or *dore* [which of more than two] when asking a question involving a comparison:

Nagoya to Kyooto de wa dochira no hoo ga chikai desu ka?	Which is nearer— Nagoya or Kyoto?
Tenisu to gorufu to suiei no naka de dore ga ichiban omoshiroi desu ka?	Which is the most interesting—tennis, golf, or swimming?

h. Use *hodo* (to show approximate degree) and a negative predicate when making a comparison between two things that are not quite alike:

Nagoya wa Oosaka hodo tooku arimasen. — Nagoya is not as far as Osaka.

Tanaka-san wa Yamada-san hodo kanemochi ja arimasen. — Ms. Tanaka is not as rich as Mr. Yamada.

i. Also use *hodo* to describe situations resulting in extreme, intense, or severe effects:

Kimochi ga waruku naru hodo takusan tabemashita. — I ate so much that I began to feel sick.

Onaka ga itaku naru hodo waraimashita. — I laughed so much that I began to get a stomachache.

j. Use *no yoo ni* [in the likeness of, in the manner of] or *kurai* (or *gurai*) [more or less] when making a comparison between two things or situations that are pretty much alike:

Yamada-san wa Eigo ga Amerikajin no yoo ni yoku dekimasu. — Mr. Yamada knows English as well as [just like] an American.

Yamada-san wa Eigo ga Amerikajin gurai dekimasu. — Mr. Yamada knows English as well as [just like] an American.

17. THE CLASSES AND FORMS OF VERBS

a. Verb classes:

There are three classes of verbs in Japanese:

Class I—consonant verbs: includes all verbs except those in Class II and Class III.

Class II—vowel verbs: includes the majority of verbs that, in their plain present form, terminate in *-eru* or *-iru*.

Class III—irregular verbs: *kuru* [come] and *suru* [do].

The base of a *consonant* verb is that part left over after the final *-u* has been dropped from the plain present affirmative form (= dictionary form). The base always ends in a consonant except where there is another vowel before the final *-u*.

The base of a *vowel* verb is that part which remains after the final *-ru* has been dropped from the plain present form. It always ends in either *-e* or *-i*.

b. *-Masu* forms:

-Masu forms (= polite present affirmative forms) are formed in the following ways:

Consonant verbs: Drop the final *u* of the dictionary form and add *-imasu*.

Vowel verbs: Drop the final *ru* of the dictionary form and add *-masu*.

DICTIONARY FORM	→	-MASU FORM	
consonant verb			
kaku		*kakimasu*	write
yomu		*yomimasu*	read
vowel verb			
taberu		*tabemasu*	eat
miru		*mimasu*	see

-Masu forms of some respect verbs are formed irregularly:

DICTIONARY FORM →	-MASU FORM	
irassharu	*irasshaimasu*	go, come, be
ossharu	*osshaimasu*	say
kudasaru	*kudasaimasu*	give
nasaru	*nasaimasu*	do

These respect verbs are consonant verbs. Notice that in their *-masu* forms, *r* is dropped. For example, the *-masu* form of *irassharu* is *irasshaimasu*, not *irassharimasu*.

c. The tenses:

In Japanese, a verb form referred to as a "tense" actually describes the *mood* of the action or state.

(1) The present tense (or *-u*-ending form) expresses an *incomplete* action or state and may have several English translations:

Hanashimasu	I speak; I do speak; I will speak
Tabemasu	I eat; I do eat; I will eat

(2) The past tense (or *-ta* form) expresses a *completed* action or state. It, too, can have several English translations:

Hanashimashita	I spoke; I have spoken
Tabemashita	I ate; I have eaten

The plain form of the past tense is formed from the plain present as follows:

(a) For consonant verbs:
    (i) When the final syllable in the plain present is *-u*, *-tsu*, or *-ru*, drop it and add *-tta:*

PRESENT	PAST	
Kau	*Katta*	I bought
Tatsu	*Tatta*	I stood
Toru	*Totta*	I took

    (ii) When the final syllable in the plain present is *-mu*, *-nu*, or *-bu*, drop it and add *-nda:*

Nomu	*Nonda*	I drank
Shinu	*Shinda*	He died
Yobu	*Yonda*	I called

    (iii) When the final syllable is *-ku* or *-gu*, drop it and add *-ita* in place of *-ku* and *-ida* in place of *-gu:*

Kaku	*Kaita*	I wrote
Isogu	*Isoida*	I hurried

    (iv) When the final syllable is *-su*, drop it and add *-shita:*

Hanasu	*Hanashita*	I spoke
Kasu	*Kashita*	I lent

(b) For vowel verbs:
Drop the final syllable *-ru* and add *-ta:*

Taberu	*Tabeta*	I ate
Miru	*Mita*	I saw

(c) For irregular verbs:

Kuru	*Kita*	I came
Suru	*Shita*	I did

The polite form of the past tense is formed from the polite present (the *-masu* form) by replacing the final syllable *-su* with *-shita*.

POLITE PRESENT	POLITE PAST	
Ikimasu	*Ikimashita*	I went
Tabemasu	*Tabemashita*	I ate
Mimasu	*Mimashita*	I saw

(3) The tentative (polite: *-mashoo;* plain: *-oo* or *-yoo*) expresses an action or state that is not certain, definite, or completed. It can have several English translations:

Yomimashoo.	I think I will read. Let's read.
Yomimashoo ka?	Shall we read?

The plain tentative is formed from the plain present as follows:

(a) For consonant verbs:
Drop the final *-u* and add *-oo:*

PRESENT	TENTATIVE	
Hanasu.	*Hanasoo.*	I think I'll speak/talk. Let's speak/talk.
Yomu.	*Yomoo.*	I think I'll read. Let's read.

(b) For vowel verbs:
Drop the final *-ru* and add *-yoo:*

Taberu.   *Tabeyoo.*   I think I'll eat. Let's eat.
Miru.   *Miyoo.*   I think I'll see it. Let's see it.

The polite tentative is formed from the polite present by dropping the final *-su* and adding *-shoo*.

POLITE PRESENT	POLITE TENTATIVE	
Hanashimasu.	*Hanashimashoo.*	I think I'll speak/talk. Let's speak/talk.
Tabemasu.	*Tabemashoo.*	I think I'll eat. Let's eat.

d. *-Te* forms:

(1) The *-te* form is formed exactly like the plain past affirmative [see Section 17-c-(2)] except that the final vowel is *-e*. A *-te* form actually has no tense; the "tense" feeling is determined by the "tense-mood," that is, the ending *(-u, -ta, -yoo)*, of the terminal verb.

Kusuriya e itte kusuri o kaimashita.   I went to a drugstore and bought some medicine.

Normally, when there is more than one verb in a sentence, the *-te* form is used for all but the last verb. The pre-*masu* form is sometimes used instead of the *-te* form, but this is considered "bookish."

*Kusuriya e itte kusuri o   I went to the drugstore
    katte uchi e kaette   and bought some
    sore o nonde sugu   medicine and re-
    nemashita.*   turned home and
                               took it and went to
                               bed right away.

(2) The *-te* form is also used:

(a) Adverbially, to modify a verb or adjective:

Isoide ikimashita.   He went hurriedly.
Naite hanashimashita.   He spoke in tears.
Yorokonde shigoto o   She took on the job
    hikiukemashita.   gladly.

(b) With *kudasai,* to form a request:

*Kesa no shinbun o katte   Please buy me this
    kudasai.*   morning's paper.

(c) With *imasu,* to form the progressive:

Hanashite imasu.   I am speaking.
Tabete imasu.   I am eating.

(d) To form the "stative," which expresses the
     state resulting from a completed action, (i)
     add *arimasu* to the *-te* form, or (ii) add
     imasu to the *-te* form. The latter kind is
     identical with the progressive in form, but
     not in function. Usually, *arimasu* is used
     after the *-te* form of a transitive verb, and
     imasu after the *-te* form of an intransitive
     verb.

| *Te de kaite arimasu.* | It's handwritten. [It is in the state of his having written it by hand.] |
| *Moo kekkon shite imasu.* | She is married already. [She is in the state of her being married since she got married.] |

PLAIN PRESENT AFFIRMATIVE (DICTIONARY FORM)

CLASS I VERBS (CONSONANT VERBS)	CLASS II VERBS (VOWEL VERBS)	CLASS III VERBS (IRREGULAR VERBS)
hanasu	*taberu*	*suru*
speak	eat	do
will speak	will eat	will do

PLAIN PAST AFFIRMATIVE

hanashita	*tabeta*	*shita*
spoke	ate	did
have spoken	have eaten	has done

POLITE PRESENT AFFIRMATIVE (-MASU FORM)

hanashimasu	*tabemasu*	*shimasu*
speak	eat	do
will speak	will eat	will do

POLITE PAST AFFIRMATIVE

hanashimashita	*tabemashita*	*shimashita*
spoke	ate	did
have spoken	have eaten	have done

PLAIN PRESENT NEGATIVE

hanasanai	*tabenai*	*shinai*
do not speak	do not eat	do not do
will not speak	will not eat	will not do

PLAIN PAST NEGATIVE

hanasanakatta	*tabenakatta*	*shinakatta*
did not speak	did not eat	did not do
have not spoken	have not eaten	have not done

POLITE PRESENT NEGATIVE

hanashimasen	*tabemasen*	*shimasen*
do not speak	do not eat	do not do
will not speak	will not eat	will not do

POLITE PAST NEGATIVE

hanashimasen deshita	*tabemasen deshita*	*shimasen deshita*
did not speak	did not eat	did not do
have not spoken	have not eaten	have not done

EXTRA-POLITENESS

NEUTRAL	RESPECT	HUMBLE
hanasu	*ohanashi ni naru, hana-sareru*	*ohanashi suru*

PLAIN -*TE* FORM[1]

hanashite	*tabete*	*shite*
speak and . . .	eat and . . .	do and . . .
will speak and . . .	will eat and . . .	will do and . . .

POLITE -*TE* FORM[2]

hanashimashite	*tabemashite*	*shimashite*

[1] See Section 17-d-(2) for additional meanings.
[2] The polite -*te* form is only used in the most formal conversations. Furthermore, the polite -*te* form is unacceptable in the usages described in 17-(2)-d.

Note that in the following groups, the "a" lines show the plain form of the verb, and the "b" lines show the polite form.

PRESENT PROGRESSIVE AFFIRMATIVE

a. *hanashite iru*   *tabete iru*   *shite iru*

b. *hanashite imasu*   *tabete imasu*   *shite imasu*
he is speaking   he is eating   he is doing

PAST PROGRESSIVE AFFIRMATIVE

a. *hanashite ita*   *tabete ita*   *shite ita*

b. *hanashite imashita*   *tabete imashita*   *shite imashita*
he was speaking   he was eating   he was doing

PRESENT PROGRESSIVE NEGATIVE

a. *hanashite inai*   *tabete inai*   *shite inai*

b. *hanashite imasen*   *tabete imasen*   *shite imasen*
he is not speaking   he is not eating   he is not doing

PAST PROGRESSIVE NEGATIVE

a. *hanashite inakatta*   *tabete inakatta*   *shite inakatta*

b. *hanashite imasen deshita*   *tabete imasen deshita*   *shite imasen deshita*
he was not speaking   he was not eating   he was not doing

PRESENT STATIVE AFFIRMATIVE

a. *Hanashite aru.* — *Tabete aru.* — *Shite aru.*

b. *Hanashite arimasu.*
The matter has already been mentioned to him. [The matter is in the state of my having spoken about it.]

Tabete arimasu.
The meal is finished. [The meal is in the state of my having eaten it.]

Shite arimasu.
It's done. [The work is in the state of my having done it.]

PAST STATIVE AFFIRMATIVE[1]

a. *Hanashite atta.* — *Tabete atta.* — *Shite atta.*

b. *Hanashite arimashita.*
The matter had been mentioned to him.

Tabete arimashita.
The meal had been eaten.

Shite arimashita.
The work had been done.

PRESENT STATIVE NEGATIVE

a. *Hanashite nai.* — *Tabete nai.* — *Shite nai.*

b. *Hanashite arimasen.* — *Tabete arimasen.* — *Shite arimasen.*
It is not

---

[1] Usually translated into English using the past perfect.

The matter has not been mentioned.	The meal is not finished.	done.

PAST STATIVE NEGATIVE

a. *Hanashite nakatta.*   *Tabete nakatta.*   *Shite nakatta.*

b. *Hanashite arimasen deshita.*   *Tabete arimasen deshita.*   *Shite arimasen deshita.*

The matter hadn't been mentioned.   The meal hadn't been finished.   It hadn't been done.

PROVISIONAL AND CONDITIONAL

hatarakeba	*tabereba*	*sureba*
hataraitara	*tabetara*	*shitara*
hataraku to	*taberu to*	*suru to*
hataraku nara	*taberu nara*	*suru nara*
hataraite wa	*tabete wa*	*shite wa*
if I work	if I eat	if I do

18. PARTICLES USED WITH VERBS

The following particles that are used with verbs can also be used with adjectives or the copula. (See also Section 10-g of the Summary of Japanese Grammar for particles used with nouns.)

a. *Bakari*[1] *desu* =

    (1) (Following a *-u* form) does nothing but (something); does only . . .

Sotsugyoo o matsu bakari desu.	I am just waiting for graduation. (I have no more school work to do.)

    (2) (Following a *-ta* form) has just done (something); did only (something):

Gohan o tabeta bakari desu.	I have just finished eating.

b. *Dake*[2] = that is just about all; that is just about the extent of it; only; just:

Mita dake desu.	I just took a look at it.
Hanashi o suru dake desu.	I am just going to discuss it. (I won't make any decision yet.)

c. *Ga* = but; in spite of the fact stated above (when preceded by either the plain or polite forms):

Ikimashita ga aemasen deshita.	I went (there), but I couldn't see him.
Kaimashita ga mada tsukatte imasen.	I have bought it, but haven't used it yet.

d. *Ka* = a spoken question mark:

---

[1] *Bakari* is sometimes classified as an adverb instead of a particle.
[2] *Dake* is sometimes classified as an adverb instead of a particle.

Kyoo wa oisogashii   Are you busy today?
   desu ka?

e. *Kara* =

  (1) (Following a -*te* form) after doing (something); since doing (something):

Mite kara kimemasu.   I will decide after taking
                     [having taken] a look
                     at it.

  (2) (Following any sentence-ending form— -*u*, -*ta*, -*i*) and so, and therefore:

Omoi desu kara watashi   It's heavy, so I will carry
   ga omochi shimashoo.   it.

f. *Keredo(mo)*[1] = in spite of the fact stated before; but; however; although:

Isoida keredo ma ni   I hurried, but couldn't
   aimasen deshita.   make it.
Yonda keredomo yoku   I read it, but I didn't
   wakarimasen deshita.   understand it well.

g. *Made* = up to the time of (something)'s happening; until; so far as:

Yamada-san ga kuru   I will stay here until
   made koko ni ori-   Mr. Yamada gets
   masu.   here.

---

[1] The use of *mo* is optional.

h. *Na* =

    (1) (Following a plain present affirmative form) don't do (something). Note that this is never used in refined speech; instead, *-naide kudasai* is used:

Hairu na!	Don't enter!
Hairanaide kudasai.	Please don't enter.

    (2) (Following a sentence-ending form) yeah, that's what it is (used only by men in colloquial speech):

Ii tenki da na!	What fine weather!
Genki da na!	You are in good shape! (You look fine!)

    (3) (Following a verb and used with *ka*) should I? I wonder if I should? (used in colloquial speech):

Dekakeyoo ka na?	Let's see. Shall we go now?
Eiga de mo miyoo ka na.	I guess I will see a movie or something.

i. *-Nagara* = (following a pre-*masu* form, showing that two or more actions or states take place or exist concurrently) while; in the course of:

Arukinagara hanashimashoo.	Let's talk as we walk (to that place).
Hatarakinagara benkyoo shite imasu.	He is studying while working (he is supporting himself).

j. *Nari* =

(1) (When used in a parallel sequence) either . . .
or . . . ; whether . . . or . . . :

Denwa o kakeru nari tegami o kaku nari shite minna ni shirasemashita.	She informed everybody either by phoning or writing a letter.

(2) (When *not* used in a parallel sequence) as soon
as; the moment (something) has taken place:

Kao o miru nari naki-hajimemashita.	He burst into tears the moment he saw me.

k. *Ni* = the purpose of the "going" or "coming" that is
expressed (when it follows the pre-*masu* form of a
verb):

Kaimono o shi ni iki-mashita.	He went shopping. [He went in order to shop.]

l. *Node* = (following a sentence-ending form) and so;
and therefore:

Totemo tsukareta node sukoshi yasumitai desu.	I got very tired, so I would like to [take a] rest.
Okane o harawanakatta node okutte kimasen deshita.	I didn't send the money for it; that's why it didn't come.

m. *Noni* = despite that; but; although; and yet:

Yonda noni henji ga nai.	I called her, but there was no answer.
Itta noni awanakatta.	Although I went there, I didn't see her.

n. *To* =

(1) (Following a present form) whenever:

Hima da to sanpo shi-masu.	Whenever I am free, I take a walk.

(2) Acts as an "end quote" when it precedes a verb meaning "say," "hear," "ask," "think," "believe":

Itsu kimasu ka to kikareta.	I was asked [as to] when I would be coming.

(3) (When it follows a tentative and is in turn followed by *shita*) to be on the point of doing (something); to try to do (something):

Uchi o deyoo to shita tokoro e tomodachi ga kimashita.	Just as I was about to go out, a friend of mine came (to visit me).

o. *-Tari . . . -tari suru* =

(1) Sometimes does (something); at other times does (something else):

Nihon to Amerika no aida o ittari kitari shite imasu.	She travels back and forth between Japan and the United States.

(2) Does (one thing) and (another):

Hito ga nottari oritari shite imasu.	Some people are getting on, some are getting off.

p. Terminal particles:

(1) *Ne* = isn't it? doesn't it?

Erai hito desu ne?	He is a great man, isn't he?

(2) *Sa* = sure it is so (used only by men, slang):

Shitte iru sa!	Of course I know it.

(3) *Wa, wa yo* = a diminutive used only by women:

Sanji ni denwa o kakeru wa (yo).[1]	I will phone you at three.

(4) *Yo* = an exclamatory particle:

Kyoo wa okyakusan ga arimasu yo!	We are going to have a visitor today!

(5) *Zo* = an emphatic particle (used only by men, slang):

Naguru zo!	I'll hit you!

---

[1] The use of *yo* is optional.

19. NEGATIVES

a. Used with verbs:

(1) Plain negative present—formed from the base of a consonant verb plus the suffix *-anai*, or the base of a vowel verb plus *-nai:*

Kaku.	I write.
Kakanai.	I don't write.
Taberu.	I eat.
Tabenai.	I don't eat.

Notice that a verb like *kau* [buy] or *warau* [laugh], whose plain present affirmative ends in two vowels, appends an extra *w* before adding *-anai:*

Kawanai.	I don't buy (it).
Warawanai.	She doesn't laugh.

(2) Plain negative past—formed from the stem of the negative present (the form without the final *-i*) plus *-katta* (like the plain negative past of an adjective):

Kaita.	I wrote.
Kakanakatta.	I didn't write.

(3) Plain negative tentative:
  (a) For a consonant verb, use the plain present affirmative plus *-mai*.
  (b) For a vowel verb, use the pre-*masu* form plus *-mai*.

(c) For the irregular verbs, use *komai* and *shimai*.

Kakoo.	I think I'll write it.
Kakumai.	I don't think I'll write it.
Tabeyoo.	I think I'll eat.
Tabemai.	I don't think I'll eat.

b. Used with a copula:

(1) Plain forms:

... *da*	It is ...
... *de aru*	It is (formal, "bookish") ...
... *ja nai* ... *dewa nai*	It is not ...
... *datta*	It was ...
... *ja nakatta* ... *dewa nakatta*	It was not ...
... *daroo*	It is probably ...
... *ja nai daroo* ... *dewa nai daroo*	It is most probably not ...

(2) Polite forms:

... *desu*	It is ...
... *ja arimasen* ... *dewa arimasen*	It is not ...
... *deshita*	It was ...
... *ja arimasen deshita* ... *dewa arimasen deshita*	It wasn't ...
... *deshoo*	It is probably ...
... *ja nai deshoo* ... *dewa nai deshoo*	It is most probably not ...

c. Used with *i*-adjectives:

(1) Plain forms:

Takai.	It is expensive.
Takaku nai.	It is not expensive.
Takakatta.	It was expensive.
Takaku nakatta.	It wasn't expensive.
Takai daroo.	It may be expensive.
Takaku nai daroo.	It is probably not expensive.

(2) Polite forms:

Takai desu.	It is expensive.
Takaku arimasen.	It is not expensive.
Takakatta desu.	It was expensive.
Takaku arimasen deshita. *Takaku nakatta desu.* }	It was not expensive.
Takai deshoo.	It is probably expensive.
Takaku nai deshoo.	It is probably not expensive.

d. Other negative expressions (used with negative predicates):

zenzen	not (at all)
hitotsu mo	nothing
dare mo	no one
doko mo	nowhere
nani mo	nothing
dochira mo	neither . . . nor
kesshite	never
Zenzen wakarimasen deshita.	I did not understand it at all.

20. WORD ORDER

There are two very important rules to remember for word order in declarative sentences:

a. A predicate word (the copula, verb, or adjective used as a predicate) is placed at the *end* of the clause or sentence except when a sentence-ending particle such as *ka* (the question mark particle) or *ne* [isn't it? doesn't it?] is used, in which case the predicate word is usually placed *immediately before* such a particle.

b. A modifier *always precedes the word or clause it modifies:*

   (1) An adjective or adjectival phrase (a noun plus *no*) always precedes the noun it modifies.
   (2) A demonstrative always precedes the noun.
   (3) An adverb or adverbial phrase always precedes the adjective, adverb, verb, or copula it modifies.
   (4) A modifying clause always precedes the noun it modifies.

For example:

akai booshi	a red hat
ano hito	that person
ano hito no booshi	that person's hat; her (his) hat
ano hito no akai booshi	that person's red hat; her red hat
ookina booshi	a big hat
ano hito no ookina akai booshi	that person's big red hat
katta booshi	the hat she bought
kinoo katta booshi	the hat she bought yesterday

kinoo Matsuya de katta booshi	the hat she bought at Matsuya yesterday
kanojo ga kinoo no gogo Matsuya de katta booshi	the hat she bought at Matsuya yesterday afternoon
kanojo ga kinoo no gogo Matsuya de katta ookina akai booshi	that big red hat she bought at Matsuya yesterday afternoon
kanojo ga kinoo no gogo watakushi to issho ni itte Matsuya de katta ookina akai booshi	that big red hat she bought yesterday afternoon with me at Matsuya

21. QUESTIONS

The word order for questions is the same as for declarative sentences. The question particle *ka* may or may not be added at the end to show that a question is being asked. For instance:

When *ka* is used, it is not necessary to use the rising intonation. The intonation may remain similar to that of a declarative sentence, even though a question is being asked. When a question is being asked and *ka* is not used, however, the rising intonation must be employed, and the last syllable should be pronounced with a distinct rise in pitch. (See Lesson 13.)

Ikimasu.	I am going.
Ikimasu?	Are you going?
Ikimasu ka?	Are you going?

See the following section for other words that are used in formulating questions.

22. QUESTION WORDS

There are several words that are used to form questions. Study the following list to learn what the words are and how they are used.

QUESTION WORDS	MEANING	NOTES
nan, nani	what thing? what? how many?	For the usage of *nan,* see Lesson 32. The meaning "how many?" applies only when the word is used before a counter.
nannin	how many people?	
ikutsu	what number? how many?	The answer must be a number.
iku-	how many . . . ?	A prefix used only with a counter.
itsu	what time? when?	When used adverbially, it may sometimes be used without a particle.
Itsu kimashita ka?	When did it arrive?	
Itsu hajimar- imasu ka?	When does it begin?	

Itsu ga ii desu ka?	When would it be good for you?	
dare	which person? who?	*dare no:* whose? *dare ni:* to whom? *dare kara:* from whom? *dare to:* with whom?
dore	which thing? which?	Used when there is a choice of more than two.
dochira	which of these two? which direction? which place (polite)?	Used when there is a choice of only two.
dochira e	where to?	
dochira kara	where from?	
dotchi	see above	A (more informal) variant for the first two meanings of *dochira*.
doko	which place? where?	
Doko ni arimasu ka?	Where is it?	
Doko de tabemashita ka?	Where did you eat?	

| *Doko kara kimashita ka?* | Where did you come from? |
| *Doko ga itai desu ka?* | Where does it hurt? |

dono	which	A demonstrative used when there is a choice of *more than* two. Use *dochira no* when there is a choice of *only* two.
donna	what sort of?	A demonstrative used when you are interested in the kind or type of thing being discussed.
doo	how? in what manner?	An adverb.
ikaga	how (polite)?	An adverb; same as *doo* (above), but used in refined speech.

23. SOMETHING, EVERYTHING, NOTHING, ANYTHING

Each of the question words appearing in the first column of this table undergoes a change in meaning when it is used together with one of the particles appearing in the other columns. The new meaning is shown for each combination.

TABLE III

QUESTION WORD	+ ka	+ mo (used with affirmative predicate)	+ mo (used with negative predicate)	+ de mo	+ -te mo
nani, nan = what	nani ka = something or other	nani mo ka mo = everything	nani mo = nothing	nan de mo = anything	nani . . . te mo = whatsoever, no matter what
dore = which one	dore ka = one or the other; anyone	dore mo = all, any	dore mo = no one, not anyone, not a one	dore de mo = whichever it may be; any at all	dore . . . te mo = whichsoever, no matter which
dochira = which of the two	dochira ka = either one	dochira mo = both	dochira mo = not either one, neither one	dochira de mo = whichever it may be, either one	dochira . . . te mo = whichever, no matter which
dotchi[1] = which of the two	dotchi ka = either one	dotchi mo = both	dotchi mo = not either one, neither one	dotchi de mo = whichever it may be, either one	dotchi . . . te mo = whichever, no matter which
doko = which place	doko ka = somewhere or other	doko mo = everywhere; all places	doko mo = not anywhere, nowhere	doko de mo = wherever it may be, any place at all	doko . . . te mo = wherever, no matter where
dare = which person	dare ka = somebody	dare mo = everybody	dare mo = not anybody, nobody	dare de mo = whoever it may be, anybody at all	dare . . . te mo = whoever, no matter who

[1] *Dotchi* is more informal than *dochira*.

TABLE III

QUESTION WORD	+ ka	+ mo (used with affirmative predicate)	+ mo (used with negative predicate)	+ de mo	+ -te mo
itsu = what time	*itsu ka* = sometime or other	*itsu mo* = always	*itsu mo* = not anytime, never	*itsu de mo* = whenever it may be; anytime at all	*itsu . . . te mo* = whenever, no matter when
doo = how	*doo ka* = somehow or other; please, by some means or other	*doo mo* = in every way, very	*doo mo* = somehow; not; in no way	*doo de mo* = however it may be; anyway at all	*doo . . . te mo* = however (one does); no matter how
dooshite = why	*dooshite ka* = somehow or other, for some unknown reason	*dooshite mo* = by all means, under any circumstances	*dooshite mo* = somehow or other . . . not; however one tries . . . not	*dooshite de mo* = by all means; at all costs	—
ikutsu = how many	*ikutsu ka* = some number, several	*ikutsu mo* = any number	*ikutsu mo* = not many, no great number, not much to speak of	*ikutsu de mo* = however many it may be; any number at all	*ikutsu . . . te mo* = however many (one may); no matter how many
ikura = how much	*ikura ka* = some amount	*ikura mo* = any amount; ever so much	*ikura mo* = not much; no great amount	*ikura de mo* = whatever amount it may be	*ikura . . . te mo* = however much it may be (one may); no matter how much

24. EVEN IF, EVEN THOUGH

a. Affirmative:
   Use *-te* plus *-mo:*

Ame ga futte mo iki- masu.	I'll [still] go, even if it rains.
Takakute mo kaimasu.	I'll [still] buy it, even if it's expensive.

b. Negative:
   Use *-nakute* plus *mo:*

Ame ga yamanakute mo ikimasu.	I will go [anyhow], even if it doesn't stop raining.
Yasuku nakute mo ka- maimasen.	I don't care, even if it's not cheap.

c. Permission:
   Use *-te mo ii desu* for "you may [you have my permission to]"; use *-nakute mo ii desu* for "you don't
   have to [you have my permission not to; even if you
   don't, it is all right with me]":

Itte mo ii desu.	You may go.
Ikanakute mo ii desu.	You don't have to go.

d. No matter how, no matter who, no matter how
   much:
   Use a question word plus *-te mo:*

Donna ni yasukute mo kaitaku arimasen.	I don't want to buy it, no matter how cheap it is.
Dare ga shite mo kekka wa onaji desu.	No matter who does it, the result will be the same.
Ikura yonde mo imi ga wakarimasen deshita.	I couldn't understand it, no matter how many times I read it.

25. HEARSAY

To express the ideas "I hear that . . ." or "They say that . . ." in Japanese:

a. For the affirmative:
Use a plain affirmative form of a verb, an *i*-adjective, or the copula plus *soo desu:*

Kyoo wa Yamada-san ga kuru soo desu.	I hear that Mr. Yamada is coming to visit us today.
Sapporo de wa yuki ga futta soo desu.	I hear that it snowed in Sapporo.
Takai soo desu.	I understand (that) it's expensive.
Tanaka-san wa byooki da soo desu.	I hear Ms. Tanaka is sick.

b. For the negative:
Use a plain negative form of a verb, an *i*-adjective, or the copula plus *soo desu.*

Rajio no tenki yohoo de wa kyoo wa ame wa furanai soo desu.	According to the weather forecast, it's not going to rain today.
Yamada-san wa konakatta soo desu.	I hear that Mr. Yamada didn't come.
Takaku nai soo desu.	I hear (that) it's not expensive.
Furansugo wa joozu ja nai soo desu.	I hear she is not good at French.

26. SEEMING

You can express the idea of "it seems" or "it seems to me that . . ." in several ways in Japanese:

a. For the affirmative:

    (1) Use a plain affirmative form plus *yoo desu:*

Moo shitte iru yoo desu.	It seems to me that he already knows it.
Chotto muzukashikatta yoo desu.	It seems that it was a little difficult.
Minna genki na[1] yoo desu.	It seems that everybody is fine.

    (2) Use a plain affirmative form plus *rashii desu:*

Moo shitte iru rashii desu.	It seems to me that he already knows it.
Ano hito wa Amerika e kaetta rashii desu.	It seems that he has gone back to the United States.

[1] The copula *da* (present affirmative) becomes *na* before *yoo desu.*

It is more likely, however, that the sentence with *rashii desu* will be interpreted with the meaning of "hearsay" like *soo desu* in Section 25 than with the meaning of "it seems."

(3) Use an *i*-adjective without the final -*i* or a *na*-adjective without the copula plus -*soo desu:*

Kurushisoo desu.	It seems that he is finding it painful.
Genki soo desu.	It seems that she is fine.

b. For the negative:

(1) Use a plain negative form plus *yoo desu:*

Mada shiranai yoo desu.	It seems that he is unaware of this.
Amari takaku nai yoo desu.	It seems that it is not very expensive.

(2) Use a plain negative form plus *rashii desu:*

Mada shiranai rashii desu.	It seems that he is unaware of this.
Kare wa Nihon e konakatta rashii desu.	Apparently [it seems that] he didn't come to Japan.

(3) Use a negative *i*-adjective without the final -*i* or the negative copula without the final -*i* plus -*sasoo desu:*

Kurushiku nasasoo desu.	He is apparently [it seems that he is] not finding it painful.

*Are wa Nakamura-san   That does not seem to
    ja nasasoo desu.   be Ms. Nakamura.*

27. IMMINENCE

To express the idea "it appears that . . . will soon happen":

a. For the affirmative:
   Use the pre-*masu* form of the verb plus *-soo desu:*

*Ame ga furisoo desu   It looks like rain,
    ne.   doesn't it?
Yamada-san wa yame-   It looks as if Mr. Ya-
    soo desu.   mada is ready to quit.*

b. For the negative:
   Use the pre-*masu* form of a verb plus *-soo ja arimasen:*

*Ame wa furisoo ja ari-   It doesn't look as
    masen.   though it will rain soon.
Nedan wa yasuku nari-   It doesn't look as
    soo ja arimasen.   though the price is
                               going down.*

28. OBLIGATION AND PROHIBITION

To convey the idea of obligation or impulsion (expressed in English by "should," "must," "ought to," "have to"):

a. For the affirmative:

   (1) Use the negative *-ba* form of a verb, an *i*-adjective, or the copula, plus *narimasen* or

ikemasen [if you don't do it, it won't do; if not (something), it won't do].

(2) Use the negative *-te* form plus *wa* plus *narimasen* or *ikemasen*.[1]

Ikanakereba narimasen.	
Ikanakereba ikemasen.	I should (must, have to,
Ikanakute wa nari-	ought to) go.
masen.	
Ikanakute wa ikemasen.	
Yoku nakereba narimasen.	
Yoku nakereba ike-	
masen.	It should (must, has to,
Yoku nakute wa nari-	ought to) be good.
masen.	
Yoku nakute wa ike-	
masen.	

b. For the negative:

(1) Use the affirmative *-te* form of a verb plus *wa* plus *narimasen* [if you do (something), it won't do; if it is (something), it won't do]:

Itte wa narimasen.	I should not (must not, ought not) go.

(2) Use the affirmative *-te* form of a verb, an *i*-adjective, or the copula plus *wa* plus *ikemasen* or *dame desu:*

Koko de asonde wa ikemasen.	You should not (must not, ought not) play here.

[1] Notice the use of a double negative.

| *Yasashikute wa dame desu.* | It should not be easy. |
| *Kono kaban de wa dame desu.* | You should not use this bag. [It should not be this bag.] |

c. *Beki desu* [should], *beki ja arimasen* [should not]: *Beki* is a form remaining from classical Japanese.

(1) For the affirmative, use the plain present of a verb plus *beki desu:*

| *Iku beki desu.* | I should (must, have to, ought to) go. |
| *Iku beki deshita.* | I should have gone. |

(2) For the negative, use the plain present affirmative of a verb plus *beki ja arimasen:*

| *Iku beki ja arimasen.* | I should not go. |
| *Iku beki ja arimasen deshita.* | I shouldn't have gone. |

(3) For warning or prohibition (seen in public signs only), the plain present affirmative of a verb is used with *bekarazu* [don't]:[1]

Hairu bekarazu!	No admission!
Tooru bekarazu!	No trespassing!
Sawaru bekarazu!	Don't touch!

---

[1] *Bekarazu*, which is a derived form of *beki*, is becoming obsolete in public signs. *-Nai de kudasai* [Please do not—] is now preferred.

29. PERMISSION

To express the granting of permission, use -*te* plus *mo* plus *ii desu* [you may, it's all right to]:

Kaitakereba katte mo ii desu.	If you want to buy it, you may (buy it).
Uchi e motte kaette mo ii desu.	You may take it home if you wish.
Takakute mo ii desu.	It may be expensive. [Even if it is expensive, it is all right.]
Kono jisho de mo ii desu.	This dictionary will do. [It is all right to use this dictionary.]

30. ALTERNATIVES

In statements setting forth a choice of alternatives, use:

a. -*Tari* . . . -*tari shimasu* (the -*ta* form plus *ri* followed by the -*ta* form plus *ri suru*):

Kyoo wa ame ga futtari yandari shite imasu.	Today it has been raining off and on.
Kare wa chikagoro gakkoo e ittari ikanakattari shimasu.	He has been irregular recently in (his) attendance at school.
Nichiyoobi no gogo wa shinbun o yondari terebi o mitari shimasu.	On Sunday afternoons, I spend my time doing such things as reading newspapers and watching television.

Hito ga detari haittari shite imasu.	People are going in and out.

b. *-Tari shimasu* (a single *-tari* followed by *suru*):

Eiga e ittari shima-shita.	Among the various things (I did), I went to the movies. I spent my time going to the movies and doing things like that.
Miyagemono o kattari shimashita.	I bought souvenirs and did (other) things like that.

31. PASSIVE, POTENTIAL, AND RESPECT

A verb made up of its base plus *-areru* or *-rareru* may be any one of the following: (1) passive, (2) potential, or (3) respect. (Use *-areru* with a consonant verb and *-rareru* with a vowel verb.) The exact meaning of such a verb is determined by the context in which it is used.

a. Passive:

Watashi wa keikan ni namae o kikare-mashita.	I was asked my name by a policeman.

b. Potential:

Nihon no eiga wa Amerika de mo mi-raremasu.	Japanese movies can be seen in the United States, too. [One can see a Japanese movie in America, too.]

c. Respect:

Itoo-sensei wa kinoo Amerika kara kae-raremashita.	My teacher, Mr. Ito, came back from the United States yesterday.

The passive of some Japanese verbs—most particularly the passive forms of intransitive verbs—means "(something) happened when it wasn't wanted," or "I underwent (something)," or "I suffered from the interference of (something)":

Densha no naka de kodomo ni nakarete komarimashita.	We were embarrassed by our child, who cried continuously while riding on a train.
Ame ni furarete sukkari nurete shimaimashita.	We were drenched by the rain.

32. CAUSATIVE

To form the causative of a verb, add *-aseru* to the base of a consonant verb and *-saseru* to the base of a vowel verb. The causative forms of the irregular verbs are (for *kuru*) *kosaseru* and (for *suru*) *saseru*.

Causative verbs may be used to express the thought that:

a. X *causes* (makes, forces) Y to do (something)

b. X *allows* (permits, lets) Y to do (something)

Notice that in each instance the element Y is marked by the particle *ni*.

Tanaka-san wa Yamada-san ni den-poo o utasemashita.	Ms. Tanaka had Mr. Yamada send a telegram.
Kodomo ni kimono o kisasete kudasai.	Please have the children put on their clothes.
Kyoo wa itsu mo yori ichijikan hayaku kaerasete itadakitai desu.	I would like to have your permission to go home one hour earlier than usual. [I would like to have you make me go home . . .]

A causative can be combined with a passive ending. If the causative ending comes first, the combination means "be made," not "be allowed."

*Ik**aserare**mashita.*	I was made to go.
*Tabes**aserare**mashita.*	I was made to eat it.

33. DESIDERATIVES

The desiderative is the grammatical term for verbal expressions that signify a desire to do something.

a. To say, "I want to do (something)," use the pre-*masu* form plus *-tai:*

Kyoo wa kaimono ni iki-tai desu.	I want to go shopping today.
Ima wa nani mo tabe-taku arimasen.	I don't want to eat anything now.

b. To express the idea, "one shows that he/she wants to do (something)," add *-tagaru* to the pre-*masu* form:

Kodomo ga soto e ikitagatte imasu.	The children can't wait to go outside.
Uchi no kodomo wa sono kusuri o nomitagarimasen.	Our child doesn't like to take that medicine. [Our child shows that he doesn't like to take that medicine.]

c. Use the stem (the form without the final *-i*) of an *i*-adjective plus *-garu* to express the meaning that "someone[1] shows outwardly that he/she feels . . .":

Samugarimashita.	He showed that he felt cold.
Hoshigarimashita.	He showed that he wanted to have it.

d. To say, "I want you to do (something) for me," use the *-te* form of a verb plus *itadakitai desu:*

Kono tegami o Eigo ni yakushite itadakitai desu.	I would like you to translate this letter into English for me.
Kore o katte itadakitai desu.	I would like you to buy this for me.

[1] Usually not the speaker.

34. To Do (Something) for . . .

a. To say, "Somebody does (something) for me," in the respect form, use *-te kudasaimasu;* in the neutral form, use *-te kuremasu:*

Sono koto wa Yamada-san ga shirasete kudasaimashita.	Mr. Yamada was kind enough to inform me about it.
Shirasete kudasai.[1]	Please let me know.
Ani ga katte kure-mashita.	My older brother bought it for me.

b. Use *-te agemasu* to say "I (or others) do (something) for you (him, her)." In the humble form, use *-te sashiagemasu.* You can use *-te yarimasu* when the recipient of the favor is an animal or plant. When the recipient of the favor is a person who is inferior to the speaker, such as a child, *-te yarimasu* can be used, but it is not always appropriate. For this reason, it is safer not to use *-te yarimasu* when the recipient of the favor is a person.

Sore wa anata ni katte ageta no desu.	I bought it for you.
Anata ni katte sashiage-mashoo.	I'll buy it for you.
Inu ni katte yarimashita.	I bought it for our dog.

c. Use *-te itadakimasu* to say, "I (or others) have you (him, her) do (something)" in the humble form, and *-te moraimasu* in the neutral form:

Yamada-san ni katte itadakimashita.	I had Mr. Yamada buy it for me.

[1] *Kudasai* is a request form of *kudasaimasu.*

Tomodachi ni yakushite moraimashita.	I had a friend of mine translate it for me.
Yamada-san ni yakushite itadaite kudasai.	Please have it translated by Mr. Yamada.

35. MAY, PERHAPS, PROBABLY

To say, "something may (might) happen," add *kamoshiremasen* after a plain form of a verb, an *i*-adjective, or the copula.

Ame ga furu kamoshiremasen.	It may rain (but I can't tell for sure).
Shiken wa muzukashikatta kamoshiremasen.	The test might have been difficult.
Tanaka-san wa tenisu ga joozu kamoshiremasen.[1]	Ms. Tanaka may be good at tennis.

36. IF AND WHEN

a. The use of *to:*

(1) Use *to* between two clauses to show that the second clause follows as a natural result of the first clause. The particle *to* in such a case comes at the end of the "if" or "when" clause:

Ame ga furu to anmari hito ga takusan kimasen.	When it rains, not too many people come.

[1] The copula *da* (present, affirmative) is deleted before *kamoshiremasen*.

| *Kippu ga nai to haire-* *masen.* | If you don't have tick- ets, you can't get in. [If there isn't a ticket . . .] |
| *Atarashii to takai desu.* | When it's new, it's expensive. |

(2) Note that the predicate before *to* is *always* in the present form regardless of the tense of the rest of the sentence:

| *Ie ni kaeru to dare mo* *imasen deshita.* | When I got home, nobody was there. |

(3) The predicate before *to* usually appears in the plain present form. When *to* is used for "if" or "when," the predicate of the main clause (that is, the one following the clause ending in *to*) must be the *-u* or *-ta* form; it can *never* end in *-masyoo* or *-te kudasai*.

b. The use of *-tara*:
 To introduce a condition or a supposition, add *-ra* to the *-ta* form of a verb, adjective, or copula:

Ame ga futtara iki- *masen.*	If it rains, I won't go.
Denpoo ga kitara *denwa o kakete* *kudasai.*	If you get a telegram, please phone me.
Anmari samukattara *mado o shimete* *kudasai.*	If it's too cold (for you), please shut the window.
Nihonjin dattara dare *de mo ii desu.*	Anybody who is Japanese will do. [If it's Japanese, anybody will do.]

c. The use of *nara:*
   Use *nara* with a plain form of a verb, an *i*-adjective, and the copula to express "if."

Byooki[1] *nara yasunda hoo ga ii desu.*	If you are sick, you had better rest.
Shiranai nara oshiete agemasu.	If you don't know, I'll teach you.
Yasui nara kaimasu.	If it is inexpensive, I'll buy it.

d. The use of *-ba:*
   The *-ba* form is used only for unconfirmed situations. The *-ba* form is formed in the following ways:

   Consonant verb:
   Drop the final *-u* of the dictionary form and add *-eba*.

furu → *fureba*

   Vowel verb:
   Drop the final *-ru* of the dictionary form and add *-reba*.

miru → *mireba*

   Irregular verb:

kuru	→	*kureba*
suru	→	*sureba*

---

[1] For present affirmative, the copula is deleted.

i-adjective:
Drop the final *-i* of the dictionary form and add *-kereba*.

takai	→	*takakereba*

Negative of a verb, an *i*-adjective, the copula: Drop the final *-i* and add *-kereba*.

furanai	→	*furanakereba*
takaku nai	→	*takaku na-kereba*
shizuka ja nai	→	*shizuka ja nakereba*

Ame ga fureba ikimasen.	If it rains, I won't go.
Ame ga furanakereba ikimasu.	If it doesn't rain, I will go.
Mireba sugu wakari-masu.	If I take a look at it, I can readily identify it.
Takakereba kaimasen.	If it's expensive, I won't buy it.
Shizuka ja nakereba ikitaku arimasen.	If it is not quiet, I do not want to go.

e. The use of *-te wa:*
   This expression for "if" is most often found in an expression denoting "must" (e.g., "if you don't do . . . , it won't do"):

Soko e itte wa dame desu.	You must not go there. If you go there, it will be no good.
Okane ga nakute wa kaemasen.	If you have no money, you can't buy it.

Yoku benkyoo shi-　　　If you don't study hard
　nakute wa ikemasen.　(you must!), it won't
　　　　　　　　　　　do.

37. WHETHER ... OR ... , IF ... OR ...

a. The uses of *ka:*

(1) Use *ka ... ka* in a sentence conveying the
meaning "whether or," "if or":

Okane ga aru ka nai　　I don't know if he has
　ka shirimasen.　　　　money or not.
Takai ka yasui ka shiri-　I don't know if it is
　masen.　　　　　　　expensive or not.

For present affirmative, the copula is deleted:

Suki ka kirai ka kiite　　Please ask her whether
　kudasai.　　　　　　she likes it or dis-
　　　　　　　　　　　likes it.

(2) Use *ka doo ka* to express "whether or not," "if
or not":

Okane ga aru ka doo　　I don't know if he has
　ka shirimasen.　　　　money or not.
Takai ka doo ka　　　　I don't know if it's
　shirimasen.　　　　　expensive or not.
Iku ka doo ka　　　　　I don't know whether
　shirimasen.　　　　　she is going or not.

(3) Use *ka* in a sentence having the sense of
"either ... or":

Suiyoobi ka Mokuyoobi ni kimasu.	She will come on Wednesday or else on Thursday.
Yoshida-san ka mata wa Kida-san ni kite moratte kudasai.	Please have either Mr. Yoshida or Mr. Kida come.

38. INDEFINITE PRONOUNS

Indefinite pronouns appear at the end of a clause and convert that entire clause into a noun equivalent. For example:

a. *No* = the one (the time, the person, the place); the act of:

Kesa hayaku uchi ni denwa o kaketa no wa Tanaka-san de- shita.	The person who phoned us early this morning was Ms. Tanaka.
Kinoo mita no wa Amerika no eiga deshita.	The one we saw yester- day was an Ameri- can movie.
Kyooto e itta no wa Shigatsu deshita.	It was in April that we went to Kyoto. [The time when we went to Kyoto was April.]
Mainichi yoru osoku made hataraku no wa karada ni warui desu.	Working until late at night every day is bad for your health.

b. *Koto* = the act of; the experience of:

Hokkaido e itta koto ga arimasu.	I have been to Hokkaido. [The experience of having gone to Hokkaido exists.]
Nihongo wa hanasu koto wa dekimasu ga yomu koto wa dekimasen.	I can speak Japanese, but I can't read it.

39. IN ORDER TO

a. To say, "one goes or comes in order to do (something)":

(1) Use the pre-*masu* form plus *ni* plus a verb of locomotion such as *ikimasu* or *kimasu:*

Mi ni ikimasu.	I am going there to see it.
Gohan o tabe ni ikimashita.	He went to eat.
Amerika no shinbun o yomi ni kimashita.	I came to read American newspapers.

(2) Use a noun describing an action, plus *ni* plus a verb of locomotion:

Kaimono ni ikimashita.	He went out to shop [for shopping].
Ryokoo ni dekakemashita.	He set out on a journey.

b. To indicate, "one does (something) for the purpose of doing (something else)," the predicate verb can be any verb, including a verb of locomotion.

(1) A present-tense verb plus the indefinite pronoun *no* plus *ni* plus a verb:

Kono megane wa hon o yomu no ni tsukaimasu. — I use these glasses for reading books.

Kono basu wa shita-machi e iku no ni benri desu. — This bus is convenient for going downtown.

(2) A present-tense verb plus *tame ni* plus a verb:

Kuruma o kau tame ni okane o karimashita. — I borrowed some money to buy a car.

Tomodachi o miokuru tame ni eki e ikimashita. — He went to the station to see a friend off.

40. REQUESTS, COMMANDS

There are several ways to express a request, command, or wish in Japanese. You can use:

a. *-Te kudasai* = please do (something):

(1) For the affirmative:

Hayaku kite kudasai. — Please come early. Come early.

Yukkuri hanashite kudasai. — Please speak slowly.

(2) For the negative:

Hayaku konaide kudasai. — Please don't come early.

Yukkuri hanasanaide kudasai.	Please don't speak slowly.

b. *O kudasai* = please give me:

Rokujuunien no kitte o kudasai.	Give me a sixty-two-yen stamp, please.
Mizu o kudasai.	Please give me some water.

c. *Ga hoshii desu* = I want to have (preceded by the noun showing the thing desired):

Puroguramu ga hoshii desu.	I would like a program.
Osake wa hoshiku arimasen.	I don't want any sake.

d. *-Te itadakitai (no)* desu *(ga)*[1] = I would like to ask you to:

Kore o yonde itadakitai desu.	I would like to ask you to read this for me (but do you have time or would it interfere, etc.).
Eigo de kaite itadakitai no desu ga.	Would you mind writing (may I trouble you to write) this in English?

e. *Yoo ni shite kudasai* = be careful (not) to, try to:

Kono tegami wa hayaku dasu yoo ni shite kudasai.	Please make every effort to send this mail out early.

[1] The use of *no* and *ga* is optional in this construction.

| *Kore wa otosanai yoo ni shite kudasai.* | Please be careful not to drop this. |

f. *-Te choodai* = please do (something):
This request form is used (primarily by women) in an intimate, informal, or relaxed situation.

| *Katte choodai.* | Please buy it. |
| *Sore o totte choodai.* | Please pick it up. |

g. The plain imperative of a verb:
Each verb has a form called the "plain imperative," which is constructed by adding *-e* to the base of a consonant verb and *-ro* to the base of a vowel verb. The imperative of the irregular verbs is *koi* for *kuru* [come] and *shiro* for *suru* [do].

| *Ike!* | Go! |
| *Miro!* | Look at it! |

Take note, however, that the plain imperative is used *only* in "rough" speech, and *should not* be used in everyday conversation.

41. ADVERBIAL EXPRESSIONS

a. Formation of adverbial expressions:

(1) Many adverbs are formed by adding *-ku* to the stems (the plain present affirmative minus *-i*) of adjectives:

ADJECTIVE		ADVERB	
takai	expensive	*takaku*	expensively
yasui	cheap	*yasuku*	cheaply

yasashii	easy	*yasashiku*	easily
karui	light	*karuku*	lightly

(2) Some adverbial expressions are formed from *na*-adjectives by using *ni* following the *na*-adjective:

ADJECTIVAL PHRASE		ADVERBIAL PHRASE	
kantan na	simple	*kantan ni*	simply
benri na	convenient	*benri ni*	conveniently
tokubetsu na	special	*tokubetsu ni*	especially
joozu na	skillful	*joozu ni*	skillfully

b. Comparison of adverbial expressions:
   Adverbial expressions can be compared like adjectives (see Section 16 of the Summary of Japanese Grammar):

POSITIVE	COMPARATIVE	SUPERLATIVE
takaku = expensively	*motto takaku* = more expensively	*ichiban takaku* = most expensively

c. Adverbial expressions of place:
   Use *ni* when the verb is *arimasu*, *imasu*, or *sunde imasu*. Use *de* for most other cases.

koko ni, koko de	here
soba ni, soba de	at the side, near
mae ni, mae de	before, in front
ushiro ni, ushiro de	behind
ue ni, ue de	on top
shita ni, shita de	underneath
naka ni, naka de	inside

soto ni, soto de	outside
doko ni mo, doko de mo	everywhere *(with an af-firmative verb)*
doko ni mo, doko de mo	nowhere *(with a nega-tive verb)*
tooku ni, tooku de	far
chikaku ni, chikaku de	near
doko ni, doko de	where
soko ni, soko de	there (nearby)
asoko ni, asoko de	there (far off)

d. Adverbial expressions of time:

kyoo	today
ashita, asu, myoonichi	tomorrow
kinoo, sakujitsu	yesterday
ototoi, issakujitsu	the day before yesterday
asatte, myoogonichi	the day after tomorrow
ima	now
sono toki	then
mae ni	before
moto	once, formerly
hayaku	early
sugu	soon, presently
osoku	late
tokidoki	sometimes, from time to time
itsu mo	always
nagai aida	for a long time
. . . tari . . . tari shimasu	now . . . now, some-times . . . sometimes (See Section 30 of the Summary of Japanese Grammar.)
mada	as yet, still

moo	already *(with an affir-mative)*
moo	no longer *(with a nega-tive)*

e. Adverbial expressions of manner:

yoku	well, frequently, studi-ously, hard
waruku	ill, badly
konna ni	thus, so
onaji yoo ni	similarly
hantai ni	otherwise, conversely
issho ni	together
taihen	much, very
yorokonde	willingly
toku ni	especially
waza to	on purpose, expressly

f. Adverbial expressions of quantity or degree:

takusan	much, many
juubun (ni)[1]	enough
sukoshi	little
motto	more
hidoku	extremely, excessively
amari, anmari	too, too much, too many
sonna ni	so much, so many

42. THE WRITING SYSTEM

The Japanese writing system contains four types of symbols that are usually used together:

[1] The use of *ni* is optional.

a. One set of 46 phonetic symbols called *hiragana*

b. One set of 46 phonetic symbols called *katakana*

c. 1,945 basic ideographic symbols called *kanji*

d. The letters of the English (or Roman) alphabet, called *Roomaji*, together with the Arabic numerals, which are called *arabiya suuji* or *san'yoo suuji*

Each of the symbols in *hiragana* and *katakana* represents *one syllable*, and each of the forty-six basic syllables of the Japanese language is written with a single symbol, whether in *hiragana* or *katakana* (see Tables IV and VIII, which follow). *Hiragana* symbols are considered to be standard, and are most widely used. Katakana symbols are used primarily for (a) writing "borrowed" words (words derived from Western languages), (b) giving special emphasis to certain words within a sentence, in much the same way that italics are used in English, and (c) writing certain onomatopoeic words.

(1) The hiragana symbols:
Study the charts of *hiragana* symbols on pages 399–403. Compare these charts with Chart I of Table I on page 310. (The syllables in parentheses are only for *katakana*.) Note that the *sound* or *syllable* for each symbol appears in the corresponding square of that chart. For instance, at the point of intersection of vertical and horizontal columns 1 in the chart that follows this section, the symbol stands for *ka*.

SPECIAL NOTES FOR
THE *HIRAGANA* SYMBOLS

(a) Note that the first vertical row of symbols (headed "O") shows the symbols for the *vowel syllables only*. In all of the other columns (except the last), each consonant (or semi-vowel)-plus-vowel combination has a new symbol, as each stands for a different syllable.

(b) Note, too, that there are *two* symbols for the vowel syllable *o*. The one in column 9 (を) is used *only* to write the particle *o* (the thing acted on, or the direct object); it is *never* used to represent anything else.

(c) Some symbols have a dual function:

    (i) The symbol for *ha* (は) is also used to write *wa* in the following cases:

particle *wa*	これは	kore wa
Konnichi wa.	こんにちは	Hello.
Konban wa.	こんばんは	Good evening.
dewa	では	well then
negative of copula	しずかでは ありません	It is not quiet.

    (ii) The symbol used for *he* (へ) is also used to write the particle *e* [to, toward]. The symbol for the vowel *e* (え) (which appears in the 0 column) is used to write all other *e*'s.

(d) Write syllables other than the forty-six basic syllables covered in the above table as follows:

(i) Syllables listed in Chart II of Table I (see page 311) are written using the basic symbols plus a diacritical mark (" or °) on the upper right shoulder of each symbol, as in Table VI, on page 403.

Table V shows the number of strokes that are necessary to write each of the *hiragana* symbols. In each chart within the table, the first vertical column shows the completed symbol; the following columns show the strokes that make the symbol. Match these left-hand columns against the symbols in Table IV to read the symbols. The charts are numbered to correspond with the vertical columns in Table IV.

(ii) Syllables that have a *y* in the middle, e.g., *kya, kyu, kyo, gya, gyu, gyo,* etc., are written with special combinations of two syllables (see Table VII, page 403). This is true also of the syllables *cha, chu, cho, sha, shu, sho, ja, ju, jo.* Thus, in writing *kya,* you combine the symbol for *ki* with the symbol for *ya.* Note that in forming these special combinations, the symbols for *ki, shi, chi, ni, hi, mi,* and *ri* are used as if they were symbols just for the initial consonant, and not for the consonant-plus-vowel syllable. And so, to write *kya,* you would use the symbol for *ki* (き), which here would represent the consonant *k,* plus the symbol for *ya.* Remember, too, that the second symbol in a special combination must always be one of the following three: *ya* (や), *yu* (ゆ), or *yo* (よ), and that this second member of the combination is usually written smaller than the first and is typically placed slightly to the right of center in a text written from top to bottom. Study Table VII for examples of these special combinations, and compare with Chart III, Table I, for sound values.

TABLE IV
THE BASIC HIRAGANA SYMBOLS

		0	1	2	3	4	5	6	7	8	9	10
		vowel	k	s	t	n	h'	m	y	r	w	n
v	1. a	あ	か	さ	た	な	は	ま	や	ら	わ	ん
o	2. i	い	き	し	ち	に	ひ	み		り		
w	3. u	う	く	す	つ	ぬ	ふ	む	ゆ	る		
e	4. e	え	け	せ	て	ね	へ	め		れ		
l s	5. o°	お	こ	そ	と	の	ほ	も	よ	ろ	を	

TABLE V

CHART 0

Vowels	1	2	3	4
a あ	₹	比	办	あ
i い	小	い		
u う	う	う		
e え	込	え		
i' お	₹	诗	お`	お

CHART 1

k				
a か	プ	功	が	
i き	₹	₹	寺	ほ
u く	父			
e け	屯	に	け	
o こ	る	に		

CHART 2

a	さ	二	七	は		
i	し	ル	つ			
u	す	つ	す			
e	せ	ホ	せ			
o	そ	ツ	そ			

CHART 3

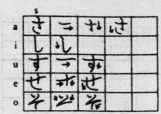

a	た	二	た	た	た
i	ち	二	ち		
u	つ	つ			
e	て	二	て		
o	と	こ	と		

CHART 4

a	な	二	た	な	な
i	に	い	つ	に	
u	ぬ	い	ぬ	ぬ	
e	ね	し	ね	ね	
o	の	ル	の		

CHART 5

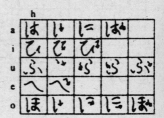

a	は	し	に	は	
i	ひ	び	ぴ		
u	ふ	つ	ふ	ふ	ふ
e	へ	べ			
o	ほ	し	に	に	ほ

CHART 6

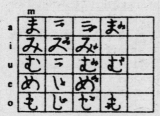

a	ま	二	三	まみ	
i	み	ズ	みぃ		
u	む	二	むぃ	む	
e	め	い	め		
o	も	じ	じ	も	

CHART 7

a	や	わ	じ	や	
i					
u	ゆ	ゆ	ゆ		
e					
o	よ	ら	よ		

CHART 8   CHART 9

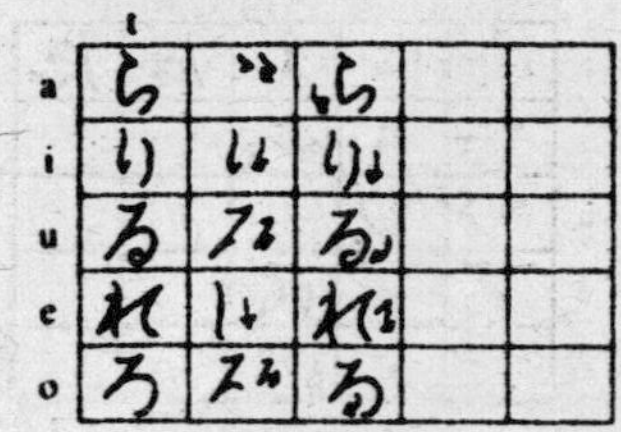

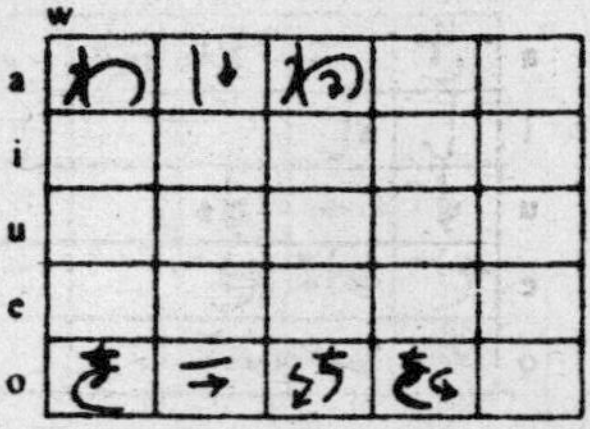

CHART 10

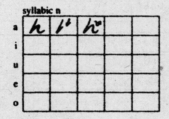

(iii) To write a double consonant other than *nn* in Japanese, you *always* need to use the symbol for *tsu* (つ) for the first letter, *regardless of the sound that is being doubled*, whether *kk*, *ss*, *ssh*, *tt*, *tch*, *tts*, or *pp*. Note that the symbol for *tsu*, when used in this way, is frequently written smaller than usual and placed to the right of center in text that is written from top to bottom. In text written horizontally from left to right, however, the symbol for *tsu* is placed either a little above or below the center.

Study the examples below. See how the *tsu* symbol is written in place of the first letter in a doubled consonant, which appears here in boldface type:

*Cho***tto**	ちょっと	a little
*Ke***kkon**	けっこん	marriage
*I***sshuukan**	いっしゅうかん	one week
*I***ppun**	いっぷん	one minute

(iv) See the examples of double vowels:

aa (a-a)	ああ	Oh!
okaasan (*o-ka-***a**-*sa-n*)	おかあさん	mother
oishii (*o-i-shi-***i***)	おいしい	delicious
kuuki (*ku-***u***-ki*)	くうき	air
oneesan (*o-ne-***e**-*sa-n*)	おねえさん	older sister

There is one exception to this rule: to write *oo*, you almost always use the symbol for the vowel syllable *u* in place of the second *o*, as illustrated below.

kooshoo (*ko-***o***-sho-***o***)	こうしょう	negotiation
Tookyoo (*to-***o***-kyo-***o***)	とうきょう	Tokyo
*moo (mo-***o***)*	もう	more, not any more (with a negative)
*doozo (do-***o***-zo)*	どうぞ	please
*doozoo (do-***o***-zo-***o***)*	どうぞう	bronze statue

TABLE VI
HIRAGANA WITH DIACRITICAL MARKS[1]

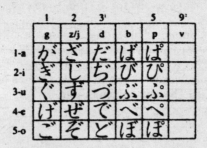

	1	2	3[1]	5	9[2]
	g	z/j	d	b	p	v
1-a	が	ざ	だ	ば	ぱ	
2-i	ぎ	じ	ぢ	び	ぴ	
3-u	ぐ	ず	づ	ぶ	ぷ	
4-e	げ	ぜ	で	べ	ぺ	
5-o	ご	ぞ	ど	ぼ	ぽ	

TABLE VII
COMPLETE LIST OF THE SPECIAL COMBINATIONS

	1	2	3	4	5	6	7	8	9
	k	sh	ch	n	h	m		r	
1.	きゃ	しゃ	ちゃ	にゃ	ひゃ	みゃ		りゃ	
3.	きゅ	しゅ	ちゅ	にゅ	ひゅ	みゅ		りゅ	
5.	きょ	しょ	ちょ	にょ	ひょ	みょ		りょ	

	g	j			b p				
1.	ぎゃ	じゃ			びゃぴゃ				
3.	ぎゅ	じゅ			びゅぴゅ				
5.	ぎょ	じょ			びょぴょ				

[1] ち and づ are ji and zu, respectively, just as with じ and ず. Usually, じ and ず are used, except for special cases.

[2] Traditionally, Hiragana characters are not used to represent the "V" sound.

(2) The katakana symbols:
All the rules used for writing *hiragana* apply to *katakana* except for the following cases:

(a) Some syllables that are not traditionally Japanese syllables can be used for borrowed words, which are written in *katakana*. Such syllables are shown in parentheses in Table I. They are written as follows:

ti	ティ	fa	ファ
tu	テュ	fi	フィ
tse	ツェ	fe	フェ
		fo	フォ
di	ディ		
du	デュ	va	ヴァ
		vi	ヴィ
she	シェ	ve	ヴェ
che	チェ	vo	ヴォ
je	ジェ		

(b) For the second vowel of a double vowel, use a bar —. In text written vertically, write |. (When *katakana* symbols are used for giving special emphasis to certain words, a bar is not used. Instead, *katakana* symbols are used in the manner of *hiragana*.)

kaado (ka-a-do) カード   カードド   card

biiru (bi-i-ru)   ビール   ビール   beer

suupu (su-u-pu) スープ   スープ   soup

keeki (ke-e-ki)   ケーキ   ケ
|
キ   cake

booto (bo-o-to)   ボート   ボ
|
|
ト   boat

Table IX shows the number of strokes that are necessary to write each of the *katakana* symbols. In each chart within the table, the first vertical column shows the completed symbol; the following columns show the strokes necessary to produce the symbol. Match these left-hand columns against the symbols in Table VIII to read the symbols. The charts are numbered to correspond with the vertical columns in Table VIII.

TABLE VIII
THE BASIC KATAKANA SYMBOLS[1]

	0	1	2	3	4	5	6	7	8	9	10
	vowel	k	s	t	n	h	m	y	r	w	n
1. a	ア	カ	サ	タ	ナ	ハ	マ	ヤ	ラ	ワ	ン
2. i	イ	キ	シ	チ	ニ	ヒ	ミ		リ		
3. u	ウ	ク	ス	ツ	ヌ	フ	ム	ユ	ル		
4. e	エ	ケ	セ	テ	ネ	ヘ	メ		レ		
5. o*	オ	コ	ソ	ト	ノ	ホ	モ	ヨ	ロ	ヲ	

[1] Note that in *katakana*, as in *hiragana*, there are two symbols for the letter *o*.

Table IX

Chart 0

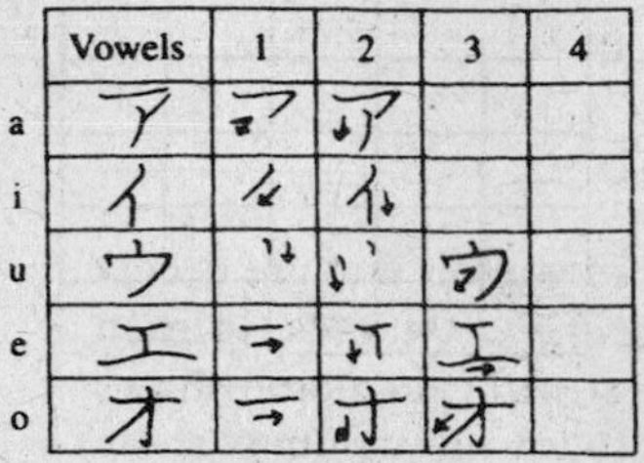

Chart 1

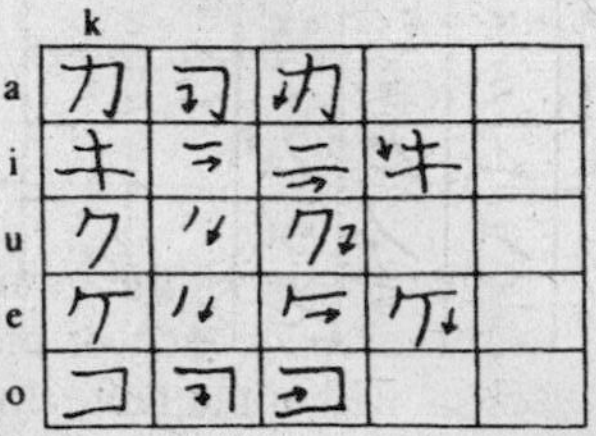

Chart 2

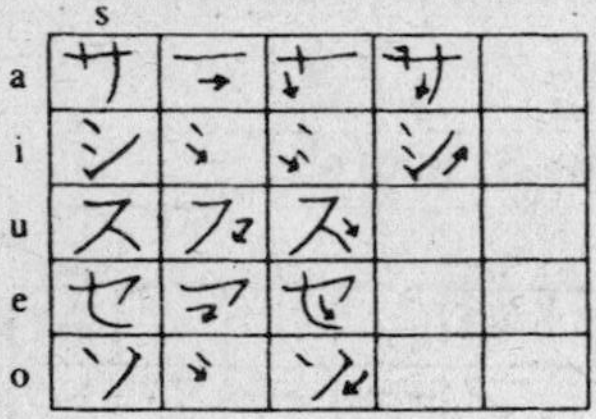

Chart 3

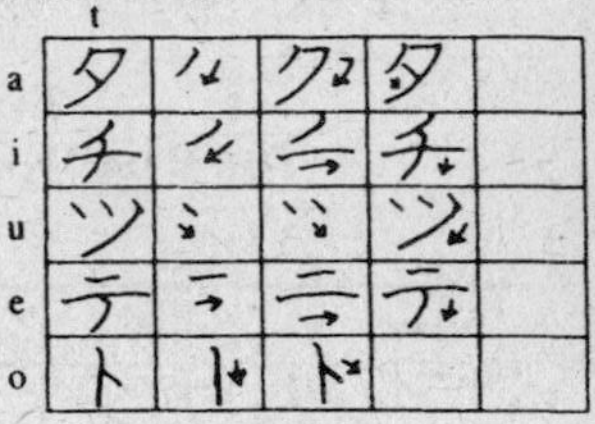

Chart 4

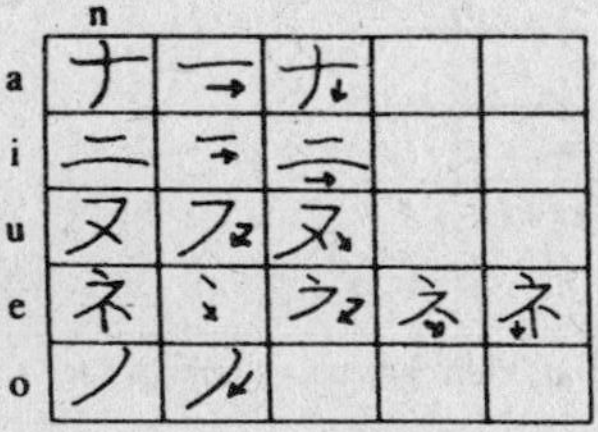

Chart 5

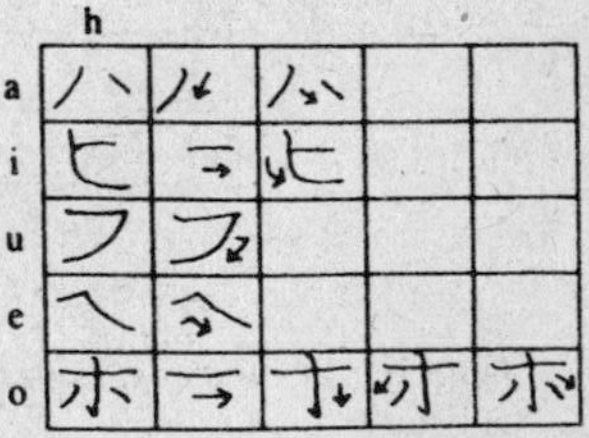

CHART 6

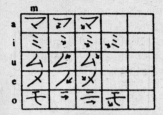

CHART 7

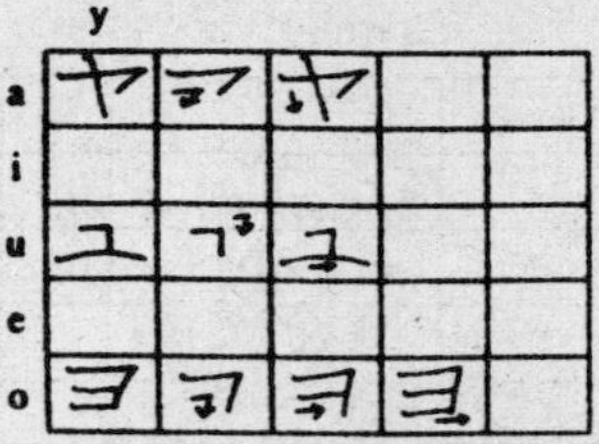

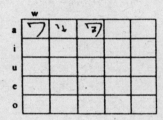

CHART 8

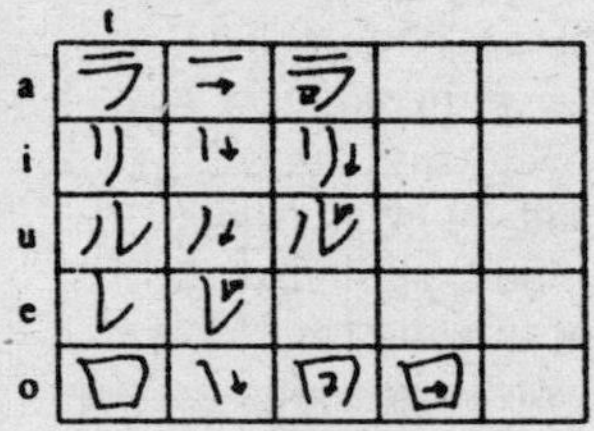

CHART 9

CHART 10

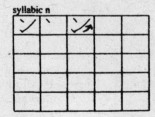

(3) Ideographic symbols (*kanji*):

A few of the most frequently used ideographic symbols are shown below. These are called *kanji* or, in English, "Chinese characters," because the vast majority of these characters are of Chinese origin, unlike the *hiragana* and *katakana* symbols, which were created in Japan.

SYMBOL	READING	MEANING AND CONTENT
日	*hi* *nichi* *bi* *jitsu*	the sun; a prototype was a stylized picture of the sun: ⊙ This symbol is also used to write -*nichi* in *mainichi* [everyday], *nichi,* and -*bi* in *Nichiyoobi* [Sunday]; it also occurs in many other words pertaining to the sun, day, day of the week, etc. Write this figure in the order shown by the arrows:

ㅓ　ㄷ　ㅂ　ㅂ

| 月 | tsuki
gatsu
getsu | the moon; a stylized picture of the moon; its prototype was more like a crescent: |

ⅅ

This symbol is also used for many other words pertaining to

the moon, such as
month (as a duration
of time) or name of
the month, etc.
The order of writing is:

丿 几 月 月

木   ki   a tree; a picture of a
    moku   tree; its prototype
    boku   had the branches and
                    roots more pictori-
                    ally drawn: 业

The order of writing
is: 一 十 才 木

一   hitotsu   one: "oneness" is
    ichi   depicted by one line,
                    "two" is 二 ,
                    "three" is 三 ,
                    but beyond three it is
                    not this simple.
                    The stroke is written
                    from left to right: ⇀

LETTER WRITING

Formerly, letters were written in accordance with rather rigid forms, but today, these forms are seldom used except in formal announcements, such as weddings, births, and deaths. Instead, ordinary personal correspondence is written without adhering to any particular form.

1. FORMAL LETTERS

a. Salutation:

    (1) In a formal letter, it is customary to begin with one of the following highly stylized salutations:

        (a) *Haikei:* corresponds to "Gentlemen," "Dear Sir(s)," or "Dear Madam" [I humbly state . . .]

        (b) *Kinkei:* corresponds to "Gentlemen," "Dear Sir(s)," "Dear Madam" [I reverently state . . .], used mainly by men

        (c) *Haifuku* (used only in reply to a letter): "Gentlemen," "Dear Sir(s)," "Dear Madam" [I reply humbly . . .]

    (2) The addressee's name does not appear until the very end of the letter, where it is written in the following order:

        (a) The family name.

        (b) The given name.

        (c) The proper honorific (the most common and useful of which is *-sama,* a formal variation of *-san* [Mr., Mrs., Miss]). (See also the next section on complimentary closings.)

(3) When a letter in Japanese is written in the English alphabet, it customarily follows the form for an English letter; thus, the addressee's name is used with the honorific *-sama,* and the formal salutation word [see Item (1) above] is omitted.

b. Complimentary closing:

(1) First, use one of the following stylized closing remarks:
   (a) *Mazu wa oshirase made.* = Just to inform you (of) the above.
   (b) *Mazu wa goaisatsu made.* = Just to extend my greetings to you.
   (c) *Toriaezu gohenji made.* = Just to answer your letter in a hurry.

(2) Then add one of the following complimentary closings:
   (a) *Keigu.* = Respectfully yours. [I have respectfully stated.]
   (b) *Soosoo.* = Sincerely yours. [In a hurry. Hurriedly.]
   (c) *Kashiko.* = Sincerely yours. [In awe (used by women only).]

(3) After signing your name, place the addressee's name with the proper honorific on a separate line, either flush with the left margin or slightly indented:
   (a) *Yamada Yoshio-sama* = Mr. Yoshio Yamada.

(b) *Yamada Yoshio sensei*[1] = Mr. Yoshio Yamada (used for a minister, priest, doctor, schoolteacher, etc.).

(c) *Yamada Yoshio-dono* = Mr. Yoshio Yamada *(used in official letters)*.

(d) *Yamada Yoshio Shichoo-dono* = (Mr.) Mayor Yoshio Yamada (used for writing to someone we would address as "the Honorable," e.g., a distinguished officeholder: consists of the addressee's name plus his or her official title plus the honorific *-dono* or *-sama*).

---

[1] *Sensei*, unlike *-san* or *-sama*, may be used by itself as a term of address (somewhat like our word "sir"), and consequently is not always appended to the name as a suffix.

2. BUSINESS LETTERS

LETTER 1

Peter Paine[1]
104-0005
Tookyoo-to, Chiyoda-ku Marunouchi 1-2-3
Marunouchi Hoteru
Heisei 16 nen[2]
9 gatsu 25 nichi

104-0045
Tookyoo-to, Chuuoo-ku
Tsukiji 5-3-2
Asahi Shinbun Sha

Japan Quarterly Onchuu:[3]

Japan Quarterly ichinenbun no koodokuryoo to shite yonsen yonhyaku nijuu en no yuubinkawase o ookuri itashimasu. Ouketori kudasai.

> *Piitaa Pein*
> *(Peter Paine)*[4]

---

[1] It is customary to retain the English name of the writer in the Japanese heading.

[2] *Heisei 16 nen* = the sixteenth year of the Era of Heisei, corresponding to the year 2004.

[3] *Onchuu* is used when the addressee is a group, such as a company.

[4] Normally, the English name would be signed as in the parentheses.

Marunouchi Hotel
1-2-3 Marunouchi Chiyoda-ku, Tokyo 104-0005
September 25, 2004
Japan Quarterly
Asahi Shinbun Sha
Tsukiji 5-3-2, Chūō
Tōkyō 104-0045

Dear Sir/Madam:[1]

Enclosed you will find a money order for ¥4,420 for a year's subscription to your magazine *Japan Quarterly*.

Very truly yours,
Peter Paine

LETTER 2

104-0061
Tookyoo-to, Chuuoo-ku
Ginza 4-choome, 2-10
Sakata Shookai
Heisei 17 nen
8 gatsu 16 nichi

100-0006
Tookyoo-to, Chiyoda-ku
Yuurakuchoo, 1-choome 3-15
Tanaka shookai Onchuu

Haifuku:

Otoiawase no shinamono wa saru 8 gatsu 13 nichi ni machigainaku kozutsumi de hassoo itashimashita.

Mazu wa oshirase made.
Sakata Yukio

---

[1] In Japanese, it is not necessary to use such a salutation.

Sakata and Co.
4-2-10, Ginza
Chūō-ku, Tokyo 104-00061
August 16, 2005

Tanaka and Co.
1-3-15, Yūrakuchō
Chiyoda-ku, Tōkyō 100-0006

Dear Sir/Madam:

In reply to your recent letter, we wish to advise you that the merchandise was mailed to you parcel post on August 13.

Very truly yours,
Yukio Sakata

3.   INFORMAL LETTERS

a. Salutation and content:

(1) Do not use one of the formal salutations described in the preceding section on formal letters.

(2) It is customary to mention the recent weather and climate in your locality.

(3) Inquire into the health of the person to whom you are writing as well as that of his/her family.

(4) Address whatever other topics you want to bring up.

b. Closing:

(1) Instead of using any of the complimentary closing remarks described in Item b-(2) of the preceding section on formal letters, close with a stylized remark such as:

(a) *Dewa mata.* = Well, then again.

(b) *Gokigen yoo.* = Wishing you good health.

(c) *Okarada o odaiji ni.* = Keep well. Take good care of yourself.

(d) *Minasan ni yoroshiku.* = Regards to everyone.

(2) Sign your name on a new line.

c. Examples:

Study the informal letter and thank-you note that follow.

INFORMAL LETTER

Heisei 18 nen
3 gatsu 15 nichi

Azusa sama:

Otegami ureshiku haiken shimashita.

Minasama ogenki na yoo de nani yori ni omoimasu.

Sate watakushidomo no Kyooto hoomon no koto desu ga Shigatsu no hajime ni jikkoo suru koto ni shimashita. Nishuukan taizai no yotei desu. Minasama ni ome ni kakareru no o tanoshimi ni shite imasu.

Kanai no Irene mo issho ni mairimasu. Shoobai no hoo mo okagesamade umaku itte imasu. Kore ga tsuzuite kureru to ii to omoimasu. Chotto muri na onegai ka mo shiremasen ga Azusa san mo Shigatsu ni haittara sukoshi te o yasumete issho ni ikuraka asoberu yoo ni shimasen ka.

Konoaida Nomura kun ni attara Azusa san wa doo shite iru daroo to itte imashita. Kare mo shigoto wa umaku itte iru rashii desu.

Daiji na koto o wasureru tokoro deshita ga Gurando Hoteru ni heya o yoyaku shite moraemasen ka? Shigatsu itsuka desu. Onegai shimasu.

Ja kyoo wa kore de shitsurei shimasu. Otayori o matte imasu. Okusan ni yoroshiku.

Jakku
(Jack)

March 5, 2006

Dear Azusa:

I was very happy to receive your last letter. I'm glad to hear that all of you are doing well.

First of all, I expect to spend two weeks in Kyoto at the beginning of April, and I'm looking forward to seeing you and your family.

My wife, Irene, is coming with me. Business is pretty good right now. Let's hope it keeps up. Try not to be too busy during the month of April so that we can have some time together. I suppose that's a little difficult for a busy man like you.

The other day Nomura asked about you. His business is going well.

I almost forgot the most important thing. Can you reserve a room for me at the Grand Hotel for April fifth? You'll be doing me a great favor.

I'll stop writing now. I hope to hear from you soon. My best regards to your wife.

Yours,
Jack

THANK-YOU NOTE

Yamada Fujiko-sama:

Kono tabi wa taisoo rippa na okurimono o choodai itashimashite atsuku orei mooshiagemasu. Hanga ni wa watakushi mo higoro kyoomi o motte ori sono ue ni kondo itadakimashita oshina wa kyakuma ni yoku choowa itashimasu node hontoo ni yorokonde orimasu. Arigatoo gozaimashita.

Mazu wa on-rei made.

Robaato Sumisu
(Robert Smith)

Dear Fujiko Yamada,

I would like to thank you for your delightful present. I have long had an interest in woodblock prints, and I'm glad that the one you gave me matches the other things in my parlor perfectly.

Thank you ever so much.

(Sincerely yours,)[1]
Robert Smith

---

[1] Note that in Japanese there is no formal closing in a note of this kind.

4. Electronic Mail

E-MAIL MESSAGE 1 (SOMEWHAT FORMAL)

Yamada-san:

Tookyoo honsha de no kaigi no hookokusho o sooshinshite kudasari, doomo arigatoo gozaimashita. Sassoku shitenchoo o hajime buchoo, kachoo, soshite ta no shain ni mo tensooshite okimashita. Kyoo wa, nyuuyooku shisha no kongetsu no eigyoohookoku o tenpushimasu kara me o tooshite kudasai. Moshi tenpufairu ga hirakenakattara renrakushite kudasai. Dewa, mata.

> *Piitaa Pein*
> *ABC Software Co. Eigyoobu*
> *500 Broadway, Suit 1011*
> *New York, NY 10003*
> *Tel (212) 555-5555 Fax (212) 555-3333*

Dear Mr. Yamada:

Thank you very much for sending me the report of the meeting at the Tokyo headquarters.

I promptly forwarded it to our branch manager as well as the division manager, the section manager, and other employees. Today I will attach this month's business report from the New York branch, so please have a look at it. Please let me know if you cannot open the attachment file. I will talk with you later.

> Peter Paine
> Sales Department, ABC Software Co.
> 500 Broadway, Suit 1011
> New York, NY 10003
> Tel (212) 555-5555 Fax (212) 555-3333

E-MAIL MESSAGE 2 (INFORMAL)

Yumi-san,

Konnichi wa. Ogenki desu ka? Senjitsu wa nyuuyooku de issho ni totta shashin o tenpushitekurete doomo arigatoo. Jitsu wa uirusu no mondai no tame itsukakan mo meeru ga jushin dekinakatta n desu. Sorede henji ga okurete shimaimashita. Ukkari sakujoshite shimau to taihen da kara, sassoku tenpufairu o hozonshite okimashita. Mata shuumatsu ni meeru o okurimasu ne. Jaa, mata.

Piita

Dear Yumi,

Hello. How are you? Thank you very much for sending me by attachment the picture that we took together in New York. I wasn't able to check e-mails for five days due to virus problems, in fact. That's why I couldn't reply to you sooner. Since it would have been a shame if I had accidentally deleted it, I immediately saved the attachment file. I will send you an e-mail again this weekend.

Talk to you later.

Peter

5. ADDRESSING AN ENVELOPE

For a letter using the Roman letters:

Peter Paine
3-2-15 Oiwake-chō
Bunkyō-ku, Tōkyō 112-0000

    Tanaka Tarō Sama
    Kyōto Daigaku Igakubu
    Sakyō-ku, Kyōto-shi
    Yoshida-Konoe-cho,
    Sakyo-ku, Kyoto 606-8315

In Japanese writing and using a Japanese envelope:

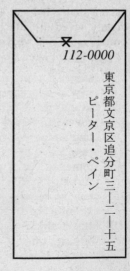

606-8315

京都市左京区吉田近衛町
京都大学医学部
田中太郎様

112-0000

東京都文京区追分町三－二－十五
ピーター・ペイン

6. INTERNET RESOURCES

1) www.yahoo.co.jp
   Japanese version of Yahoo. It is a popular search engine. Online shopping, auctions, yellow pages, etc., are available. It also provides current world and domestic news.

2) www.asahi.com
   Homepage of a popular Japanese newspaper.

3) www.yomiuri.co.jp
   Homepage of a popular Japanese newspaper.

4) www.amazon.co.jp
   Homepage of Amazon.com Japan. One can purchase Japanese books, CDs, DVDs online.

5) http://dictionary.goo.ne.jp
   English-Japanese dictionary, Japanese-English dictionary, and Japanese dictionary are available.

6) www.wanogakkou.com
   This site introduces Japanese culture and industry. English site is available for culture section.

7) www.metro.tokyo.jp
   Official site of Tokyo metropolitan government. English site is available. It provides a variety of information related to Tokyo.

8) www.us.emb-japan.go.jp
   Official site of Embassy of Japan in the U.S.A. It provides a variety of information including traveling and visa.

9) www.pia.co.jp
   Homepage of a popular Japanese information journal. It provides entertainment information, such as movies, concerts, music, theaters, art exhibitions, sports, and restaurants.

10) http://webjapanese.com
    This site offers a variety of information for students of Japanese.

ULTIMATE JAPANESE
Beginner-Intermediate or Advanced

Equivalent to two years of college-level study, this comprehensive program covers reading, writing, grammar, conversation, and culture. Includes a coursebook and eight 60-minute CDs.

Beginner-Intermediate
CD/Coursebook program • 1-4000-2113-8 • $79.95/C$110.00
Coursebook only • 1-4000-2112-X • $18.00/C$26.00

Advanced
CD/Coursebook Program • 1-4000-2069-7 • $79.95/C$120.00
Coursebook only • 1-4000-2067-0 • $18.00/C$27.00

BUSINESS COMPANION: JAPANESE

The 416-page handbook contains more than 1,000 general business phrases and vocabulary for over 25 specific industries, plus a two-way glossary, useful addresses, and more. The audio CD contains more than 500 phrases used in realistic, current business dialogues.

Handbook/CD program • 1-4000-2042-5 • $21.95/C$32.95
Handbook only • 1-4000-2044-1 • $12.95/C$19.95

IN THE KNOW IN JAPAN
The Indispensable Guide to Working and Living in Japan

Fit right in by understanding Japanese etiquette, navigate through everyday life with tips for the whole family, and get an insider's perspective on the social and business environment. 272-page book with a bonus audio CD featuring key expressions and business terms.

0-609-61114-3 • $22.95/C$34.95